PRAISE FOR *CRYPTO ISLAND* . . .

"Vulnerable and unrestrained about the realities of reinvention, *Crypto Island* might be the how-to-manual—or treasure map—midlife mavericks who dream of trading security for a sandy beach have been searching for!"

—**BRIDEY THELEN-HEIDEL**, author of *Bright Eyes*

"The joy of reading this memoir is discovering the healing power of how Georgine faced fear . . . and ultimately encountered a new relationship with herself, something all of us hope for in midlife."

—**DR. LINDA JOY MYERS**, founder of the National Association of Memoir Writers and author of *Don't Call Me Mother* and *Song of the Plains*

"Both a cautionary saga and an awakening to adventure make *Crypto Island* a page turner as the author faces a reckoning of the past and navigates her way through to an innovative future."

—**RITA M. GARDNER**, author of *The Coconut Latitudes*

CRYPTO ISLAND

CRYPTO ISLAND

A MEMOIR OF MIDLIFE RELOCATION TO PUERTO RICO

GEORGINE HODGKINSON

SWP

SHE WRITES PRESS

Published in 2026 by
She Writes Press, an imprint of The Stable Book Group

SWP

1569 Solano Ave #546
Berkeley, CA 94707
https://shewritespress.com
Library of Congress Control Number: 2026907211
ISBN: 979-8-89636-148-0
eISBN: 979-8-89636-149-7

Interior Designer: Tabitha Lahr

Printed in the United States

Names and identifying characteristics have been changed to protect the privacy of certain individuals.

For my daughters Eden, Raeanne, Abigail, and Olivia—
being your parent is the best adventure of all.

AUTHOR'S NOTE

This memoir draws on written journals and voice recordings I created during the first year I lived in Puerto Rico, helping me to recreate scenes and dialogue with accuracy. Stories from my youth, however, were constructed from memory. While I believe they capture the essential truth—both emotional and factual—exact details may be imperfect. Names and identifying characteristics have been changed for all individuals except family members and speakers at public cryptocurrency events. Any similarities between the reconstructed characters portrayed and real people not identified in this work are unintentional.

CONTENTS

PREFACE

I grew up poor, reckless, and too fast. In adulthood I washed myself of these sins in the rivers of academia, marriage, and motherhood. So, to tell me that I'd move to Puerto Rico at age fifty, learn to trade cryptocurrency, and take chances with family, love, and money? I would have said that you're nuts. I didn't know much about digital assets. I'd heard the word "cryptocurrency," but it sounded senseless to me. I wasn't a gamer or someone who purchased goods off the dark web. I was a regular person: a wife, a busy mom, and a college professor. I managed a household, not a crypto Ledger wallet. I wondered who wanted coins or tokens that only existed in a digital universe?

It turned out that lots of folks did. At the height of the COVID-19 pandemic, the cryptocurrency market was highly unstable and unpredictable, but it grew in popularity. Whether this shift in public regard was the result of new trends in policymaking, quantitative easing, a need for improved international payment and transaction systems, escape from pandemic tedium, or outright fraud, more people than ever before engaged with cryptocurrency. The global user base of cryptocurrency increased by almost 200 percent between 2018 and 2020. Bitcoin, along with other cryptocurrencies, skyrocketed in price and social acceptance.

No place experienced the impact of this sudden cryptocurrency popularity like Puerto Rico. The arrival of Brock Pierce (a former Disney child actor turned billionaire turned playboy) and other Brock-wannabe crypto leaders resulted in new legislation, redevelopment, and myriad activities related to crypto. The island was even given nicknames by the crypto community like Crypto Rico and Puertopia. Of course, not everyone (including 90 percent of the locals) thought the growing crypto community was a blessing. Change is often linked to controversy, and from what I witnessed, this adage applied to Puerto Rico.

My name is Georgine Hodgkinson and I have a confession: I'm an unlikely person to trade cryptocurrency since I don't have a background in technology or finance. I'm a professor of communication studies and I also coordinate a program on my college campus that supports formerly incarcerated students. If you want to know about interpersonal relationships, or services available to help someone recently released from prison, I'm your gal. But expertise on decentralized finance and blockchain? Not so much—*until* I moved to Puerto Rico.

During the first year of the pandemic, I studied and traded cryptocurrency for three reasons. First, I was bored. Like other people whose work life changed dramatically when the world went remote, I was looking for new ways to challenge my intellectual curiosity. Teaching classes on Zoom all day left me hungry for cerebral nourishment. Second, in 2020, my husband and I relocated to Puerto Rico as members of Act 20 & 22, legislation that rewarded residency with tax advantages (Act members paid 4 percent in federal income taxes and zero on capital gains). When we moved to the small Caribbean island, we met others who had relocated for the same reason.

However, lots of these stateside transplants did work in crypto and other forms of finance, and they introduced us to a thriving crypto community. Third, I hoped to make some money—which I did! I wasn't always blessed with the middle-class life that being a tenured professor provided. I was raised by a single mom who struggled to make ends meet, so the part of me that hated growing up poor got pretty darn excited about the chance to make some extra cash.

I also learned about the cryptocurrency community in Puerto Rico by attending their regular weekly gatherings called Crypto Tuesdays (a pseudonym used throughout this book). At these events, cryptocurrency insiders shared their stories and strategies. They networked and pitched products. They organized parties and weekend retreats. This smart, creative, and hedonistic group of transplants formed an island family, a wild social circle that triggered memories from my carefully hidden past. Interacting with this community taught me about crypto, but that wasn't all I learned. My time with this group, comprised mostly of white, rich men, got me thinking about power and the ways in which wealth and entitlement work. As Ralph Waldo Emerson said, "Money often costs too much."

This story is about cryptocurrency, and it isn't. Crypto, and the cryptocurrency community in Puerto Rico, played a significant role in my life during 2020 and 2021, but my story is as much about love as it is about money. The relationships I had with myself, my daughters, and my husband, Mark, changed dramatically in the early 2020s. During this unusual time in our history, my personal life took some unexpected turns. I became an empty nester, grew frustrated by the pandemic and my remote teaching load, learned to trade crypto, joined new financial communities, and experienced emotional triggers resulting from a chaotic childhood and scandalous adolescence.

Research tells us that a willingness to take risks, to make ourselves vulnerable, is required to deepen bonds of love and connection. In order to build trust, vulnerability is key. I knew this intellectually, but it wasn't until I experienced that vulnerability—until I gave up the life in California that made me feel secure—that I personally learned of vulnerability's challenges and rewards. Given all the time I've spent in the classroom, I could talk the talk, but this story is about learning to walk the walk.

In this book I share the things I learned about, like trading crypto, but I also explore the topics to which I've dedicated my life's work: the complicated relationships we have with others and with ourselves. I have been teaching classes on identity, love, and relationships for twenty-five years, but when I moved to Puerto Rico, these topics challenged my life. Writing this memoir was an opportunity to explore the way that my past informed my present. It was also a chance to heal old wounds and release buried shame. I learned that novel experience and vulnerability do more than make life interesting—they change who we know ourselves to be. They also, I believe, create endless possibility for who we might become.

CHAPTER 1:

NINE FLOORS UP

I was kicked by an invisible foot that sent me flying to the edge of the bed. I grabbed the nightstand to stop my fall, then sat up. Blackout curtains made it impossible to see so I reached out for my husband, Mark, and slammed my knuckles into the headboard.

"Earthquake," Mark said, sitting up next to me. His voice surged with adrenaline. "Let's move."

"It's big!" My hand throbbed and I felt dizzy. "It nearly tossed me out of bed."

I kicked off the tangle of sheets around my legs and followed Mark. I expected to hear crashing—the smash of water glasses as they hit tile or the sharp crack of picture frames launched from walls—but there was only silence. It was the anticipation of danger that made me creep on tiptoe until I stood in a narrow-framed space, a bathtub on one side and a suitcase, perched atop a luggage rack, on the other.

I'd been here before. California was home so I knew that earthquakes were noisy, that they rumbled, clapped, and groaned. The quiet in our hotel room made me fear this quake was just getting started. Mark and I braced ourselves for more.

"Oh my God." The floor shook and I grabbed the doorframe to stop my fall. My heartbeat accelerated and bile rose from my stomach.

Mark wrapped his strong arms around me, steady and fixed, but the ground kept rolling. We balanced ourselves like surfers hugging on a longboard, cresting a wave.

"Let's get the hell out of here before the next one hits," Mark said.

I flipped on a light. We slid into the previous day's clothes, rushed out the door, and joined a hallway full of hotel guests desperate to get down from the ninth floor of the Sheraton in San Juan, Puerto Rico. Fathers carrying sleepy toddlers and mothers holding the hands of pajama-clad children pushed toward the exits. It wasn't until our elevator doors shut that I realized we were supposed to take the stairs. I turned toward Mark to voice my concern but his trance-like stare kept me silent. When the green *L* chimed and the doors opened, I took a deep breath and whispered a prayer of thanks.

"What if we just sleep out here?" Mark asked. We sat in the dark on a cement bench between the hotel and a magnificent glass-encased convention center. The air was warm and my face moist from humidity.

"Well . . ." I considered. "I'm not sure that's any better."

I pointed to the glass-faced building. The shape of a waxing moon was reflected in its shiny panes.

"If we stay here, I'm thinking we'll die for sure, impaled by falling shards." I tilted my head, closed my eyes, and stuck my tongue out the side of my mouth to make Mark laugh but he didn't even crack a smile so I put my hand on his knee.

All around us confused vacationers hugged and huddled. I supposed they were also weighing the options: die by glass spike when the convention center windows shattered or be buried alive inside the hotel.

What the hell am I doing in Puerto Rico? I asked myself. Again. The thought played on a continuous loop since we'd landed on the island. I knew about danger, about how life could turn scary in an instant, and I avoided those situations. My childhood had been turbulent, filled with earthquakes of one kind or another, and that influenced the type of adult I'd become—a woman who liked her feet on solid ground.

It turned out that earthquakes were common in Puerto Rico. This little island was located where the Caribbean and North American tectonic plates met, compressed between mantle and crust like a bit of puzzle that got pinched between misaligned pieces. We didn't know any of this on the night we escaped from the Sheraton, only a few days into our relocation trip.

Our life was in Northern California, but my husband needed a second place to live for work. We had recently agreed that Mark would move his law practice to Puerto Rico. He had been accepted into Act 20 & 22—a tax program in Puerto Rico that offered incentives to relocate businesses—which meant he would split his time between the West Coast and the Caribbean. I didn't like the idea since my job kept me tied to Sacramento, but I couldn't argue with his logic. Relocation under Act 20 & 22 meant that he'd only pay 4 percent in income tax and zero on capital gains. As a small business owner, the sole proprietor of a law firm, these tax advantages were significant. Plus, the last of our four daughters was about to leave for college and now that we were both in our fifties, saving for retirement was essential. We were in San Juan to find Mark housing and office space.

The morning after our sleepless night we learned from news reports that a 6.4 magnitude quake along the southern coast was the culprit. Unlike hurricanes, which were limited to a season, earthquakes could happen at any time and aftershocks continued for weeks. Over coffee in the hotel lobby, we watched a stream of disaster images on TV. Houses whose stilts snapped and destroyed cars parked below, concrete walls of city buildings that had crumbled into rubble, and a giant hole that was once the infamous Punta Ventana ("Window Point") kept us glued to a muted television screen as we tried to figure out our next steps.

Even though it had been decades since I brushed up against the shadowy feelings of death, I recognized them instantly during the quake. The ghost that haunted my past—the one that whispered death was near when I was sick or in danger—showed up the night the earth turned violent in Puerto Rico. Its sinister presence raised the hairs on my arms, and its ghoulish warning foretold that my predictable, carefully managed life had taken a wrong turn.

My early recollections of the ghost—the eerie presence I associated with death—always occurred in the black of night. I was a small child then, five, maybe six, and I struggled to breathe, shallow gasps the only way to get oxygen into my lungs. That's when I first saw the faceless ghost. It was floating near the ceiling of my bedroom like sheets blowing in a gentle breeze. I watched its translucent form hover above my bed and wondered if I was having a bad dream.

"Wake up, Georgine," my mother said, tapping my shoulder and brushing the damp curls on my forehead toward the sides of my face.

She put her ear to my chest and then propped me up on pillows.

"Nick, it's bad!" Mom screamed to Dad. He was scrambling around in another part of the house. "Her lips are blue."

"I'm looking for her inhaler," Dad replied. "Just give me a minute." Cupboard doors banged from the bathroom down the hall.

Mom scooped me out of bed and into her arms. "There's no time. I'm taking her. Now."

I tried to wrap my arms around my mom's neck as she carried me down the hallway but my limbs wouldn't obey. They flopped around lifeless like puppet parts dangled from string.

Mom carried me straight to the car, laid me down on the back seat, and sped toward the hospital.

Flashing lights from oncoming traffic danced in our car and I wondered if the ghost had followed us out of the house and flew behind the green Pinto she drove.

"Stay awake, Georgine. Come on now," Mom coaxed. "Nice slow breaths."

My lungs were heavy as cement, hard and unmoving. I tried to follow my mom's instructions, but the task was impossible. My breathing was shallow and narrow. The only option was to sip air through a tiny invisible straw.

"Mom . . ." I tried, but couldn't finish the sentence and coughed. The force was a sledgehammer that pounded at the cement in my chest, and bubbling mucus-filled debris exploded from my mouth.

"Don't try to talk. Just be calm."

From the back seat, I could see Mom gripping the steering wheel with both hands.

"You're going to be just fine. You know your father had asthma when he was a little boy and he survived. You will too because you're tough. You're strong. Remember, it's always mind over matter."

I wiped the phlegm from my mouth with the back of my hand.

"Okay. We're almost there." Mom stopped the car in front of the emergency room entrance. "Let's get you inside."

She scooped me back into her arms and walked me to a nurse sitting behind a desk near the entrance.

"Sorry to see you both again so soon," the nurse said.

My mother answered questions as another hospital employee brought a wheelchair around to the front of the nurse's desk. I was deposited in the chair, wheeled behind a curtain, and placed onto a bed. A different nurse hooked me up to a Bird Machine, a type of 1970s nebulizer, that pumped medication into my lungs and relaxed my inflamed bronchial tubes. I slept in an oxygen tent that night and was given a course of steroids. By the following day, the emergency was over and I'd forgotten about my ghost, and about looming death, until the next time I was rushed to the hospital because I couldn't breathe.

Asthma had almost killed my father when he was a boy. Nobody thought he'd survive his childhood in the 1940s, especially the doctors who treated him. The 1970s doctors who treated me said I'd inherited my asthma from my father. Just like my dad, I survived a sickly childhood, but that didn't spare me from those scary, unexpected nights of near suffocation.

Asthma attacks weren't the only thing that invited the feathery touch of death into my young life. I faced other brushes with the dark shadow force growing up. At ten I was attacked by a dog and almost lost my right eye. At sixteen I rolled down a mountain in a car, drunk as a skunk, and stayed trapped upside down under the steering column until a farmer (whose fence I destroyed on my way down the mountain) came to help me escape. At nineteen I got tangled up while bungee jumping off a train trestle and the cords designed to keep me from hitting the ground broke my arm before stopping my fall.

The ghost of death also visited me in college, the time of life I drank heavily and used drugs. Long weekend benders called forth the dark figure, a warning that my grip on life was tenuous. Too hungover to move, I'd lie on the floor of my apartment and look up at the ceiling, watching the apparition taunt me from a semi-conscious state and praying it might end my misery.

* * *

A few days after the earthquake in San Juan, Mark and I were looking at office space to rent in the city's historic district. The list of possible options Mark had compiled took us up and down narrow streets and past brightly painted Spanish-style buildings that were more than four hundred years old.

"I think I saw a ghost in our hotel room the night of the earthquake," I said to Mark.

I stared at the ground as I walked, careful not to trip on the cobblestones under my feet.

"I wouldn't be surprised. San Juan is the oldest city in the United States. These buildings are definitely haunted."

Mark laughed and then stopped to look for an address on the colonial architecture.

"This city is gorgeous," he said, and continued walking. "All the history and the vibrant colors—I've never seen any place quite like this."

I still don't want to live here, I thought.

"I'm serious," I said. "When I was a kid, this weird ghost appeared whenever I was in danger."

"That's called your guilty conscience. It's the price you pay for breaking all the rules and having all the fun."

I furrowed my brow and followed him around the corner of a building painted sky blue.

Then he turned around to look at me with a smile. "I'm just jealous," he teased. "My altar boy stories are boring compared to your colorful youth."

We walked past a mass of raspberry bougainvillea petals that poured from a balcony above like a waterfall.

"There," Mark said, pointing across an open plaza. "That's our next office space appointment. Piloto 151."

Whatever I saw the night of the earthquake, it left me feeling uneasy. What the hell was I thinking when I agreed to Mark's relocation plan? My inner voice sounded nervous. *Be strong. Be tough. Mind over matter*, it chanted. But I couldn't shake my fear.

There was a Hindu belief that proclaimed we received signs of things to come in the form of *nimitta*. Since nimitta portend the future, it was said, they should guide us as encouragements or warnings. After the earthquake in San Juan, I feared violent shifts in the earth's crust were a nasty message from the ancients. Was it a nimitta that my stable, coveted life was about to crack wide open?

We walked across the plaza, entered the office complex, and were greeted by a salesperson.

"*Buen día*, Mr. and Mrs. Redmond," said a woman with glossy black hair. "Right this way."

"Perfect," Mark said after the tour. Then he handed over his credit card to an administrative assistant sitting at reception. "I'm happy to prepay the lease for one year."

My jaw clenched to control the objections in my throat while my inner voice screamed, *Stop!*

CHAPTER 2:

DETOURS

A few months before the earthquake in San Juan, when Mark first shared his interest in applying for the Act 20 & 22 program, I was dumbstruck. We were sitting at the dining table in our Sacramento River home drinking red wine. Dinner warmed in the oven, an eggplant dish that Mark loved, and I could smell the mix of garlic and tomatoes coming from my kitchen.

Orange flames of clouds filled the sky in the large window behind Mark as we started our daily ritual: admire the sunset over the river, share events from our day, reconnect. The rhythm of our life synchronized each evening with highlights. Inevitably these included the troublesome antics of our dog, Lucy. Most often she had rolled in something unmentionable during Mark's afternoon walk. Then I'd share an anecdote about a student, Mark would update me on one of his legal cases, and we'd talk about our mothers, both of whom were widowed, in their seventies, and living alone.

Some might consider these conversations boring, but they felt like my favorite pair of slippers and I looked forward to them all day.

"Maybe they could be roommates, or better yet, each other's life coach," I joked about our mothers. "My mom would encourage yours to go to cocktail parties and your mom might get mine to slow down. Combined, they would make the perfectly balanced parent."

Our mothers had opposite personalities. My mom was a social butterfly, and Mark's was solitary and private, but they shared a fierce independence. I dreaded the day we would need to take away their car keys or hire caregivers.

Instead of a smile, or a sassy retort, Mark looked at the darkening sky. The set of his eyebrows suggested that something was weighing on him. They were heavy with thought, an expression usually associated with a stressful workday. His long lashes blinked slowly and his voice steadied with practiced calm.

"I've been thinking about this for a while," Mark began. "About a year ago I noticed some of the macroeconomists I follow online reside in Puerto Rico. At first I just thought it was a weird coincidence, but when I dug deeper, I learned about the tax advantages of relocating to the island."

Then Mark repeated what I already knew: 2020 was an important year for him professionally since a large class action case, one he'd spent almost a decade working on, was likely to settle.

"You've been thinking about moving to Puerto Rico for a while?" I asked.

The air in the room shifted.

"Applicants who get accepted into the program are only required to pay four percent in income taxes. Can you believe it? *Four* percent."

"Is that legal?" My face felt hot. "You're an attorney who practices law in California for God's sake. Why would you qualify for a Puerto Rican tax rate?"

Mark said that the Puerto Rico tax incentives were created for people who owned their own businesses and could work remotely. The government there wanted new residents whose enterprises in the states could be managed from the Caribbean. As a US territory, Puerto Rico was not beholden to the federal tax laws that governed other states, but unlike other tax-incentivized Caribbean islands, a move to Puerto Rico didn't require us to relinquish our US citizenship or pay repatriation taxes if we decided to move back home.

The commonwealth of Puerto Rico passed the first legislation of this kind in 2008; Act 73 was established to promote economic development. In 2012, Act 20 & 22 passed to clarify criteria and incentives. Resident transplants managed their new and established business ventures in things like social media, Internet sales, finance, legal services, and manufacturing from Puerto Rico. They contributed to the local economy by buying houses, offices, cars, entertainment, food, and services. Residency requirements—sometimes called the Teddy Bear clause—mandated that Puerto Rico was the primary home to Act beneficiaries. Participants had to live on the island at least six months and a day each year. Between the personal spending, mandatory yearly donations to approved charities, and the need to hire local employees, Act advocates argued that they were economic aids who injected money into the cash-strapped island.

What I didn't yet know was that the Puerto Rican tax legislation was also controversial. While politicians touted this creative tax loophole as a blessing for the commonwealth, the majority of Puerto Rican people believed it exacerbated the growing economic divide between indigenous inhabitants and wealthy foreign transplants.

"Anyone who owns their own business potentially qualifies," Mark explained. "Georgine, this is a *fantastic* opportunity."

Mark talked like someone planning a great adventure. He articulated dates and details. He had executed phone interviews with accountants and attorneys. He knew the names of neighborhoods where Act 20 & 22 residents lived. Since our youngest daughter was leaving for college in the fall, he said, we were no longer tied to Sacramento. This relocation would maximize the profits he'd worked for years to achieve at a stage in life when strategic financial planning was critical.

The smell of eggplant churned my stomach.

"But what about *my* job?" I asked. "I'll be teaching in a Sacramento classroom this fall. I'm not even close to retiring, and you would have to live in Puerto Rico for 183 days of the year. Are we just going to live in separate places?"

I didn't ask in what universe he could justify keeping all this from me until now, but he must have seen the hurt in my eyes.

"Look," he said gently, "this only has to be a one-year experiment. If I get accepted into the Act 20 & 22 society it could save us a significant amount in taxes next year. You have a pension when you retire, but I don't. A tax savings like this would be a game changer."

I believed this experiment could change more than our financial situation; I feared it would change us. I liked our life in Sacramento. We had stability. Our jobs and finances were solid. We were decent savers and had college accounts for our daughters. We avoided debt. We moved slow but steady and did not need tax incentives to get to the finish line.

In the weeks that followed I hypothesized a mountain of reasons to explain why my husband would consider shaking up our life like a Christmas snow globe. A lead contender was that Mark's Puerto Rico plan was connected to his dead father, a man Mark still wanted to please. It had to be more than money that motivated my husband to live far away from *me*. Right? And this proposal was the kind of financial decision that Michael, my deceased father-in-law, would have admired.

Mark's father, Michael, had quite a history and legacy. He was born Nathaniel Mitchell Moskowitz in 1939 to parents Minnie (Sadie Weitzman) and Pop (Irving Moskowitz). Pop immigrated to New York in 1915, just before World War I. He was an orphan from Europe and headed to New York via Ellis Island, sponsored by a relative and in search of a better life. He found a job as a loader for Birds Eye Food on the train docks in New York City and according to family lore, fell in love with Minnie. She was the only daughter in the Weitzman family hanger business and older than Pop. She married him in 1936. At thirty-one, Minnie became Mrs. Moskowitz and a few years later gave birth to their only son, Nathaniel.

As an only child, Nathaniel was deeply loved and fretted over. Nathaniel was bright and good-natured, but born with hemophilia, a blood-clotting disorder. He spent month-long stints in the hospital as a child. Every bump and fall led to internal bleeding and other medical complications. Mark believed that these long lonely visits fueled his imagination. Once we found a box of his dad's childhood effects that included a View-Master toy loaded with hazy pictures of the Grand Canyon and the plastic kaleidoscope he played with during hospital stays. Nathaniel, who was never allowed to play sports, was a dreamer.

When Nathaniel left the East Coast to find his better life at twenty-six, he headed west. First, he went to Las Vegas, inspired perhaps by View-Master clicks. He got a job as a comptroller for casinos and then found his way to Los Angeles, where he became an independent agent; he sold financial planning products and insurance. By the time he arrived in California, however, he was no longer Nathaniel Moskowitz. He had changed his name to Michael Redmond in an attempt to stop the racism he experienced over his Jewish heritage.

In contrast, Mark's launch into adulthood started with college. He attended Pepperdine University on a debate scholarship and graduated with a degree in business in 1989. When he couldn't find a job, Michael encouraged him to go to law school, the career he always wished he might have had. Mark's undergrad experience confirmed a love of philosophy. Mark's dad was Jewish but his mom, Mary Ann, was a devout Catholic. Mark grew up an altar boy with eclectic religious tastes. He wanted to attend graduate school and study comparative world religions, but to please his father, went to law school instead.

Five days before Mark's graduation from law school, his father suffered a massive heart attack and died.

Perhaps relocation was some inherited genetic proclivity in Mark's DNA like asthma was for me. After all, my husband was the son and grandson of men who had traveled great distances to reinvent themselves; they had reshaped their destinies through geographic risk-taking. Was it possible that his immigrant blood was to blame, a fate written in the stars long before he was born?

A chapter in the book, I told myself, but not the whole story. Mark had talked about leaving the law since we first met. The act of becoming an attorney for a father who died—right before parental expectation turned into sweet admiration—left Mark with persistent low-level professional resentment. I suspected that relocating to Puerto Rico was Mark's chance to get two things he desperately wanted: imagined approval from his dead father and enough money to finally leave the law.

On the night of the big Puerto Rico reveal, my curiosity over Mark's motivation didn't exist. Instead, the nauseous feeling in my stomach was compounded by anxiety as the image of living 3,500 miles away from my husband started to take shape. What was it I saw? A middle-aged woman, forlorn when she returned from work each day, wandering the rooms of a big empty house. She ate stale crackers straight out of a box for dinner in smelly pajamas. She obsessed over the cold, unslept-in side of the bed and winced at the night-time sounds her house made. Her life looked isolated. Empty.

Almost four years before, when our youngest daughter started high school, Mark and I sort-of-joked/sort-of-fantasized about becoming empty nesters. I imagined that the pending quiet in our kid-less house would give way to falling in love, again, like the other times that followed major shifts in our marriage. Our romantic life was a partnership of discovery and reinvention, but most often executed behind the walls of our home. Time together was sacred. We promised. This was a second marriage for both of us, the one we chose consciously, as fully formed adults. I wanted to spin a cocoon around us and share long mornings in bed to commemorate the next chapter of our lives, not live in separate houses. I expected empty nester love jail, not solitary confinement.

These were the sorts of things I told myself in the days that followed Mark's Puerto Rico proposal. Sometimes I conjured explanations for his behavior that prompted empathy, but other times I hit replay on line after line of woeful lamenting that painted me as the loving spouse and him as the selfish husband. These thoughts stitched my nauseated guts together with threads of dread. I felt helpless and needy. And then, *pathetic*. In an instant I had become one of those tragic women I despised in my youth, the kind that seemed unmoored without a man around. My distress commingled with shame over the weakness and disappointment I embodied.

The night Mark confessed to his Act 20 & 22 hopes, the wine burned my throat. He seemed determined, focused on growing his bank account and unfazed by the possibility of a long-distance marriage. He was in legal mode, building a case for a future I couldn't fathom. Did he trust in our marriage more, or care about it less?

"I don't like it," I said after Mark explained his plan. "Who cares about money if we're living a miserable life apart?"

"I think you're being a little dramatic, George." Mark took a slow drink of his wine and looked away.

Heat from my face had traveled down my neck and filled my body.

"*I* think I'm being realistic," I countered.

"I'm not asking you to sign on the dotted line this minute, but I would like you to at least consider what I've shared." Mark started to say more but stopped himself. "Just think about it," he said finally, his voice tight and controlled.

I paused, knowing that we were headed for a doozy of a fight.

"Okay." I took a breath. "Okay. I'll think about it."

Risk-taking had grown less appealing for me with age. Teeth-rattling roller coasters were a thing of the past, and visions of shadowy figures looming around my bedroom ceiling long gone. Since geographic distance strained marriages and family relationships, I preferred to pass on this ride. If I worked in California, I'd miss my husband, and if I spent my vacations with my husband, I'd miss my daughters. The equation made me long for a simple, uncomplicated year, but instead I heard the eerie clacking of rickety tracks beneath wheels.

CHAPTER 3:

CONDITIONS

"I want to be clear," I said. "I am only agreeing to your Puerto Rico plan for a single year." I tried to say the words with calm but my voice cracked. I tapped my fingers on the table in rapid succession and felt a small vibration on my skin that corresponded to the pounding against my ribcage.

"Understood," Mark replied. "One year is all I need."

"I hope you're right," I said. My fingers stopped tapping but my heart still raced.

How do married couples navigate a chasm of disagreement, wherein one spouse wants to move to Puerto Rico and the other doesn't want them to go? For us, the process involved yellow legal pads with pro and con lists, tension-filled morning walks where silence replaced hand holding, and conversations about short-term sacrifices for long-term gains.

We were sitting at the kitchen table, the same place I first learned of Mark's Act 20 & 22 plan, when I outlined my conditions for support.

"It's important to me that all four daughters visit whenever they want," I continued. "Not a one can afford the airfare, so that extra cost is on us."

I glanced around my kitchen. Pricey stemware gleamed from a high shelf and I thought of all the chipped cups that had lined my childhood kitchen cupboards.

"Agreed."

"And finally," I looked directly into my husband's eyes. "No matter what, I don't want to sell the house. This is our forever home."

Mark gave me a smile of understanding and took my hand in his. "Okay," he said, his voice like expensive velvet.

The house was important to me for many reasons, but the biggest were sentimental. And therefore, impractical. My whole life, I'd never lived in a house as long as I'd lived in this one: ten years. I knew that Mark was right, that the feeling of home wasn't just a place, but the nostalgia of our current home on River Acres Drive conjured images of working in the garden with my daughters, memories of Easter egg hunts, and family swims in the Sacramento River, the banks upon which our house sat. I had a long way to go before retirement and if I had to be in Sacramento—especially without my husband—I wanted to do so living within the walls of my beloved home.

Houses were a touchy subject in my marriage. This was our third home but the only one that didn't symbolize failure. Our first attempt to live together was a disaster. The Perkins Way house was charming but way too small for six people. It was a rental I had snapped up while getting divorced from my daughters' father. The Perkins Way house was old and rickety but sat in a charming neighborhood called Land Park. It was close to the girls' school and made sense for the three of us but felt like a cage once Mark moved in with his two daughters. Built in the 1940s, there was no closet space, the kitchen was the size of a postage stamp, and single-pane windows left you to freeze in the winter. Still, location, location, location, so we had decided to give it a try thirteen years ago when we first moved in together.

Mark and I had made the mistake of thinking "cozy" was a perfect way to start our life of cohabitation. We knew it was tight living quarters, but we were in love! Big mistake. We soon learned that blending families required more space, not less. This was the first serious relationship for both of us since splitting from our first spouses, and we needed entire rooms for our divorcee emotional baggage alone.

Before Mark and I first moved in together, one of my divorced friends gave me a warning. We had met for coffee and she responded to my big news—that Mark and I wanted to cohabitate—with concern.

"Don't agree to live together unless you have a space that works for everyone," she said. "The odds are stacked against stepparents—something like 70 percent of blended families end in divorce. My advice is to slow down. This family merger will throw all sorts of curveballs at you."

Did I listen? No way. It was intoxicating to be in love after a painful, lonely marriage, and a subsequently awful divorce. I should have proceeded with greater caution; fast-paced, passion-filled decision-making was a surefire way to torpedo your future with potential husband number two.

When I started having sex with Mark, I literally lost my mind. Like a starving woman invited to feast at an exquisite buffet, I spent many sleepless nights stuffing my face. Some days I couldn't think about anything else except his hands on my skin, the warm honey in his voice, and the taste of his mouth. It's one thing to fall in love at twenty and another thing entirely at almost forty. The force with which I fell in love as a grown-up person was exponentially stronger and required better guardrails than I initially erected. Not surprisingly, we stumbled a few times on our way to the altar.

The second house resulted from our first living together failure. After moving out of the Perkins Way house, Mark bought his own house a few miles down the road on Derrick Way. Since he made this decision during our brief Valentine's Day breakup, when we weren't speaking to each other, I dubbed this residency 123 Fuck You Way. After we reconciled and then married, my daughters and I let go of Perkins Way and moved into Mark's house on Derrick. I stopped with the nasty moniker, but this house never felt right either. Even with more space, the fact that Mark bought this house solo, immediately following a red-hot Valentine's Day fight—well, the house and I didn't really get along.

River Acres, in contrast, always felt like home. It wasn't my sad divorcee rental or my husband's I'll-show-you impulse purchase; it was unexpected and inspired by our love of baseball. After two years of marriage, driving to meet friends at a San Francisco Giants game, we started one of those couples conversations about where we might live when all the kids went to college and we transitioned into retirement. For us, the dream involved a second home on the California coast where I could write, Mark could play golf, and we could both enjoy the ocean. Maybe in Sea Ranch, Mendocino, or San Diego, we fantasized. As we drove in annoying bumper-to-bumper Bay Area traffic, our conversation took a left turn.

"Do you think we would actually spend time in a second home on the coast if it meant driving there in this mess?" I asked.

Cars inched along in bright sunshine. Angry-looking drivers avoided eye contact as they squeezed in front of one another, forcing entry into the crowded lanes, and further slowing the vehicles that followed.

"Doubtful," Mark agreed. "You know, there are beautiful places in Sacramento by the river. Maybe we should check out options?"

When we returned from our baseball game weekend, Mark showed me an online ad for a home that was within bike riding distance. At this time, we lived in the Derrick Way house (no longer referred to as 123 Fuck You Way) and were trudging through the muddy waters that constituted blending families. In a span of five years, our daughters had endured the divorce of their biological parents, been squeezed together in the Perkins Way house, watched me and Mark break up, get back together, get married, and then were reshuffled into the Derrick Way place. Everyone was tired.

Mark pulled our bikes out of the garage, put the address in his phone, and we rode along the Sacramento River until we arrived at River Acres. The large white house was beautiful and boasted a top-to-bottom remodel on the For Sale sign. Views of the river from the front deck were mesmerizing. Large windows on the second floor invited scenes of nature right into the living room. The property had once been a walnut orchard and old beautiful trees dotted the landscape. It wasn't the oceanfront fantasy we had talked about, but it was close, and owning it meant living in nature and by water. At long last, I had the man *and* the house of my dreams. *No more earthquakes*, I thought.

When we moved into the River Acres home, our family let out a collective sigh of relief. Finally, we had ample living space.

So, all these years later when Mark and I negotiated the finer points of his PR plan, more than a decade into our marriage, I knew the importance of proceeding with caution. The River Acres house was a sticking point but thoughtfulness around living spaces mattered in our marriage and ultimately Mark agreed that we could keep the River Acres house *and* take advantage of Act 20 & 22 in Puerto Rico. River Acres symbolized love and perseverance—it was our *family* home. Once he committed to stretching financially, I agreed to stretch geographically. It was marital yoga, the kind that forced us to twist into uncomfortable positions and made us sweat.

The morning of the kitchen-table talk, after Mark and I hammered out the PR plan details, I felt a mix of emotions. I was glad to be on the other side of the decision, but dreaded living apart from my husband. At the end of the conversation, I grabbed my car keys.

"I'm going to head over to my mom's," I said. "I won't be gone long. She needs me to help her get some crafting boxes down from the rafters in the garage."

I felt grateful for the excuse to end the conversation. Mark's excitement over moving to Puerto Rico added to my nervousness.

"Give her my best," Mark said.

On the drive to my mom's house, I thought about all the work it took to reach our agreement—like training for a marathon—exhausting and invigorating at the same time. It hurt, but in a good way. The process of figuring out the we'll-try-it-for-one-year deal made us feel like a team. Inwardly, however, I struggled. I found myself worried in ways I hadn't been before. Mark's PR plan made me question who I had become.

"Hi there!" Mom greeted me when I opened the front door. Her little dogs, Maggie and Zoey, barked and bounced around my feet, wagging their tails.

I gave Mom a long hug and a kiss on the cheek. After a morning of negotiations with Mark, the comfort of Mom's arms made me weepy.

"Are you okay?" Mom asked once we separated.

"Mostly," I said. "There's something I need to tell you."

I walked into the kitchen and turned on the kettle for tea.

"You look like you did at seven when your hamster died. What's going on?"

Mom put her hands on her hips and gave me a curious look.

"Nobody has died, I'm happy to report. But Mark is moving to Puerto Rico for six months and I'm feeling . . . conflicted."

I told Mom the whole story—that Mark's class action case was likely to settle, the tax benefits of Act 20 & 22, the hours of marital wrangling I'd stomached, how much I didn't want to live alone, and that in the end, I had agreed.

"We haven't told the girls yet," I said. "I imagine they're going to be pretty upset."

We sat on the couch, warm mugs in our hands.

"I wouldn't be so sure," Mom replied. "Georgine, Olivia's your baby and she's almost eighteen. She's going to be away at college next year, and Abby, Raeanne, and Eden? They're off doing their own thing."

"You sound like my husband." I took a sip of tea and looked at Maggie and Zoey, who had both curled up on my mom's lap, a black-and-white bundle of Havanese fluff.

"I understand that this is going to be hard on you—I know how connected you are to Mark—but this opportunity sounds smart to me. It might be different if the girls were little, but they're not. You don't have children anymore; you have adult daughters. Be careful not to project your upset on them. Besides, all they want at their ages is the freedom to live their own lives."

Mom's freedom comment landed on me like a bee sting. *They still need guidance and support*, I thought. *Just because you were too busy partying when I was a teenager doesn't mean I didn't need you.*

"Even adult kids need their mom," I said. "Someone who'll rush to their side when there's an emergency. What if something terrible happens and I'm in Puerto Rico with Mark?"

"You'll call me for help and then jump on a plane. Sweetheart," Mom said, "you raised those girls to be self-sufficient. You've done the parenting work. And you and Mark are solid—you can get through a challenging six months. Take it from me, you might even enjoy living alone."

Mom smiled and tussled Zoey's ears.

"Maybe," I said.

"Life is short. Who knows what excitement awaits you and Mark in Puerto Rico? Don't pass up the chance at a little adventure."

"Thanks, Mom," I said. "I really do appreciate your optimism."

"Plus, with Mark out of town, we'll have an excuse to go out and cause some trouble."

I shot her an accusatory glance.

"Don't worry! I do the Uber now. I got the app for my phone."

Mom feigned innocence and then looked at me with love. Her blue eyes sparkled.

"Okay," I laughed. "You got it. Now let's take care of the boxes in your garage before I head home."

As I drove back to River Acres, I considered living life as an adventure. They say that we're on a journey but omit that the traveler of said roads morphs into completely different versions of herself along the way. Life doesn't change, we do. Life just is. I was wild in my teens and twenties. I believed I was invincible and controlled my own destiny. I was certain, stubborn, and full of bravado. I was also angry. After my mother kicked me out of the house for the final time at seventeen, I felt abandoned and didn't think I owed anyone anything.

When I considered this version of me, the one that existed during my teens and twenties, I felt ambivalent. All that willfulness gave me a zest for life, a sort of vibrancy that was alive and juicy, but those memories also left me feeling embarrassed. At those ages I was self-centered. I drank heavily. And I had a drug problem.

When I was a kid, I watched a cartoon that characterized the duality of one's conscience. The portrayal showed up as both angel and devil, perched on each of Fred Flintstone's shoulders, debating yet-to-be-made choices and giving advice. Naughty options were dispensed from the little man holding the pitchfork, while sweet obedience flowed from the mouth of a halo-wearing winged figure. The poor choices I made when it came to sex, drugs, and employment in my youth had left me with deep-seated shame in adulthood.

When I got serious about college and decided to exercise restraint around men and substances, a make-believe character landed on my shoulder, just like Mr. Flintstone's. She was the personification of my early adult conscience, the me that was trying to grow up. She wasn't heavenly, or hellish, just clear and careful. I imagined her as a tiny crossing guard, ready to take over decision-making when life got messy. She wore a pressed blue uniform under a bright neon vest. Her work boots were black and shiny. She carried a stop sign in her hand and a whistle around her neck. She made sure that my life moved forward in a safe and orderly fashion.

By the time I was twenty-nine, married to my first husband, working as a tenure-track college professor, and pregnant with my first child, my crossing guard blew her whistle and directed my life's activities by pointing in easy-to-see directions. Even when I got divorced in my mid-thirties, and became a single mom with two young children, my crossing guard kept me moving along.

After marrying Mark, tired narratives of single-parent suffering and scarcity were replaced by the chronicles of blending families. My crossing guard still kept watch, but the nature of my need for her counsel lessened.

But once Mark was accepted into the Puerto Rico tax program and we had negotiated the details, I couldn't seem to stop the internal hand-wringing. I didn't give my complaints airtime—at least not much—yet inside I was a hamster who couldn't get off the anxiety wheel. I told myself to stop acting like a spoiled child. Wasn't safeguarding our economic future also a way to fight for our marriage and our family? Wasn't I the kind of wife who trusted and supported my husband? Wasn't the foundation of our marriage and family solid? I sifted through the dichotomous layers of internal choice and tried to rationalize my way to acceptance, but below the surface of my PR plan agreement, a fear of change remained.

The 6.4 magnitude earthquake that threw me out of bed in the middle of the night happened on our first trip to the island. While that night rattled my confidence in Mark's PR relocation plan, it wasn't the only experience that shocked me to my core. During this time period—when Mark and I were making arrangements for his relocation to PR—I went to visit my high school home, the same home from which I was banished by my mom at seventeen. If the earthquake rattled my sense of safety, seeing this house again sliced into scar tissue that covered an old ugly wound.

CHAPTER 4:

SECRETS

In the midst of our PR relocation negotiations, I enrolled in a writing workshop where the instructor discussed the topic of memory. "If you are struggling to access a memory, old photos, music, and letters from that time may help unlock what's been lost or repressed," she said.

I was working on a story that investigated my tumultuous high school relationship with my mother, and I was struggling to get it right. I didn't have old photos of us from that time, but I knew the name of the street we lived on. Maybe if I saw that house, the memories would shake loose? Mark agreed to join me for the drive and we headed toward a small town about an hour from our River Acres home in Sacramento.

"Slow down, this looks familiar," I said to Mark, scanning the residential street in Roseville, California, where I once lived. The late afternoon sun had softened as dusk inched closer. "Okay. Stop here. This is it."

The house was familiar yet strange and a wave of nostalgia washed over me. More than thirty years had passed since I had laid eyes on Sierra Gardens, the modest rental I lived in during high school. The last time I saw the little house was the night I left for good after a blowout fight with my mother. I was seventeen, angry, ill-prepared, and determined to make it on my own.

"It's held up," Mark said innocently. "It's small but kind of sweet looking."

The single-story house had received a creamy coat of light peach paint and was brightened by daisies that bulged out of a reconfigured wine barrel near the front door.

Mark pulled the car closer to the curb and turned it off. He put his hand on my shoulder, knowing a few stories I'd told him about this place, but not knowing all of the details. Entranced, I stared out the window.

"It looks better than I remember." My hands fidgeted. I rubbed the bed of each nail, pushing back its cuticle.

When I was growing up here between the ages of fourteen and seventeen, Sierra Gardens sported yellow, stained peeling paint and spikes of dead grass in the front yard. The bottom of the garage door was black with rot because the creek behind the house flooded its banks in heavy rain, and the landlord never fixed it. The updated version I saw from my car window was a big improvement. The garage door looked new, and the place seemed cared for. The house mirrored my life—the me then, and now.

"They finally got AC," I said, pointing to the shiny box on the roof. "When I lived in the house, I'd crawl out of bed in the middle of the night and sleep in the hallway to stay cool. We had a swamp cooler, but it only blew cold air down the hall."

Remembering my teenage self, who looked for relief from the summer heat, was dreamlike. I could hear the whir of the swamp cooler and feel the drips of condensation that landed on my bare feet during those hot summer nights. I could smell the mossy creek that ran behind the fence in the backyard and see the ugly mustard paint on the bathroom wall.

"How does it feel to be back after all these years?" Mark asked.

I tried to find words as my stomach twisted. "Weird. Like a gate just got unlocked in my mind, and things I haven't thought about in ages happened as if it were yesterday."

I remembered that next to the kitchen sink, there was a long galley counter where my cat, Sophie, would jump up and eat scraps of food. My mind flashed to the long line of bloody paw prints she left after devouring a pound of raw hamburger meat my mom defrosted one night for dinner. She had licked her pink paws incessantly for a week afterward until they turned back to their snowy white state.

"Where does that door go to?" Mark asked, pointing to a side entrance on the house.

It was smaller than the front door, positioned to the right of the main entryway. The sight of the door caused a large boulder to form in my stomach. I suddenly felt sick and my shoulders grew tense.

"An in-law unit. My mom rented the house and sublet the in-law unit."

Mark must have sensed my discomfort, because he took my hand while I kept staring at the little door. He sat by my side in silence while more memories arose.

* * *

My mom was thrilled when she found the Sierra Gardens house to rent for our little family—my mom, my brother, and me.

"We couldn't normally afford a place this nice," she told me, "but since I can rent out the in-law unit, I can make it work." The Sierra Gardens house had a small, self-contained studio adjacent to the main house. The owner had built it for his mother to live in during the last years of her life.

Mom gave me a big hug. The year was 1983 and I had just started attending a new private high school on a scholarship. Sierra Gardens, she told me, was more proof that our life was looking up.

"You and your brother will make friends here and I already have our first tenant!"

Our first tenant was Sharon. My mom and Sharon were work friends. They waitressed together at the Carrows coffee shop up the street. My mom, my brother, and I lived in the main house, and Sharon lived in the studio. This arrangement worked well until Sharon decided to move out and my mom had to find another renter to sublet the space. His name was Pat.

Pat told us that he worked in construction. He was tall and had sandy blond hair that framed a long, tan face. His muscled arms stretched the openings of his T-shirt sleeves, and I couldn't help but notice how much stronger his body looked than the bodies of the boys at my high school. Pat always wore the same thing—Nike sneakers, 501 blue jeans, a T-shirt, and a baseball cap pulled tight over his bushy hair. He was quiet and mostly kept to himself, but his girlfriend Kelly would visit him often, and she and I had started to become friends. When Pat and Kelly wanted a change of scenery, or were feeling cooped up in the studio, they would knock on the door to the main house and I'd invite them in to watch TV. Sometimes we'd visit while I made dinner or took a break from doing homework. I was sixteen and since my mom worked most evenings, I appreciated the company while I babysat my little brother. Even though Pat and Kelly were both in their late twenties and I was in high school, they treated me like their friend, like someone their age. They'd talk about their jobs and the cool bars where they'd meet their besties for happy hour. They made me yearn for my twenty-first birthday.

One night when Pat knocked on my door, he was by himself. I looked around behind him and asked, "Where's Kelly?"

"Out drinking with girlfriends. What are you doing?" His clothes were dusty and I suspected he'd only just returned from work.

"Just watching TV. Come on in." Sometimes he visited me when I was there alone, but usually my brother was there too. Tonight, my brother was at a friend's house and I was waiting for my mom to get home from her work shift.

The Cosby Show was on and I had finished my homework.

"Cute pj's," Pat joked as we sat down on the couch. Pat had never seen me in pajamas before.

I felt my face turn red and wished I had picked out something different to wear after my shower. The Snoopy nightshirt I'd selected was my favorite, but in front of Pat, I felt embarrassed by my childish taste. I reached over, grabbed a throw blanket that was slung across the arm of the couch, and pulled it over my lap. Just as I was arranging it to cover the Snoopy decal on my chest, Pat's face was next to me, and suddenly he was too close, and kissing me.

What the hell is happening? His kiss was so unexpected that for a second, I thought I was imagining it.

Pushing away from him on the couch, I said, "Pat, you shouldn't do that. I have a boyfriend. Danny. And you have Kelly. She's my friend."

"That's why we can't tell them." He smiled and moved in to kiss me again, but I turned my face away from his mouth.

"I don't want to cheat on my boyfriend. Or on Kelly."

My body tensed up and my heart beat fast. Fear coursed through me.

I saw Pat was not listening to me, just staring at my chest and moving closer. That made it difficult for me to think or talk, but I managed to move away and say, "Pat, you need to stop kissing me."

"Come on, I know you have a crush on me." He grabbed my wrists, pulled my arms over my head, and used his full weight to press me down on the couch.

I begged, "Pat, stop. Please, stop!" I struggled under him, but he was too heavy.

Pat frantically tried to kiss my mouth, moving his lips all over my face and neck as his body pressed harder against me.

No, he couldn't, surely he . . . I started to cry. I couldn't escape the full weight of his body pressing into me and the strength of his hands around my wrists. My cotton nightgown slid up until it was a belt around my waist. I squirmed under his muscled frame. I could hardly breathe and had to try to escape.

"I don't want to do this," I pleaded.

The side of my face mashed into the woven fabric of the couch. Pat's shaggy hair was caught between us, scratching my other cheek. His eager breath smelled sour and his T-shirt reeked of dirt and sweat. My eyes burned with tears as I stared into the place where the back of the sofa met the seat cushions, a dark line of space that offered escape.

I cried out—maybe someone would hear me—but it was useless. It was surreal, what he was doing. I couldn't believe it even while it was happening.

"Shhhh, Georgine," he tried to quiet me. "Shhhh . . ."

Some part of me wanted to scream, but instead I lay there, my body frozen, my voice choked with tears as he raped me. I felt hollow, a paralyzed shell of nothing. I imagined climbing out of my body and into the couch, into the safety of the cushions, the crevasses, the dark places inside the sofa where I could hide, where nobody would find me.

Finally, Pat pushed himself off me and stood up, buttoning his jeans. He picked up the baseball hat that had fallen to the ground and secured it with a satisfied tug.

"Since you have a boyfriend and I have a girlfriend, I think you already know we shouldn't tell anybody about us."

I heard Pat's words, but I was empty. I had nothing to say. I pulled the blanket back up over my body and turned away from him, curled into a ball.

"People make mistakes," he said, standing above me. "But let's not burden Danny and Kelly with ours."

After he left, I rubbed my face on the couch cushions to dry my tears. Then I walked into the kitchen and opened the cupboard where my mom kept the liquor. I grabbed the vodka, unscrewed the top, and took a long drink. The fiery liquid burned my throat, causing me to cry just a little. I took another drink. And a final swig for good measure. I added an inch of water to the bottle from the sink, carefully put it back in its spot, and quietly went to bed before my mother ever got home.

* * *

Two days later there was a knock on the door. When I opened it, Pat and Kelly were standing on the other side. My eyes grew wide and wild horses stampeded right through me. I was stunned, caught between an impulse to run or to freeze.

"We have something to tell you," Kelly said, walking inside without being invited. Then Pat walked right past me, behind his girlfriend, and into my house.

Pat and Kelly sat next to each other on the brown couch. My face felt warm and my throat, constricted. My guts twisted around the shards of glass still digesting in my stomach from Pat's last visit. Why would he come back over after what happened? What did Pat tell Kelly? What was Kelly going to accuse me of?

I stood in the kitchen, my arms folded tight across my chest. I was terrified of what was about to happen, of what I'd be forced to say out loud, of needing to defend myself. I took a deep breath, wishing that my heart would slow down, and prepared to tell Kelly the truth—that Pat was a liar and that he forced himself on me.

"We're engaged!" Kelly cheered, raising her left hand to show off a diamond ring.

"What?" I didn't understand.

Kelly grinned and babbled on. "It just happened. Pat took me to Strings for dinner and ordered champagne with dessert. When I looked at my glass, the ring was inside. I said yes before he could even ask! I couldn't wait to tell you—we're getting married!"

Pat was silent but Kelly's voice exploded with excitement. She chattered about wedding plans as I floated away, nodding but not listening. I stared at the black couch line where I had tried to take refuge until Kelly's voice faded from my ears. I became weightless and turned into air, nothing more than a whisper. I floated across the room and vanished inside the sofa cracks. My body was standing in the kitchen, but the real me, my essence, was alone in the dark behind the sofa cushions.

Right before I disappeared, I almost told Kelly that Pat was a terrible man, but I couldn't find the words in my ghostly state. Feeling the threat of Pat's eyes on me, I stayed hidden, traveling further away. I wasn't sure how long they stayed, Kelly's voice talking nonstop, but after they left, I went straight to bed, curled into a tiny ball, and hid under my blankets. Fading into unconsciousness, I dreamed of Pat's violence taking shape in my bowels, angry pustules attaching to my intestinal membranes.

The next night, I waited up for my mom to get home from work.

"Hey, Mom," I began. I was sitting at the kitchen table, pretending to read a book. I hoped I could convince her to find a different renter for the in-law unit.

"Hmmmm."

I sounded uncertain, distracted. "Pat has been making me feel a little uncomfortable lately."

My mom pulled a wine glass from the cupboard and reached for the half-empty bottle of red on the counter.

"He's such a sweet guy. Just a little shy. Sorry he made you feel uncomfortable, but it doesn't matter."

I looked down at my book. I wanted to tell her that she had no idea what she was talking about, that she had no idea what kind of man Pat was, but I wanted my privacy more.

"He called me this morning to say he's moving out," she continued. "He and Kelly are getting married. They already found a place that works better for the two of them."

I pretended to read, silent, until my mom picked up her wine and left the room.

* * *

Now, sitting in the car with Mark, staring at the Sierra Gardens house and the door to Pat's studio, the old wounds reanimated in my gut. The shame I'd experienced at sixteen was morphing into something new—anger. It stabbed at old intestinal scars, the place in my body where secrets were hidden. Why hadn't I called the police? Why hadn't I told my mom, or a friend, or someone, what had happened? Why did I protect Pat with my silence?

My sixteen-year-old self had felt ruined and alone. She worried no one would believe her and she was so full of disgrace that keeping the secret seemed her only choice. But my fifty-year-old self, the one who sat in the car with her husband, felt white-hot fury.

I was outraged at my mother for trusting this man around her sixteen-year-old daughter and livid with my voiceless young self. How could I have been so stupid? So afraid? So weak? At sixteen I knew that what Pat did to me was wrong. He was a grown man, at least ten years older than me. If I had called the police that night, maybe this secret wouldn't have stayed lodged in my guts for almost forty years. Maybe I could have protected other victims.

"Let's go," I said to Mark. "A lot of bad stuff happened in that house. I don't want to look at it anymore."

As we drove away, my hands instinctively massaged my stomach, moving the sickness through my innards like bad food. I needed it out of me.

* * *

The next morning, I told Mark I wanted to talk about what I had seen sitting in front of the Sierra Gardens house. He grabbed us coffee, and then sat next to me at the kitchen table, ready to listen. I took a breath and told Mark about Pat and what had happened to me in that house. I had to stop and start, and sip some coffee, but Mark's eyes told me to keep going. He squeezed my hand.

"I still don't understand why Pat came over the night he got engaged," I said. "Was he trying to make sure I would keep his secret? Was he crafting a narrative to discredit me in case I told on him later? Or did he take some kind of twisted pleasure in seeing my fear?"

"I don't know," Mark said.

I could see the sorrow in his eyes, and I knew I didn't have to be alone with my shame any longer.

He put his arm around me. "But I feel terrible that this happened to you. I'm so sorry, George."

"I felt completely powerless and ashamed and just shoved the secret down deep. I told myself to forget it happened.

Honestly, I can't remember the last time I thought about that night. I'm not sure I would have if I hadn't seen the door to the in-law unit."

I looked down into my coffee cup, rage rising in my chest. "I should have never opened the door in my nightshirt or invited him into my house with nobody else home."

I stopped talking, but the internal scolding continued: *I should have slapped him when he first kissed me. I should have screamed. I should have threatened to call the police when he didn't stop. I should have fought harder when he forced himself on top of me. I should have told someone. I should have done* something.

"What happened that night wasn't your fault, George." Mark put a gentle hand on my forearm and looked at me. "I need you to hear me."

My eyes filled with tears.

"I know, but there was so much more I should have done to prevent it and afterward, to make sure it didn't happen to someone else. I'm so disappointed in myself. I don't know exactly why I kept it a secret."

"Maybe that's just how secrets work," he said. "They stay hidden, and keep us trapped, until they find a way to come out. I hope you'll talk to a professional about this. It worries me to hear what happened to you followed by all the anger you feel at yourself. You're the victim here."

"I will talk to someone. Promise."

Over the next few weeks, the Sierra Gardens house hung around. It hovered in the back of my mind when I drove to work and made dinner. It prompted conversations with Mark about my past and the feelings I processed with a therapist. The conversations helped. They were healing and they deepened the bond in our marriage.

Had I been trapped by this secret? It didn't feel that way. It felt more like carrying around an illness that I didn't know existed. It was a blister that formed deep inside me, under my skin, in the lining of my intestines, and I didn't know it was there until it popped and the poison oozed into my bloodstream. What I did know is that I wanted to detox from its effects, to expel the hazardous bacteria from my body along with the anger and the shame. I wanted to give the sixteen-year-old me a voice.

CHAPTER 5:

FRIENDS

After the visit to Sierra Gardens and accompanying painful memories about Pat, I kept myself busy by helping Mark prepare for his move to Puerto Rico. I had arranged to fly out and help him get settled in his new apartment. My plan was to stay a few days, give my best show of support, then head back to work in Sacramento.

I also kept myself intentionally distracted. I graded student papers, listened to podcasts, and stared out the windows of River Acres watching the wildlife. The scenes of nature soothed me. Birds soared above the Sacramento River and foxes darted along the river trail at dawn. I watched squirrels from my kitchen window as they jumped great distances from one tree branch to another, their bushy brown tails like the sail of a boat. These little gymnasts dazzled as they flew through the sky and raced each other up and down the crusty bark of old walnut trees in my front yard. (They also ate patio furniture and decimated vegetable gardens, hiding nuts in all sorts of inconvenient places like car engines and Lucy's dog bed.)

Once Mark and I landed in Puerto Rico, I swapped neighborhood squirrel surveillance for iguana watching. Like squirrels, iguanas were as entertaining as they were destructive. I learned that green iguanas were native to Central and South America but invasive to Puerto Rico. They were introduced to the island through the pet trade in the 1970s, lived up to twenty years, and grew as large as six feet long. The color of the young iguanas amazed me, an emerald to rival jewels on royal fingers. They were social creatures and spread out like giant living paper fans across the grassy fields Mark and I walked each morning. I learned that iguanas were fearful of humans and ran at high speeds, their back legs transforming into miniature Hot Wheels, to swim in a pond or run up a coconut tree when they felt threatened. Despite their prehistoric charm and gentle vegetarian ways, they were considered an island pest. They dug burrows where homeowners wished they wouldn't. I'd even seen them hunted with air guns in my new neighborhood.

Time spent in nature helped me heal from the Pat memories and lessened my longings for home—that and the fact that Mark and I lived under the same roof. After months of fretting over living at a distance from my husband, the pandemic changed our circumstances and our lives in unexpected ways. Six weeks post-earthquake in Condado, the planet was reeling from COVID-19. Panic ignited as news reports detailed rising death tolls and medical facility chaos, first in China and then Italy. Drastic containment measures and the need for vaccine research dominated the global conversation. We developed a newfound appreciation for ventilators, hand sanitizer, and most importantly, health care workers.

In the midst of tragedy, our relocation decision had simplified. In mid-February 2020, I was in the middle of giving a lecture when my students were distracted by an emergency alert on their phones. My college campus had enacted a lockdown and we were all instructed to leave as soon as possible. Just like that, my teaching job turned remote. I didn't know how long my 100 percent online teaching assignment would last, but at least for now, I could go with Mark to Puerto Rico.

After all the apprehension and tussle about a long-distance marriage, after endless conversations that weighed opportunity and sacrifice, our circumstances changed overnight. Even though I thought I had evaluated every potentiality, I hadn't. As the sages proclaimed, control is illusory. "Humans plan and God laughs," goes one proverb, and apparently the universe believed humanity needed reminding.

We locked up our California home and moved to Dorado, Puerto Rico, a beach town west of San Juan that attracted other stateside transplants. It had a decent grocery store and none of the traffic or chaos that defined the large city of San Juan.

Mark was thrilled. If we were going to be socially distanced from our family, friends, and colleagues, why not do it together as members of the Act 20 & 22 society in Puerto Rico? Taking advantage of the tax savings granted to Act members made even more sense. Despite my concerns about pandemic travel and limited access to health care, this turn of events quieted private anguish that had lingered over Mark's PR plan. I still didn't love the idea of relocation, but instead of feeling trapped inside a hornet's nest, I was down to nursing a few stings.

One day, when Mark and I followed a creeping baby iguana like curious children, we rounded a corner and bumped into someone unfamiliar. She was dressed in black yoga pants and talking to a security guard. A blonde ponytail bounced from the back of her baseball cap.

"I'm Deborah," she said as we entered the security gate. Her voice was like her ponytail—full of pep. The woman offered us a maskless smile. "We're obviously neighbors."

I suddenly felt strange, maybe even a little scared of catching COVID. This was the first person, other than masked grocery store clerks or car rental agents, most of whom we were separated from by plexiglass, that we had met since moving to the island. I realized that I hadn't had a face-to-face conversation with someone other than my husband in months.

"Hi. I'm Mark and this is my wife, Georgine," my husband replied. The employee Deborah was talking to quietly faded back into the guard station at the entrance to our community.

"I just moved here," she said. "Isn't it amazing?"

Deborah raised her arms above her head, palms open wide, and performed an animated intake of our surroundings. It was beautiful. Wild parrots chirped in the tall palms above, their fronds swaying in the breeze, and bright red flowers floated to the ground from a flame tree nearby. Then my concerns over safety began to pick a fight with mild excitement. My Spanish was poor and pandemic isolation prohibited socializing. Deborah was my age and the thought of having a friend in the community made me a little giddy.

"I rented my place over FaceTime," she continued. "All the realtor had to do was walk onto my patio. I saw that ocean view and was sold! I moved here from San Diego. Both my kids are in college and I'm working on a screenplay, a sort of *National Treasure* meets *Indiana Jones*."

We were discussing our "what brings us to Puerto Rico" stories when Mark mentioned his membership in Act 20 & 22.

"Hey!" Deborah interrupted. "Are you guys part of the crypto community? I just got mine!"

Deborah pulled a small wallet from her pocket and removed a black plastic Bitcoin credit card.

"I'm here in Puerto Rico thanks to Bitcoin and I'm dying to meet Brock Pierce. He's on the island right now!"

Was this friendly Californian a cryptocurrency aficionado? Had she really financed her oceanfront Caribbean lifestyle with Bitcoin investments? The topic of cryptocurrency was thought-provoking, but outside my area of expertise. Like most people, I knew that crypto was a form of digital currency, considered riskier than US currency, and that when the topic showed up in the news, it was often linked to scandals since bad guys used crypto to purchase illegal goods on the dark web.

"We're not involved in the crypto community here, but we're definitely interested," Mark said. "Indirectly, it's macroeconomists I follow that brought us here. There are multiple investment guys I've been reading for years, and a while back I noticed they all have addresses in Puerto Rico. As you can imagine, one of the things often discussed is the growing strength in the crypto markets."

There it was again. Money. What was it about this topic that made ordinary people ignite like fireworks? We all needed it to survive, I got that, but for some people, like my husband, the topic was intoxicating. I once asked Mark why he specialized in large class action lawsuits. Just like crypto, they were loaded with financial risk.

"I just want to see if I can do it," Mark had responded.

Even though the potential payoff was big, these cases were expensive and precarious. Mark had invested hundreds of thousands of dollars in experts, court filings, and staff. He knew that for any given case a bad verdict meant a major loss since litigators got paid a percentage of their clients' settlement, not a retainer.

When I had suggested that a few more, slightly less expensive cases produced similar financial results with less monetary risk, he smiled.

"Of course," he had said. "But then there's no excitement. Besides, I hate the law. I don't want to work more; I just want to work smarter."

Deborah nodded agreement with Mark. "The crypto markets are on fire right now," she said, and explained that her interest in Bitcoin had lured her to Puerto Rico.

"I've been listening to crypto podcasts religiously for the last year," she confessed. "I hope to get connected to the local crypto events. I plan to join the PR crypto community, and I've got an appointment to get vetted tomorrow."

Deborah's excitement mirrored that of a teenager going to her first concert.

"Do you guys want to come with me?" she asked.

CHAPTER 6:

VETTED

We picked up Deborah in front of her villa and began the drive from Dorado to San Juan. The kind of conversation we had—where we grew up, what we did for a living, our impressions of Puerto Rico—might have seemed banal a year earlier, but not then. I felt a twinge of excitement over human interaction that resembled a pre-pandemic life.

I asked Deb to tell me more about her screenplay.

"I want to create a versatile product," she said. "So that my audience will be able to access my production as a movie or a series. One of the more unusual things I'm hoping to accomplish is to pay my actors with Bitcoin."

"Is your family involved in the crypto community?" I asked.

"Oh God no," Deborah answered. "I'm originally from Dayton, Ohio. My dad lives in Florida now, but he's a real estate developer. Probably owns more than six hundred properties. Anyway, I've tried to get him interested, but he says he's too old at eighty-eight."

Deborah was in her fifties. I was curious about how a middle-aged, single woman from California got into Bitcoin. When I asked, she explained that friends got her involved and that her only regret was that she hadn't bought Bitcoin sooner.

"People who got in on the ground floor have made billions. Bitcoin just crossed over the $20,000 mark—that's twenty grand for a single coin."

Deborah pointed to a restaurant through the car window.

"There it is," she said. "That's where we're meeting Julio. It looks like there might be parking in the back."

We found the outdoor café that Julio, Deborah's crypto community contact, chose, in spite of signage-free streets.

"Good eye, Deborah," I said. "There are no addresses anywhere."

After Hurricane Maria pounded the island in 2017, things like street signs and power lines continued to need repair.

This meeting with Julio, which preceded Crypto Tuesday, would determine future invites and community access. I was ambivalent about Crypto Tuesday attendance, but the thought of getting out of the house more regularly sounded great. If learning about crypto was going to improve my social life, I was ready to sign up.

We ordered drinks from a woman behind a window and then found a table. Soon, we were joined by Julio and Lana. Julio wore classic Puerto Rican features, dark eyes and hair, except he was built like a retired NBA player, towering over his petite date. Julio was probably ten years younger than me and dressed in a stylish button-down shirt.

We introduced ourselves and then Julio offered us some background information.

"My role in this community is to connect people and guide our community in ways that help Puerto Rico and the world," Julio said. "There is a lot of money in our group, but we are also about service and philanthropy. Right now, I am organizing the biggest toy drive this island has ever seen."

"You'll make this year's pandemic Christmas happier for lots of children," I said, admiring his pitch.

"I will," Julio agreed. "But know that toy drives are just a small example of how we help the Puerto Rican people."

"What other kinds of projects are you working on?" Deb asked, then added, "I think making a movie is a great way to create jobs and support the local economy."

"Of course," Julio said.

It was obvious that this wasn't the first time Deborah had pitched Julio on her *Indiana Jones*-meets-*National Treasure* movie idea.

"You reached out to the contact I emailed you, right?" Julio asked, and Deb nodded.

"This community is developing a makerspace designed to empower the locals," Julio continued. "We need to share what we know with the Puerto Rican people. The need for energy and food sovereignty is great. This island is beautiful, and it attracts successful people like all of you, but the local people are suffering. They don't receive the same benefits that draw stateside transplants."

"We are poor," Lana added. Her voice was soft and her eyes were large and bright. She seemed painfully shy in comparison to her extroverted partner.

"People on this island need more opportunity and it's not going to come from the government," Julio said. "Even though I take heat for fraternizing with the colonizers, I think people in this crypto space are the island's best hope."

I looked across the street at a graffiti-filled wall. The message "Yankee, go home!" was among the images, a repeat of what I'd seen on other buildings throughout San Juan. I knew that I was one of the colonizers Julio was talking about and his reference made me feel self-conscious.

Before coming to the island, I'd read books about Puerto Rican history that were filled with brutality. This was one reason that oppression and colonization continued as a common topic of conversation.

In the 1400s, the island's native Taino people endured brutal conflicts with the Carib, a raiding tribe in the Caribbean. In 1493 Christopher Columbus arrived and oppression continued at the hands of the Spanish. Other European nations fought unsuccessfully to wrestle control of the island away from Spain, all while the Indigenous people continued to be enslaved. With the Spanish-American War in 1898, the island came under military control of the United States. For many generations, Puerto Ricans had endured adversity and longed for independence. Julio's acknowledgment of power dynamics and inequality were prominent in history books as well as contemporary street art.

"Speaking of hope," Julio said, "I just had another daughter!" He was jubilant and immediately started scrolling for pictures to share from his phone.

Lana looked down at her hands, which were crossed on top of the table. She seemed uncomfortable.

"She's gorgeous," I said, gazing at the chubby-cheeked infant on the screen. "What a beautiful smile. Congratulations to both of you!"

"All that curly hair is adorable," Deborah added.

"She's at home with her mama," Julio said.

My confusion showed because he continued, "Some people might think it's weird, but Lana and I are in a polyamorous relationship and it's our other partner who just had the baby."

Lana kept looking at her hands.

"So, what can I tell you about crypto?" Julio asked, breaking the silence.

"This is all new to us," I said. "We're eager learners, but don't know much about cryptocurrency."

"Our experience is in traditional finance," Mark said. "Let's start big picture. What are the primary crypto investing categories?" he asked.

Julio launched into a rapid-fire explanation of Bitcoin, altcoins, and what he called "shit coins." He shared development narratives for cryptocurrencies named Polkadot and Tether and made utilization predictions for stablecoins and Ethereum.

I understood basic economic concepts, but Julio's machine-gun stream of crypto words left me dazed. I wondered if learning about different cryptocurrencies was like learning about stocks. Were cryptocurrencies like company IPOs? Or was a crypto coin more like art, simply valuable for aesthetic or other qualities? What was the function of a cryptocurrency? How did they come into existence? How did a person buy them? Questions tumbled like somersaults in my mind.

"When it comes to crypto," Mark asked, interrupting Julio's monologue, "what do you think the best three-to-five-year investment trends are?"

"Only one thing you gotta do," Julio said, looking directly at Mark. "Buy as much Bitcoin as you can."

I knew Julio's certainty would not comfort my husband, a man who studied economic theory for fun. Mark didn't travel anywhere without a book that had "crash" or "reset" in the title, what I called his end-of-the-world reading material. Over the years I'd come to appreciate his interest in economics. As a social scientist, I was more interested in people than forecasting charts, but you learned a lot about a person by considering their relationship with money.

For example, I considered the difference between stock market bulls and bears. Bulls were enthusiastic, they saw the market soaring, while bears tended toward conservatism and expected the market to trend down. Growing up, my dad had an endless stream of promising business ideas. He owned restaurants in Aspen, Colorado, and Newport Beach, California, and sold everything from cars to phone cards. Nothing ever worked out like he had hoped, but that didn't deter him. He survived his heartbreaks by dreaming up bigger, better business plans, but I learned that his get-rich-quick euphoria was something to be avoided.

My dad also liked to gamble. For the last twenty years he'd lived in Scottsdale, Arizona, and one of the perks of his neighborhood was Indian gaming. When I went to a casino, inevitably, I was with my dad. I got a kick out of his optimism; his hopefulness was contagious. After I lost forty dollars, which usually took me less than fifteen minutes, I stood around and just watched him play, equally convinced that at any moment he would win big. Since his stroke at the age of fifty-nine, my dad only played the nickel slot machines, but with each spin of the wheel, his eyes lit up and we sighed or cheered on cue. After his stroke, he wasn't able to move the right side of his body or speak any words except "okay," but he radiated life force when the colored sevens whirled on the electric screen. My dad never found the million-dollar business opportunity he longed for, so I hoped his jackpot destiny was linked to his favorite slot machine. If my dad had invested in the stock market, he would have been a bull.

When it came to economic optimism, my husband was the opposite of my dad. Mark was a bear. He was skeptical of the stock market, even though he admitted that this pessimism resulted in missed market rally opportunities. Mark thought the US and global economies were headed for hard times. Way before COVID hit Wuhan, Mark lost faith in the financial markets and sided with economists who predicted the inevitability of dire financial days on the horizon.

Some people would find my husband's economic cynicism depressing, but I found it sexy. His intense, authoritative nature, whether with love or money, was one of the things that attracted me in the early days of our relationship. He took financial responsibility seriously and had a low ceiling for nonsense. Unlike the men in my birth family, Mark was a disciplined saver and a smart investor. He made financial decisions with great care. Being with him made me feel safe, and feeling safe freed some piece of my heart that feared abandonment.

My dad left us as I was about to turn nine years of age, old enough to know something was wrong when my mom started sleeping on the couch. A few months before they split up, I was sitting on the porch with a friend. Janey was sleeping over and we were huddled under a blanket, looking at the stars and whispering secrets, when my dad pulled up in a car just short of our house. I was about to jump up in a surprise welcome, but my dad leaned over and started kissing the long-haired brunette driver. The woman leaned into my dad, her fingers stroking his back and her gorgeous dark mane shifting to obscure my view. I froze mid-jump and told Janey it was time to go inside.

Things got financially tight once my parents split up. Like most children of divorce, I learned how to make do with less. When the toothpaste tube was empty, you cut off the end and squeezed out another day's use. You added water to the end of shampoo bottles and cleaning products. You did not waste food. Ever. You organized coupons before going to the grocery store and looked for red day-old pricing tags in the bakery section.

During the seventies and eighties, I was raised by a single mother who both loved and resented me, or at least that's how I interpreted the bitterness she spewed about her own life circumstances—two kids, an ex-spouse who never paid child support, and few "real" job prospects. My mom was a waitress through most of my childhood, and usually worked back-to-back shifts at multiple restaurants to make ends meet. Her feet always hurt and her temper flared hot, but I never doubted her love for me and my brother. My mom believed that my father's irresponsibility and selfishness caused our suffering.

"Promise me you'll never be financially dependent on a man," she insisted. "Men can't be trusted. And life just isn't fair."

Some weeks we lived on Top Ramen and the leftovers from her shift meals, but my mother prioritized my education. She was not college educated and regretted getting married and pregnant young. When the landlord raised the rent, she moved us based on the school district. My mother told me I was smart. She wanted opportunities for me that she didn't have, so each year she encouraged me to try out for the school play. Even though she had to get someone to cover her shift at the restaurant, she never missed a performance when I was Bet in *Oliver Twist* or Joan of Arc in *Chamber Music*. The one time my mother gushed with pride was when I won an academic scholarship to attend a private high school.

Sitting at the café with Julio and Lana, our new crypto community hosts, Mark pushed for more information.

"What is the biggest fear that investors in this community have?" Mark asked.

"*Nothing!*" Julio said. Then he navigated the conversation away from financial analysis and toward social opportunity.

In another life, I thought, my dad and Julio would have been friends.

"One of the reasons that the crypto community is so awesome," Julio said, "is because we get together every month. I have thrown parties you would not believe. I've used VC money to take us to Ibiza and Malta on yachts. It's outrageous what you can do when your community is comprised of millionaires and billionaires. But things got quiet the last month. About fifty of us got COVID, so we didn't get together in November. Except we did have COVID Thanksgiving."

I hadn't been sick on Thanksgiving like Julio, but I had been sullen. Mark and I spent the day watching movies and noshing on mashed yams and pecan pie, the two holiday dishes I cooked. Without family around, the day had felt depressing.

Julio explained, "Anyone who tested positive was invited. We have a doctor who treats all our people. I'm way past it now. Plus, with the antibodies, I feel like superman."

I rolled my eyes at Julio's affirmation of Donald Trump and the president's recent hospital discharge after surviving COVID.

"What do you all do?" Lana asked.

"As you know, I'm working on trying to produce my movie. Thanks again for the contact, Julio," Deborah said.

Mark shared that he was an attorney and I explained that I was a professor of communication studies.

"But now I am partially reassigned," I elaborated. "A few years ago, I received a grant to help formerly incarcerated students navigate higher education. I've created a program on my college campus that supports their academic goals, their reentry experience and . . ."

This caught Julio's attention and he looked at me with such intensity that I didn't finish my sentence.

"I love you," he said, and then reached across the table to put his hand on top of mine.

I waited.

"I'm formerly incarcerated. I spent ten years in prison. I killed a guy who was trying to steal my drugs. I've had a crazy life. I grew up poor in New York. It wasn't until I went to prison that I figured out what kind of life I wanted to live."

Julio's voice softened as he told us the details of his arrest and lessons he learned doing hard time. He said that he wanted to start a program like mine in Puerto Rico. It wasn't until he went to prison, he said, that he started reading books. He got his GED and then took college classes. Access to higher education in prison changed the way he understood himself and the world.

I believed that access to education was life-changing for Julio, but his gentle framing of prison life was for our benefit—the three Act 20 & 22 "Yankees" sitting across from him with money to purchase cryptocurrency. It was sanitized. When I talked with formerly incarcerated students in my program about their experiences in prison, they made it clear that prison was a dangerous place, not a public library. Gangs, drugs, violence, and dirty guards made survival tough. Almost all the students in my program had PTSD from being incarcerated. Some who didn't have a drug addiction problem before they went in had one by the time they got out. I knew that a man who had lived a chunk of his life behind bars like Julio had scars.

"Hey," Julio said, shifting topics. "I really like you guys. Why don't you come to our next overnight crypto community event? It's this weekend—in the mountains!"

Julio pulled up pictures on his phone of rustic cabins by a lake. The water was glassy, and modest one-room structures on wooden posts of varying heights dotted the tropical shoreline.

"Since you will come as a couple," Julio said to Mark, "you will definitely want to rent one of the cabins. The other rooms in the main house have bunk beds for singles. We had planned to fly in a shaman so that everyone could take ayahuasca, but because of COVID, we thought a yoga-themed weekend was better. We hired a great guy who does sound healing with bowls."

Julio looked at Lana for support of our invitation and she nodded her approval.

"Have you ever taken ayahuasca?" Julio asked, circling back to the original retreat theme. "Man. It's amazing. But it takes some serious preparation. You have to cleanse for two weeks prior, and since so many of us have been sick with COVID, we're focused on healing. Our community really needs mindfulness weekends too. Anyway, this weekend will be about camping and relaxation. We'll bring the shaman over another time."

The conversation had shifted from cryptocurrency to polyamory to murder, and my risk-tolerance meter was starting to peak. *Did Julio just promote a traveling shaman and community hallucinogenic consumption?* The imaginary crossing guard that lived on my shoulder had woken up and stood by my ear at attention. She was antsy for a reason to blow her whistle and wave her red sign around.

"There are seven single cabins," Julio pivoted. "It's just a thousand dollars per couple and that includes all the activities." He smiled provocatively. "But mostly it's a chance to meet the community."

I flashed back to my twenties when a ten-dollar cover charge seemed steep and a keg sufficed as social lubricant.

"So are you free this weekend?" Julio asked.

Mark looked at me and I could tell he was intrigued by the idea of camping with the crypto community. Admittedly, so was I. Until Deborah, we had lived a friendless life in Puerto Rico.

I returned Mark's look with one of my own that said, *I'm not sure, but I'm open to having a discussion.*

Mark only deciphered the "I'm open" part of my unvocalized message because he answered, "Do you Venmo?"

"What's the address?" Deborah asked, and opened Google Maps on her phone.

"I don't ever announce the location until the day of or too many people will show up," Julio explained. "These crypto weekends are legendary."

Was Julio's claim hyperbole or did these weekends really produce infamous legends of acclaim? Either way, I liked the idea of learning more about crypto and best of all, getting to explore the island's interior. I told my crossing guard to relax and looked forward to expanding my nature-watching list. Iguanas were the first island creature I'd actively spent time observing since moving to Puerto Rico, but I was sure they weren't going to be the last.

CHAPTER 7:

THE PRICE OF ADMISSION

The car was quiet as we headed back to our condo in Dorado. I watched the brightly painted row houses from my car window. They sat perfectly positioned like a line of Crayolas in a box. Built along narrow streets, they featured decorative wrought iron on their windows and doors in Spanish designs that doubled as a security measure. Our meeting with Julio gave us a lot to process; I thought about my impressions of this crypto ambassador as Mark drove.

At last Deborah said, "If it turns out there is ayahuasca this weekend, I gotta be honest, I don't think I would be comfortable with that."

"You and me both," I said. "Something about a rent-a-shaman and group vomiting doesn't ignite my confidence. But as long as the theme is yoga, I think we'll be fine."

"The ayahuasca weekend seemed more like something we would try to talk our kids out of," Mark added. Deborah and I laughed. Like Mark and me, Deborah was the parent of adult children.

"Julio reminded me what a difference a decade makes. I love living in the sleepy little beach town of Dorado," Deborah said. "I got a kick out of his complaint that Dorado was too boring and that we should move to San Juan so we could be in the middle of all the action."

I adjusted my vent so that the stream of cold air pouring into the car blew directly at my face. Then I pulled the sweat-soaked collar of my sundress away from my neck. After sitting outside with Julio and Lana for almost two hours, I felt overheated.

"I realize we may not know exactly what we're getting into," Mark said, "but I am very interested in meeting investors within the crypto community. Regardless of party themes, it sounds like there will be opportunities for those of us who are potential investors to ask questions about crypto from people in the know."

I agreed with Mark and Deborah. A wild ayahuasca weekend wasn't in my wheelhouse either, but learning more about cryptocurrency investing intrigued me. My impressions of Julio, however, were still forming. I had a lot of respect for people who successfully forged a legitimate career path after incarceration. From working with formerly incarcerated students in my college program, I knew it wasn't easy. If Julio grew up poor, started his formal education behind bars, and successfully traversed the rampant cultural biases that existed against formerly incarcerated citizens, he had smarts and grit. Then again, his polyamory and ayahuasca enthusiasm were a little unsettling. When Julio spoke about these topics, the crossing guard that sat on my sweaty shoulder had showed signs of alarm. I knew she'd be around the next time I saw Julio.

We dropped Deborah off at her condo and headed to ours. After dinner Mark and I cleaned up and then returned to the topic of Julio's crypto weekend.

"Are you okay with this?" Mark asked.

We were sitting on the couch, ready to watch a movie.

"I definitely have COVID concerns," I admitted. "It sounds like social distancing and mask wearing is supported. And I would love a change of scenery. But are we really going to send a guy we just met a thousand dollars to camp at some unknown location we plan to leave in the event it attracts a large crowd? If that place is packed with maskless partygoers, I don't plan to stick around and catch COVID."

Our conversation was interrupted when Mark's office called. He answered his phone, listened, and responded with a series of "uh-huhs." Then he hit mute and looked at me.

"Sorry, George, I need to take this."

"No problem," I responded, and Mark stood up.

"Try not to worry," Mark added. "Just send Julio the cash—we've got nothing to lose but a few bucks and we deserve a little fun. It's already been a long pandemic."

Mark headed upstairs to the office, but I stayed seated on the couch in our living room. It had started to rain, fast and hard. I heard rolling thunder and turned toward the glass patio doors to watch. Lightning flashed above the ocean, giant bolts of ominous, jagged light that seared the night sky.

What am I doing? I deliberated, adding Julio's Venmo address to my phone. The question was reminiscent of my early days on the island when just being away from my California home during a pandemic seemed surreal. Sometimes it was difficult for me to tell if new experiences promoted personal growth or reinforced standing patterns that were tried and true. Probably both. I knew that life transitions bestowed unique lessons in hindsight, but was "cryptocurrency community member" a role I was qualified to pursue? Was it a title I even wanted?

I had traveled a long way down the road of relocation acceptance, but questions remained. While it had become easier to see the positives associated with our move to the island, sometimes I struggled to determine what part of this Act 20 & 22 experience belonged to me and what part was a performance where I played the role of the best supporting dutiful wife.

My first husband had called me a bitch. Not so much to my face, but often behind my back (if I was to believe trusted friends). As soon as our decision to divorce was public these friends told me they were not surprised to hear this news. This was to me, well, surprising. In these secondhand accounts, my first husband was the victim of my unreasonable expectations. Plus, he didn't love me anymore—this he did say to my face.

Divorce was a nasty business but my first husband was not a bad person, just a bad partner for me. He shined in group situations when I was most myself in quiet moments of intimacy. I liked close connection and he liked witty party talk. I wanted to dig into the things that caused me existential angst and he wanted to host dinner parties and join fantasy football leagues. These differences intensified as we slipped from our twenties into our thirties, had children, and launched our professional lives.

And I *was* a bitch to my first husband. At least I was toward the end when our life together started to unravel. I had just given birth to our second daughter and felt overwhelmed by the needs of a newborn, a three-year-old, and a tenured teaching job. During this period, I was demanding; the threads that organized my life were pulled too tight and had frayed. I felt desperate for support. There were days I half screamed, half sobbed with disappointment when he broke promises, almost always over time we planned to spend together. It wasn't that he got stuck late at work, again, or that he chose to spend his weekends training for his next marathon, it's that he didn't want to be with me.

I was lonely in my first marriage. I used to think this was caused by all the time we spent apart, but now that I was no longer lonely, I understood it differently. I believed that the beauty of connecting had logistical demands, but it also included tremendous internal effort. Both people had to want to do the work. Connection meant openheartedness and vulnerability in addition to showing up for family dinners. My first husband and I were friends but not romantically synced. Our relationship might have worked well had we been coworkers or attended the same fitness classes, but it made for an unsatisfying marriage.

There were many reasons we split up—that was a dramatic period of time—but for me, these experiences informed why we didn't work. The lonely bitch revelation made no real difference after I was divorced, except that sometimes I worried I was overcorrecting in my marriage to Mark. While I didn't want my bitchy side to dominate my persona, I did want to be a truthful person who owned her complicated identity and emotional states. I believed that inauthentic expressions of happiness were toxic too; nobody liked a fake.

In contrast to my first husband, Mark joked that I was the most optimistic person he'd ever met because I smiled easily and laughed often. My dad, whose disabilities kept him mostly housebound, was also abundantly positive by nature.

"Come on, Princess," Dad would whisper to wake me early on Saturday mornings, the scent of spearmint chewing gum tickling my nose. "The fish are already biting!"

Dad would grab our gear and drive us to his favorite lake while my mom cared for my baby brother.

"With luck like ours, I just know that today we're gonna catch a whopper!"

When I was little, Saturday morning fishing trips with my dad were the best.

Was disposition a matter of genetics? I didn't have much contact with my dad once my parents divorced, and yet I saw our similarities in appearance and mood. After I brushed off Mark's compliment about my optimism, I glowed, grateful that he saw this side of me. In my second marriage, I felt accepted. The roles attached to my spousal identity—cheerleader, team-player, coach—all added to the generative nature of our life together.

When Mark and I first moved to the island, my inner optimist struggled. I had stopped seeing the California therapist who helped me process memories of Pat's sexual assault and other adolescent secrets, but embarrassing thoughts lingered in the back of my mind. I still had therapeutic work to do. Olivia, my youngest daughter, had started college at UC Santa Cruz and she felt too far away. I liked Puerto Rico, but I struggled with my new empty nester status and wasn't clear on my role in Mark's PR adventure. Puerto Rico didn't feel like home and I had yet to fully comprehend the dividing line between supportive wife and compliant sidekick.

I checked many privileged boxes: white, straight, married, mother, educated, and employed. I had a breadth of advantages most others on the planet did not. I worried that adding "beneficiary of tax incentives" to this list would distance me from California friends and colleagues I had worked with for decades. Academics are thoughtful, but they have human systems too, and there was something unlikable about accumulating wealth and living in luxury while my college community struggled with COVID restrictions and online learning outcomes.

In contrast to my confusion once we moved to Puerto Rico, Mark was the happiest I'd ever seen him. He was eager for his financial coaster to climb to the top of the tracks, unapologetic, and ready to enjoy the ride.

"I just want to see if I can do it," I heard Mark say, again. Whether he was talking about winning a big case or making investment decisions, he challenged himself to think beyond traditional structures of financial success. He wasn't unrealistic or full of hubris like my father, but he did imagine a financial universe that dwarfed mine.

I wondered how our professional cultures colored our outlooks on money. I told my students that standpoint impacts perception—where you're coming from shapes what you see. In Mark's world, successful litigators peacocked in expensive suits and sports cars. They bought handmade watch winder boxes for their Rolexes. They sent each other overpriced wine baskets at Christmas. Community college professors didn't own Rolexes and instead gave Crystal Apple Awards to those who worked tirelessly on behalf of their students. We baked each other cookies for the holidays. Mark's colleagues were rich white men. Mine were middle-class and diverse, accustomed to working hours for which we were not always paid. I still didn't want a Rolex, but I was tired of working extra hours for free. If learning about Bitcoin and other cryptocurrency was lucrative, I was interested. So, with a quick tap of my finger, I sent instant cash to a formerly incarcerated self-proclaimed Puerto Rican ambassador for crypto. We were going to the crypto camping weekend even if it meant my Crystal Apple Award might get repossessed.

CHAPTER 8:

RESEARCH

Over the next few days, we prepared for Julio's crypto camping weekend. Like twentysomethings back in grad school, Mark and I consumed information with focus and discipline, and our self-curated crash course on crypto was illuminating. The use of Bitcoin as a digital currency began in 2009, but the topic didn't gain mainstream media attention until the 2010s. That's when news outlets ran a story about Bitcoin Pizza Day. A Florida man named Laszlo Hanyecz posted on a Bitcoin forum that he would pay 10,000 Bitcoins to anyone who would send him a pizza. Jeremy Sturdivant accepted Hanyecz's offer and ordered him two large pizzas from Papa John's. The Bitcoin that Sturdivant earned was valued at approximately $40. Ten years later, in 2020, that same Bitcoin exceeded $23,000 a coin (I hoped Sturdivant still owned the Bitcoins Hanyecz had paid him). The pizza challenge turned out to be a very lucky transaction.

We watched crypto analysis YouTube videos. We read crypto history books. We traded articles by economists who both deeply loved and deeply hated the world of cryptocurrency. We learned that Bitcoin existed in a class by itself; all the other forms of cryptocurrency were considered altcoins. There were also tokens, but they had a specific purpose and didn't have value outside of their application. I was swimming in facts and still didn't understand how cryptocurrency was valued or regulated given its esoteric audience and existence outside of traditional financial markets.

Mark was studious and contemplative but his computational process took time. His thoughts originated from some other universe, it seemed to me, and once he mulled them over, he shared them. Unlike my half-baked ideas that took form as I talked them through, his got articulated in a chess-piece world where pawns and knights waited patiently for his next move.

We were sitting at the kitchen table, laptops open, each of us combing through cryptocurrency data, when I asked Mark, "Philosophically speaking, how do we determine the value of something?"

I knew the basic answer to the question I posed—supply and demand—but I was thinking about how a currency like crypto, comprised of virtual tokens, mined by essentially solving math problems, could be worth such impressive amounts. Where's the demand for a *virtual* currency?

Mark looked up from behind his computer screen. He was reading across the table from me. We had started our study session with coffee and his hair was disheveled from sleep.

"Things have value when we all agree that they have value," Mark said. "Throughout history, cultures have assigned shells value, or beads, or metals, or even flower bulbs."

I thought about the dollars in my wallet, just crumpled green-and-white rectangles of paper that allowed me to buy groceries because everybody agreed that the exchange of dollars for vegetables was equitable.

"It doesn't hurt that the dollar—our fiat currency—is government issued," I added.

"True. But the rise in Bitcoin popularity makes sense," Mark continued, "because we live in a world where all it takes to create currency is a printing press and an army. Governments all over the planet print money, but that doesn't mean their dollars are worth much. Just look at Zimbabwe and Argentina."

"All the suffering a messed-up economy causes the people who live there is horrific," I said.

At this point, coffee cups had been replaced by water glasses and I took a cool drink. It wasn't quite noon, but the room was growing warm.

"So why not virtual tokens?" Mark asked. "Bitcoin isn't backed by anything, but neither is fiat currency. The important thing about Bitcoin is that people agree it has value."

We learned that Satoshi Nakamoto was the "creator" of Bitcoin. When he first released Bitcoin, a peer-to-peer electronic cash system, he claimed it would change the world. On Halloween 2008 Satoshi released an eight-page white paper on how this decentralized system could eliminate the monetary middleman from transaction processes, jump-starting the birth of cryptocurrency. Satoshi experts believed that he distrusted the banking system and wanted a way to conduct daily transactions that did not require banks. In recent years, Bitcoin had operated more as an investment than a currency, but its value was attention-getting. Satoshi's identity remained unclear. "He" or "she" may really be "they" since the name Satoshi Nakamoto was a pseudonym for the real person or group who invented Bitcoin. Satoshi vanished after 2011.

"Bitcoin is the perfect example," Mark said. "Satoshi wanted to create a measure of value that didn't require governments. His idea was to create an incorruptible, transparent system."

I relaxed into my chair and looked out at the ocean. I liked the mystery of Satoshi. It kept me curious and wanting to know more about the unfamiliar world of cryptocurrency. The fact that Satoshi could be a person, or a group of revolutionaries, or a government disguised as a tech genius added intrigue. It was like getting to the middle of a good mystery novel; the possible outcomes kept me turning pages.

Lots of online crypto posts agreed that the obscure persona of Satoshi Nakamoto was by design. However, this story of origin was not the only exciting chapter in the enigmatic Bitcoin novel. Bitcoin was mined by solving increasingly difficult math problems. A miner needed a CPU (a computer's central processing unit) to obtain promised riches; Hashcash was the proof-of-work mining algorithm. Just like panning for gold, it took luck, in addition to a powerful computer, to run Bitcoin's algorithm. In the book *Bubble or Revolution?*, Neel Mehta, Aditya Agashe, and Parth Detroja explained, "Mining Bitcoins boils down to a game of mindlessly rolling a multitrillion-sided die for decades, hoping you get a lucky roll."

I looked back at my husband.

"But unlike fiat currency that governments can just print and print forever," I said, "Bitcoin has a cap."

"Exactly," Mark said.

While governments could increase currency by passing legislation and pushing keystrokes, there was only so much Bitcoin that could be mined. This increased its value. Some analysts even argued that its limited supply created a more reliable store of value than fiat currency even though there was enormous variation in the price. During our crypto study session, Bitcoin was valued at over $20,000 a coin.

Bitcoin was the first cryptocurrency, but it soon became one of many coins traded on cryptocurrency exchanges. Other altcoins launched afterward, eager to capitalize on

Bitcoin's growing success. By 2020, there were more than five thousand altcoins available. Many of these cryptocurrency options pitched themselves as a better alternative to Bitcoin, but so far, no other coin or token had come close to Bitcoin's market value.

Mark and I swapped notes on altcoins such as Ethereum, which had held steady in the number two cryptocurrency popularity spot, and XRP, which was liked by some governments for its transaction capabilities. We surmised that if Bitcoin was digital gold and Ethereum was digital silver, Ripple's XRP was the new SWIFT, a system that enabled cross-border financial transactions. There were cryptocurrencies tied to dollars, others that were linked to gold, and still others that were linked to a basket of currencies from around the world.

We also learned that a sinister shadow element clung to the world of crypto. The Silk Road was a black market on the first modern darknet best known for selling illegal drugs. The FBI shut down the website in 2013. However, in November 2020, the US government seized more than $1 billion worth of Bitcoin connected to the Silk Road. The government's ability to seize Bitcoin sent a powerful message to the cryptoverse: "Don't think we can't take your coins if we have cause. We're watching you." This was one reason why conspiracy theories were woven into the fabric of crypto culture like multicolored yarn strands on a loom.

"Part of me thinks of crypto as something tied to gamers and criminals," I confessed. "When I watch these crypto YouTubers, I'm reminded of the Silk Road bust and an economic system that promoted the illegal sale of drugs and weapons. I'm glad they caught Ross Ulbricht, and found his Bitcoin, but I wonder how many other Ulbrichts are still out there."

"Me too," Mark replied. "But the government's ability to do the seizing is not lost on me. Political winds change. The subtext to the Silk Road story is that everyone's assets are potentially at risk. Governments can locate digital assets, just like they find and freeze bank accounts."

If this was true, the hype around crypto was all the more curious. Our research revealed an online crypto community overflowing with information. And opinion. And hope. I read pieces on decentralized finance where tokens were described like pirates' hidden treasure. Enthusiasts who operated in the crypto space were true believers. Hopeium, I learned, was a term used to describe crypto aficionados who were high on hope. They shouted hopeium slogans from atop animated milk crates that lined virtual streets. Just like Julio, there were many within this community who thought *nothing* bad could happen to Bitcoin. Were they addicted to hopeium?

"It's the hopeium that makes me feel leery," Mark said. "I wish there was a way I could sit with a bunch of crypto experts and get to the heart of what they fear most. I'd like to ask them what is likely to go wrong with cryptocurrency in the next decade and why they think those problems will or will not happen."

My husband's risk assessment process reminded me of the differences in how we experienced danger. For me, risk was like standing at the top of a giant boulder, my bare toes hanging over the edge of crumbling rock, knots of nervousness swirling in my stomach. It was that moment right before I took a deep breath and willed myself to jump, my heart racing, my body in free fall, until I plunged feetfirst into the icy water. Risk could take my breath away. The fear and exhilaration were difficult for me to untangle.

For Mark, risk was calculated. He didn't manage it wearing swim trunks but instead put on an expensive suit. Due to legal training, family scripting, or personality characteristics, Mark experienced risk distinctly different from me. Was his tolerance for risk a muscle strengthened over time, or a privilege that was fortified by gender and affluence?

"I wish Julio had been open to your line of questioning," I said. "He made it seem like there was no downside to Bitcoin."

"You really need to get all the warts on the table to understand something more honestly," Mark added, and shifted in his kitchen chair.

"Does that mean you won't consider investing in crypto until you get clarity on currency weaknesses?"

"Not necessarily," he explained. "I get the basics associated with market volatility and I'm interested in cryptocurrency as a form of insurance and speculation. In the same way that I own metals, cryptocurrency expands one's portfolio. It's speculative but compelling nonetheless."

Finally, our attention drifted back to our own computers. We sat at the table together but gave each other unspoken permission to refocus, to dig back into individualized research threads, to keep working.

I could tell that Mark was looking forward to our weekend. I imagined that he would get useful information, even if it was seasoned with hopeium. He had a way of putting people at ease while getting them to tell the truth. Cross-examination was his specialty. Plus, we were already in for a thousand dollars; a little truth telling would be a perfect return on our most recent investment.

CHAPTER 9:

EMOTIONAL TRIGGERS

When the alarm on my phone chimed, I gathered my notes from the kitchen table, closed my laptop, and stood up. Even though my mind was swimming in crypto factoids, I needed to shift gears and get ready for my real job.

"Keep going," I told Mark. "It's time for me to take a shower and get ready to teach class."

Before a weekend away with Julio and his crypto community, I had students to support.

"As soon as I finish class, I'll start packing for our weekend."

"Enjoy," Mark said, scanning articles on his computer.

One of the reasons I became a college professor was the amazing students. Teachers have the power to inspire lifelong learning, and even transform lives, but I'm convinced that teachers receive more than we give. When a kind friend told me that my students were lucky to have me as their teacher, I responded that *I* was the lucky one. My students inspired me every day, especially my Re-Emerging Scholars.

The college where I taught was located in South Sacramento and designated as a minority-serving institution (24 percent of the student population was white and 76 percent was comprised of minority populations). It was one of the most diverse community colleges in the country. Increasingly, my students expressed fears over police brutality. Two years before George Floyd was murdered, Sacramento's own Stephon Clark was shot and killed in his grandmother's backyard, right around the corner from my college campus.

In 2017, I conducted a research project that focused on institutionalized racism in California's criminal justice system and considered ways in which California community colleges were addressing the needs of justice-impacted students. After my project was complete, I applied for a grant, was successful, and started Re-Emerging Scholars (RES), a reentry program for incarcerated and formerly incarcerated students. In 2018, I was hired to run the program and split my teaching load between RES and the communication studies courses I usually taught.

When COVID turned my job 100 percent remote, I met with students in my Re-Emerging Scholars program on Zoom. This format wasn't ideal—RES students all preferred face-to-face classes—but meeting on Zoom was our only option and it helped us stay connected during COVID. Seeing students on a screen and listening to their voices still gave me important nonverbal information, something I didn't always get in an email exchange.

"Hi! Hi! Hi!" I repeated, clicking names with my mouse and admitting students into my Zoom room. "How's everyone feeling today?"

"Tired. Stressed. Fine . . ." Students turned on cameras and adjusted monitors so we could see each other.

"Let's start with highs and lows." I began the warm-up exercise that we used at the start of every class. Each student shared one thing that went well during their week and one thing that was challenging.

"Sounds like most of you had a pretty good week," I said, bringing our warm-up to a close. "Me too. Mostly. I've been productive, but this pandemic has me feeling a little isolated. It's nice to see your faces."

I paused to let my students know I was going to shift gears. "Today we are going to talk about emotional triggers. Is everyone familiar with this term?"

"You mean like what happens when my auntie won't stop bugging me about dumb stuff that doesn't even matter?" asked Elijah playfully. "Triggering me is her specialty."

Elijah had told me he moved into his aunt's house after a year in transitional housing and that he desperately needed his own place. He was sleeping on her couch until he found another option, but he didn't like being a burden.

"Sort of," I laughed. "Or that might just be called having family."

I looked at the eight faces on my screen. All men. All Brown and Black. All formerly incarcerated. This wasn't surprising because men of color were sentenced and incarcerated at disproportionate rates. In the criminal justice system, men of color were disadvantaged when compared to white men.[1] Still, my RES students had changed their narrative of failure to one of hope. Even though each of my students had grown up in poverty, and most had suffered abuse as children, today they were also successful college students. They were rewriting their lives.

"I want to share my screen with you," I said, and clicked the green icon at the bottom of my computer monitor.

Zoom squares transformed into a single PowerPoint slide.

---

1. See, for example, Michelle Alexander's book titled *The New Jim Crow: Mass Incarceration in the Age of Colorblindness*.

"Emotional triggers can catch us by surprise . . ." I summarized the words on my slide. "But sometimes, with foresight, we can anticipate the things that are going to trigger us."

New slides appeared and I talked through the content before ending my screen share.

When my students' faces reappeared, I asked, "Is anyone here already aware of an emotional trigger they try to avoid?"

Jon spoke up first. "I can't handle people walking behind me. I've been jumped more times than I can count. If I sense someone unexpected is walking up behind me, I get triggered."

"What does getting triggered mean to you?" I asked.

Jon was quiet for a moment, then said, "My heart starts beating like a million miles an hour, and I know that any second I could lose my shit."

His voice was deep and serious.

"Thanks for sharing, Jon. I get it." I thought for a moment. "It almost sounds like your body responds to the trigger before your brain may know what's happening. Is that your experience?"

"I guess so," he said, letting my question roll through his mind.

"Do you employ strategies to avoid these situations?" I asked.

"Absolutely," Jon said. "For starters, I only sit in the back of the classroom. And I like to be by the door. I have PTSD from being inside, so my counselor added this to my accommodations. Dude," he said to the other students, "if you haven't gone to the disabled students center yet, you need to. I bet most of us here probably have PTSD from prison."

"Thank you, Jon."

"I think all my worst triggers got instilled before I even went to prison," Paulo said. "Mine are connected to drugs.

I can't even hang out with my friends anymore. If they're partying, I know I'm gonna get triggered. I feel stressed out because I know if I get caught, I'm gonna violate, but the stress only makes me want to party more. The only way I stay clean is to avoid that stuff altogether."

As our Zoom class continued, other students shared experiences and support. This group was a safe space and students spoke openly about their challenges and fears.

"See you guys next week," I said when our class time was over. "You know my Zoom office hours during the week, so please reach out if anything comes up. Or just pop in to say hello and save me from pandemic boredom!"

I smiled and waved before ending our Zoom meeting.

I shut down my computer and thought about my own triggers. Like Paulo, I avoided drugs once I stopped using them in my twenties. Avoidance was the only way for me too, and even though I hadn't worried about violating parole conditions, keeping drugs out of my system meant keeping them out of my sight. Fortunately for me, that was a long time ago.

Next I grabbed a suitcase from the closet and started to pack. As I folded clothes and tucked them neatly into the small case, I considered my upcoming weekend. I was glad Julio opted for a yoga-themed crypto camping trip instead of one where campers took ayahuasca. I didn't want to be around drugs. At this stage in my life, I wasn't the least bit tempted, but drugs still weren't my scene. It was unlikely I'd be triggered by seeing others do drugs—I hadn't laid eyes on illegal substances for decades—but I was relieved to know I wouldn't have to find out on our trip with Julio and the crypto community.

CHAPTER 10:

HALF NAKED HUGS

At 2 p.m. on Friday our car was packed and we were ready for the crypto community investing weekend that Julio had invited us to join. We agreed to drive with Deborah as long as she was comfortable with mask wearing in the car. Vaccines weren't available yet in Puerto Rico and the rates of COVID on the island increased daily.

I could tell by the look on her face that Deborah thought I was being ridiculous, but my need for safety won out against my desire to appear cool and flexible. I liked to mitigate risk. (A tiny crossing guard lived on my shoulder, for goodness' sake.) The last thing I wanted was a medical emergency so far from home. The safest play was to skip this trip, to isolate, but like everyone else, Mark and I were feeling COVID safety protocol fatigue.

Julio told us that twenty or so members of the crypto community planned to attend this event and that COVID safety precautions would be enforced. How dangerous could it be? Participants would interact outside, observe mask wearing, and stay socially distanced. It wasn't perfect, but the setup seemed tolerable.

"What's the address?" I asked Deborah once she got settled in the back seat of our rental car. "I'll pull up directions on my phone."

"I don't exactly know," she said, pulling out her own phone. "It's just a Telegram pin near some lake. They don't want the address to get out yet, so we are just supposed to head toward the pin. The exact address should pop into my phone soon."

Who invited people to a weekend event but didn't tell them where they were going? I contemplated possibilities. Maybe the organizers were simply disorganized. Or less forgivable, this wasn't a real event and we were about to drive for hours to discover we had been scammed out of the cost of admission.

"Mysterious," I said instead.

"Definitely," Deborah agreed with an easy laugh.

I doubted the getting scammed scenario had pinged her radar. Deborah was good-natured, not a skeptic like me.

"Hey, on our way out of town, I need to make a quick stop at the post office."

Deborah explained that she had set up crypto accounts for her kids and wanted to mail them their wallets, which she had preloaded with Bitcoin. It reminded me of spy movies when villains coordinated clandestine ways to move money. Was an alternate financial universe something that parents should encourage their children to consider? I doubted my daughters knew the first thing about Bitcoin.

"I want to teach them how to trade and get them started on investing at a young age. And oh," she exclaimed, "I got turned on to a new crypto digital wallet by a friend last night, so I checked it out. Investors make 3 percent *a day*! You guys gotta get in on this."

Deborah's enthusiasm for Bitcoin was couched in a fantasy language where fixed rates and inevitable returns made for easy money.

"Wow," I said. "That sounds too good to be true."

Maybe my crypto naivete made me cynical, but the way Deborah talked about making money from cryptocurrency sounded like the stuff of con men. I wondered how a wallet choice—the thing a person puts their crypto inside—generated 3 percent a day regardless of investment amount when rates in traditional financial markets were at all-time lows. Deborah's claim suggested that crypto wallets rained money instead of housing it. Plus, her unbridled Bitcoin-makes-you-rich enthusiasm made me think of my dad. Every time he started a new business, he got this dreamy look in his eyes and I could hear his voice smile wide with delight. He'd give a knowing laugh and tell us that *this* idea was the one.

I thought back to when I was in college. I hadn't seen my dad in a few years and was thrilled the day he showed up on my doorstep unannounced. He said that he'd been thinking of me and happened to be in the area, so he decided to take a chance. However, the true motivation for his visit was quickly revealed.

"Everybody makes long-distance calls," my dad had said. I had invited him inside and we drank soda on my ratty garage-sale couch. "Why should the phone companies make all the money when *you* can?"

"You want me to sell phone cards to my friends?" I asked.

He smelled like spearmint gum and I sighed. "We're all broke students, Dad."

"Don't think of it as selling to your friends, think of it as helping them to save money," he explained. Then he opened his leather wallet and pulled out a shiny card imprinted with a long number he used to place long-distance calls. He handed it to me, tenderly, as if the card were made of glass.

"Every time one of your friends calls their parents back home, you'll make a kickback," Dad said. "And if your friends want to sell phone cards to their friends, they become part of your downline. You make money on the cards you sell, the calls made on those cards, *and* on the cards people in your downline sell."

"I don't know, Dad. The thought of asking my friends to discontinue their current phone service and buy these phone cards makes me feel uncomfortable."

"Don't be silly," he said. His voice shifted from jovial to serious. "How do you expect to pay back all those loans you're taking out to attend some fancy college?"

Yet here I was, diving into some technical money scheme event that I barely understood.

Despite my crypto weekend reservations, an address did pop into Deborah's phone an hour into our journey. The location was on the shore of Carite Lake, a three-hundred-acre reservoir in the mountains of Guayama, almost two hours from our condo in Dorado. It was on the southeast part of the island, and the road was winding. Puerto Rico was a small landmass, just one hundred miles long and thirty-five miles wide, but interior-island driving was slow because of narrow, pothole-filled roads. The closer we got the more Mark needed to pull over in order to let cars headed in the opposite direction pass. Our side of the road was mostly buffered by mountain; the other cars simply had nowhere else to go.

As we climbed higher, toward the center of the island, the plant life grew dense. Tree branches and vines grew over phone lines downed by Hurricane Maria three years earlier to create a dome-like canopy enveloping entire sections of our single-lane road. It looked like the mountain wore a thick green cloak around its long curvy neck. We hadn't seen a street sign in almost an hour and our navigation had stopped working. Just when I was certain we must be very lost, the flora retreated to reveal a small town. We drove by a gas station and an outdoor café that advertised mofongo, a traditional Puerto Rican plantain dish. A few locals sat behind card tables erected to sell coconuts and hats made of palm fronds.

"This is a good sign," Deborah said. "Civilization. And my nav just popped back on. I've got our address!"

Past the roadside town, our drive shifted down into a steep decline and we caught glimpses of a brilliant blue lake. We crept around corners on uneven streets and finally squeezed into the last spot on the long driveway, right behind a Mercedes SUV.

We were at the main house. It was built into a sharp mountainside and from the porch we could see the cabin roofs surrounding the lake below. The front door was wide open and the inside sounds of socializing suggested we were at the right place. I felt relief that we had made it to our destination.

"Welcome," said a young woman inside as we knocked on the doorframe. She moved from the kitchen counter, which was lined with bottles, cups, and a cooler full of ice, toward my husband.

"I'm so glad you found us. I'm Janelle," she said, and wrapped her tan arms around Mark. I stared while the young woman, naked except for her string bikini, pressed her body into his. The sides of her breasts bulged from the tiny triangles of fabric that separated her from my husband. She ran her hands, slowly, up and down the length of his back, and nestled her face just below his chin.

As the intensity of Janelle's hug registered, I was embraced and felt my own body pulled into the bare muscled torso of a young man who looked like he belonged on the cover of a surfing magazine. The tie of his swim trunks pressed firmly into my stomach, and my chest pressed against his warm skin. He smelled like salt and sunshine.

"I'm Chris," he said with a sultry voice into the N95 mask on my face. His strong hands were on my shoulders, keeping my body close to his. "I'm here to help you get bags from your car, or with anything at all."

I looked around the room. It was full of young, beautiful men and women in their twenties. Who were these people? They didn't look like the middle-aged crypto investors I'd expected. Instead they looked like reality television stars who should get cast on a dating show; their bright smiles and sexy beach bodies were shockingly attractive.

"We're looking for Julio," Mark said. "He's supposed to direct us to our cabin."

Deborah drifted from my side and made her way over to the counter. A woman (who must have been nicknamed Yoga Goddess because of her svelte body and mala beads) made Deb a rum drink.

"Can I make you something?" Yoga Goddess asked me, waving a large bottle of Don Q in the air.

"No, thanks," I answered.

If this moment was a scene in a movie, my character would have just realized that she'd unsuspectingly walked into a beach house owned by Hugh Hefner. We were standing in what I imagined was the living room—a great room that included the kitchen—but the furniture had been rearranged so that open space allowed people to mingle. Couches and coffee tables were missing. The wall directly across from us was all window and looked out across an expansive mountain range. The ceilings were high and the other walls were lined, top to bottom, with framed posters, magazine covers, and awards.

Then a man who walked with a limp and a cane appeared from around the corner to shake our hands.

"Welcome to my home!" the man said. He extended his gnarled fingers toward Mark.

We introduced ourselves and when I asked about the extensive memorabilia, Fernando told us he was a famous tennis player, a real Puerto Rican star. The deep lines on his weathered face and the braces on both knees were his proof. Fernando may not have created the real Playboy empire, but from the energy in his house, I was pretty sure he had been a playboy in his day.

When Mark and I were finally pointed in the direction of the lake to find Julio, I was relieved we had paid for our own cabin. So far, my risk reduction plan seemed silly; no one but Mark and I were wearing masks, or much of anything at all for that matter.

"At least," I said to Mark as we left Fernando's house, "the weather is nice and we can socialize outside."

"That's not the only thing that's nice," my husband said with a mischievous smile. Janelle and Surfer Boy had made an impression on him too.

The steep path to the lake was marked by rebar stakes topped with eyelets, the kind you see on docks to moor boats. A slack piece of fraying rope ran through each metal circle like a string of decorative lights placed around a patio edge at Christmastime. Cinder blocks had been shoved into the side of the mountain to create small cement steps. Damp earth that looked unstable served as the foundation for each block of concrete and made our descent slow; we had to be cautious to step in just the right spot and avoid the muddy hillside, or worse. I couldn't imagine Fernando ever descending these steps. They certainly weren't fit for limps or canes.

The cinder block stairs led us to a wide wooden deck overlooking a lake lined with cabins. Tall grasses danced along the water's edge, and a large dark bird circled above.

I had grown used to the sound of the ocean—waves crashed day and night outside our Dorado home—but at Lake Carite, the water was mostly quiet, just gentle lapping. The cabins around the lake reminded me of tree houses. Each was built on stilts and looked like something well-suited for a tree in a lucky child's backyard.

Mark and I were admiring the view when Julio approached. "I'm so glad you're here," he said.

Julio turned to the man standing behind a makeshift bar. "Let's celebrate with a shot of mezcal!"

The bartender handed each of us a red Solo cup filled with an inch of golden liquid. A woman approached and gave Julio a kiss on the cheek. Her thick black hair fell just past her shoulders.

"This is Sol," Julio introduced us. "She and her partner, Supra, are the DJs this weekend. I flew them in from Ibiza."

"Nice to meet you," Sol said with a smile.

Like Janelle, she was stunning and wore a black swimsuit my mother would have described as daring. On her bottom half, Sol also wore flowing pants made of fine black tulle, her legs draped in veil so sheer it looked like she was walking in sheets of air.

"I have some good news to share," Julio continued. "I'm going to make a movie!"

Julio tipped his head back, emptying the Solo cup contents into his mouth. Then he pumped his fist in the air and hollered with a mix of determination and joy as if he'd just reached the top of Mount Everest.

"What's the movie about?" Mark asked before following Julio's lead and consuming his shot of alcohol in one quick gulp.

"I am so stoked," Julio continued. "I just talked to one of the vice presidents of Netflix about my movie and they want me. You know about Satoshi Nakamoto, right?"

"Sure," Mark said.

"Well, I'm making the movie about his story."

First Deborah with her *National Treasure*-meets-*Indiana Jones* project and now Julio's Satoshi tale. Was everyone in the Puerto Rican crypto community working on a movie? I peered into my Solo cup but couldn't manage to take a drink. The spicy fumes filled my nose with fire.

"I thought the identity of Satoshi Nakamoto was a mystery," I said.

"It is, but I know the *real* story of Bitcoin and Satoshi. It's gonna blow your socks off!"

I knew that the look on my crossing guard's face communicated disbelief at Julio's claim. I imagined her looking at her shoes, arms crossed, and shaking her head disparagingly.

"Let's get you guys settled," Julio said. "You're in Ontario." He waved to a nearby cabin.

The deck we were standing on was being transformed into a dance floor, complete with a disco ball on a large cable, so we walked around workers on the way to our destination.

Julio pushed the door to our cabin open and reached for the Costco-sized container of candy that sat next to a bottle of red wine. "These are my gifts to you," he said.

Our cabin included a small bed and a TV tray nightstand; both were covered in dust. The windows had panel inserts that acted as shutters, but no screens. Sunlight streamed through gaps in composite two-by-fours that comprised the four walls. It wasn't just a tree house from the outside but from the inside as well. Given the modest accommodations, and the fact that Ontario Cabin sat next to the dance floor, I wondered how Julio had arrived at the $1,000 price tag.

"Now follow me," he said. "I'll show you around."

CHAPTER 11:

EXITS

Julio pointed to other cabins and stated the names and backgrounds of our weekend neighbors. He rattled off professional titles like he spewed crypto facts, bullets shot from a machine gun. Then he moved on to the weekend's entertainment.

"Tonight will be fantastic," he said. "See those rafts?"

Julio pointed to floating platforms tied up to more rebar stakes. They looked like cabin doors that had been turned into pontoons.

"Once the sun sets, the naked fire dancers will get on those rafts and float to the center of the lake; it's a fire hazard if they don't perform on the water."

With each passing moment, my understanding of the weekend shifted. It was like looking at an autostereogram, a picture within a picture. Just when you think you're looking at one image, another hidden one is revealed. Each revelation added to my growing uneasiness.

"This is where I am staying with my beautiful ladies," Julio said, leading us into the largest cabin on the lake. Julio's cabin had a refrigerator, the door of which he opened wide to reveal an impressive display of colorful fruits and vegetables. Dark leafy greens lined its shelves, and red and gold bell peppers decorated door cubbies.

"Healthy smoothies are a must for a weekend like this—I blend the magic right inside."

Then Julio reached into a cupboard and pulled out the magic on a large tray, the kind you might serve a turkey on at Thanksgiving dinner, except this one was covered with a towel.

"Ta-da!" he said, removing the towel with a quick motion.

On the tray was a large vacuum-sealed pack of mushrooms, and I knew instantly these weren't the kind you put into holiday gravy.

"And that's not all," he assured us, "I have as much Molly as you want."

The sound of a long, loud whistle screeched in my ear. Molly, or MDMA, was an illegal drug used to induce feelings of euphoria, and my crossing guard demanded to know where the exit was located.

Julio set down his tray of hallucinogenic fungi and reached into the cupboard for a gallon-sized bag stuffed with pills.

"Wow, that's a lot of party favors," I said, and inched toward the door. "Mark, we should go get settled in our cabin."

I headed for Ontario, the cabin Mark and I had been assigned, and pushed open the particleboard door. It was clear to me that Julio had choreographed an event offering far more than crypto conversation. I remembered my recent RES Zoom class and felt foolish. I hadn't outgrown being triggered by drugs like I'd imagined. What arrogance! Standing in the presence of Julio's mushrooms and Molly sent my mind whirling back to memories from my youth.

My first exposure to drugs happened at home. One of the biggest fights I ever got in with my mom happened after I found a vial of cocaine in her sock drawer when I was thirteen. I didn't have any clean socks so I decided to sneak a pair of hers without permission. After I told her what I found, and that I didn't think she should keep drugs in the house, she grounded me for a month for taking her socks without asking. She called me a thief. She told me I was selfish and didn't appreciate all the sacrifices she made for my brother and me, especially since my dad didn't want us. She told me to mind my own business if I expected to live under her roof. I felt devastated to be blamed for my mom's carelessness and flattened by her rage. I cried complicated tears of disgrace and anger, but I never stole socks again.

It wasn't until I bumped into my mom at an after-work party a few years later that I realized her own shame fueled the sock drawer rant. We both worked at a popular Mexican restaurant, me as a sixteen-year-old hostess and my mom as a thirty-six-year-old waitress, but we shared some of the same work friends. One night, as I was getting off my shift, one of those friends invited me to a party.

The party was pulsating with laughter and music when we arrived. I grabbed a beer, started to mingle, and eventually found my way to the walk-in party closet. There was my mother, bent over a dresser covered with lines of cocaine, a rolled-up dollar bill carefully placed in her right nostril. When she looked up and our eyes met, time stopped. We were locked in a vortex of awkwardness where our mother-daughter roles reversed; she was the naughty teen who had been caught red-handed and I was the adjudicating parent. The shame on her face broke my young heart. Finding drugs in her sock drawer was nothing like watching her snort lines of cocaine. The humiliation my mom felt rolled off her body with amphetamine force. She looked like she was going to cry. I'm not sure what was worse: to be revealed as the deeply flawed parent to one's child, or to be the child who discovers the deeply disturbing flaw. But at sixteen, I didn't have the words or the compassion either of us needed right then, so I turned away in silence and quickly left the party. Just like the sock fight, we never again spoke of that moment, but I felt the same devastation, the same longing for a parent who followed rules instead of breaking them.

By the time I was a senior in high school, the drugs I encountered were of my own doing, not my mom's. I drank plenty of alcohol and smoked marijuana, but cocaine was my drug of choice. My boyfriend at the time had an older brother who was a drug dealer, a familial connection I considered most convenient. We used to babysit his kids in exchange for the same white powder I had found in my mom's sock drawer during eighth grade. My boyfriend and I would fix the kids dinner, put them in their pj's, and send them to bed. Then we would help ourselves to the modest mountain of blow left on a small cutting board in a designated kitchen cupboard. By the time we cut lines onto the coffee table with a credit card, my hands perspired with desire and my heart thumped greedy beats.

It had been decades since I'd been in the presence of drugs, but seeing these in Julio's cabin kitchen triggered a river of heat under my skin. My body felt twitchy and my palms started to sweat. Just like my cocaine-babysitting nights, inexplicable eagerness molecules started bubbling in my brain.

"Should we walk back up to the car and grab the suitcases?" Mark earnestly suggested when he finally entered the Ontario Cabin.

"Are you sure that's a good idea?" I asked, thinking Mark was crazy. "Is this really *our* kind of weekend retreat?"

Mark looked confused. "Is this because of the cabin? I know there are no screens on the windows and how sensitive you are to mosquito bites, but I'm pretty sure we packed the bug spray."

"What are you talking about?" I said, exasperated. "I'm uncomfortable with the double felony-sized piles of drugs in Julio's room, the sex workers strolling around the lake half naked, and the pandemic-era orgy that's about to take place! If I'm catching COVID, it's going to be on a plane to visit our daughters, not because I accidentally attended some crypto sex party."

My husband and I had grown up in different worlds. My adolescence lacked guardrails and as a result, drugs and wild social events were hallmarks of my youth. In contrast, Mark juggled baseball practice and homework. He was also focused on helping his family once his father's health had declined. In addition to complications caused by hemophilia, his father, Michael, was the victim of a violent robbery when Mark was a sophomore in high school. Michael was beaten up, and the friend he was with got shot five times, leaving Mark's father with severe PTSD. Mark graduated from high school early so that he could be more available to support his father. This elevated level of early responsibility denied Mark a fun and carefree adolescence. He had missed out on youthful spontaneity and teenage parties.

"Oh," Mark said. "I wondered what Julio was showing us in his cabin. I've never actually seen drugs before."

I had to remind myself how innocent he was.

"Well, it's been a long time for me, but I can assure you, things are going to get a little out of control this weekend," I said, wiping sweat from my forehead.

In contrast to my husband's naivete, sticking around made me a hypocrite. How could I face students in my Re-Emerging Scholars program? How could I lecture them on the serious consequences of proximity to illegal substances? I thought of what I'd shared with Paulo the day before in our Zoom class.

"You're smart to avoid situations where people will be partying," I'd said. "And not just because you're triggered by drugs. Simply being in the presence of illegal substances or activity is a violation of your parole."

After my wild adolescence, I knew how easy it was to find yourself in the wrong place at the wrong time. I was also familiar with tendencies to make excuses, to backslide, and to do things a person would likely regret the next day.

I could hear my voice as I told my students, "You don't have to be high. You don't have to have the gun in your hand. It doesn't matter if you were only watching the fight. You can't be in the same room, the same house, or on the same neighborhood block as those things. If you find yourself in the company of illegal *anything*, get the hell out of there as fast as you can."

Given all the times I stood on that soapbox with my college students, Julio's weekend retreat made me the butt of a cosmic joke. Granted, I wasn't on probation or parole, but my professional life was dedicated to growing awareness and responsibility for one's personal choices—not just avoiding arrest.

"I just can't stay here," I said. "I'm sorry."

Mark didn't look happy but he didn't argue. He knew about my history with drug use and the efforts I'd taken not to get trapped by that life. In my twenties, I'd sworn off drugs and got serious about college.

"Okay," he said, finally.

We found Deborah and told her about my discomfort with Julio's party plans. Then I explained that we were getting back in the car to head home.

"Deb, I know we just got here," I said, "but I think you should grab your things and drive back with us."

Deborah took a deep breath and looked away from me and Mark. Her eyes scanned the lake below. After a minute, she said, "I've got too much riding on this weekend. I understand why you guys are leaving, but I'll take my chances. I have an informal meeting with a potential producer for my movie tomorrow. I'll take an Uber home if I have to, but I'm going to stick around."

There are times in a marriage when you should give your partner a shout-out for prioritizing his role as your supporter over his own desires, and this was one of those times for me. Making it home in the dark would be tricky. Our navigation was unlikely to work and the government in Puerto Rico set up random driving blockades to ensure everyone honored the nightly COVID curfew.

Deborah headed back into the main house and Mark and I started walking to the car. We never unpacked, so our suitcases were still inside our vehicle.

"I hope we don't get stopped by the police for being out past COVID curfew," I said.

"We'll be fine," Mark replied, his tone dour.

"I really am sorry I can't stay here," I said. "I know you were looking forward to the weekend."

I felt guilty about leaving Deb stranded, tired from driving to the event, and not certain we could even get back to our place in Dorado. I could tell by Mark's long face and somber mood that he preferred to stay the night and watch the show. Pandemic isolation created taxing monotony, and one night at Julio's party promised more entertainment than we had seen in a year. Maybe ever. Mark wasn't likely to take drugs, but the people-watching guaranteed five-star ratings.

"I get it," Mark said. "The weekend isn't going to be like either of us anticipated."

Then my husband got behind the wheel of our rental car and backed out of the congested driveway.

"The naked fire dancers might have been fun to see," was all he said.

CHAPTER 12:

THE RITZ

The next morning, I watched the sunrise over the ocean from our balcony and contemplated how Dorado, Puerto Rico, seemed very far away from my California home. The clouds, a rainbow of weather patterns in black, gray, white, and orange, rendered mountains of distance between me and the daughters I loved on the West Coast. Pockets of rain, far out to sea, looked like curtains of tears let loose from Poseidon. Mark and I considered ourselves blessed to live by the ocean, but California still felt like home and I missed it.

We had made it back to our condo in Playa Tortuga from Lake Carite without incident, yet my hopes of making new friends at Julio's crypto weekend were washed away. Like a bucket of ice water to the face, I felt stunned from what I'd seen and annoyed that we had wasted a thousand dollars. To lift my spirits, I grabbed a book and a towel and headed toward the beach for some wave therapy. There were many articles linking the beach to happiness and health, and I was a believer. Whether it was the negative ions in the ocean spray or the vitamin D in the morning sunshine, I had experienced physical health improvements since moving oceanside. I found myself sleeping better and able to run longer distances. At the beach, a bad mood didn't stand a chance.

En route I bumped into a neighbor, Kathy. I had seen this older woman before walking an overweight terrier in circles around the parking lot. She and her husband, Sal, lived in the building next to ours, and she looked a little lost even though she was only a hundred yards from the steps that led to her front door. Kathy asked me what my name was and introduced me to Gidget, her chubby dog. Then she looked in the direction of her condo, where she said her husband was, and switched gears. In a snap she turned from cordial to irritable.

"He's so bossy," she said, her eyes angry. "I wish that asshole would just leave me alone!"

Kathy's brown hair was streaked with gray. It fell in a tangled mess past her bony shoulders, and her oversized T-shirt made it difficult to tell if she was wearing pants. Both she and Gidget had dirt on their faces. I wondered if Kathy needed a caregiver like my father did after his stroke left him diminished.

"Kathy," a voice bellowed from behind, "put a fucking mask on!"

I turned and looked up to see Sal, Kathy's husband, sitting in an old office chair placed next to the front door of their condo. Like us, their unit was located at the ocean's edge, and they lived on a bluff at the highest point in the community. I imagined the view from their condo was spectacular, and I had silently wished for a place like that.

"Cheers!" he said when our eyes met. He thrust his drink in the air. "Wanna whiskey?" Frank Sinatra's "My Way" played from inside his house.

Sal was a big man with a booming voice, one that yelled instead of talked.

"Nine a.m. is a bit early for me, but thanks."

Mark had met Sal previously, but this was my first encounter. I turned back toward Kathy.

"Ahh . . . marriage," I offered lightly, grateful that Mark started his day with black coffee.

Sal and Kathy were original owners at Playa Tortuga, our condo community. According to Sal, he'd bought their beachfront condo—the first one sold—sight unseen in a New York diner thirty-five years ago. He claimed that his initial agreement with the builder was written on a paper napkin, when a promise and a handshake still meant something. Sal owned a whiskey and liquor distribution company. At eighty-six, he still ran his company, but he told Mark that Kathy had dementia and they were thinking it might be time to live closer to family in Florida. Mark shared all this information with me because he wanted to extend his Puerto Rican residency and he thought Sal and Kathy's condo might become available.

The month before, Mark had reached out to our landlord, curious to see whether the condo we rented might be for sale. My college announced that remote teaching and COVID safety would continue for the next academic year, so an extension of his Act 20 & 22 membership seemed possible, and sensible. The tax savings from our first year on the island were going to be significant. We figured we could isolate in Puerto Rico just as easily as in California, but I worried about housing conversations yet to come. What would buying a place in Puerto Rico mean for our California home ownership? What about my relocation stipulations? I wondered if this was the start of a much longer PR residency renegotiation.

At Playa Tortuga, owners and renters kept tabs on one another, and Sal knew we were renting our unit when he approached Mark the week before. Sal had suggested we get together and have a conversation. He wondered if we wanted to rent his unit once our current lease ended. A deal negotiated without an agent, he said, would be financially beneficial to both parties.

When Mark heard the parking lot commotion, he walked downstairs, waved to me and Kathy, and then headed toward Sal. I said my goodbyes to Kathy and continued on to the beach. When I returned home, Mark was smiling and patted the couch next to where he sat.

"Sal told me that he is willing to make a rental agreement that gives us first right of refusal. So . . ." Mark said, "if his condo goes on the market, as his renters, we would have the right to purchase before the sale went public."

This was a big deal. There were no oceanfront condos for sale in our community, and from what we had learned these places were most often inherited or else sold by word of mouth through real estate agents getting secret kickbacks from buyers in addition to the commission they made from sellers. Given Sal's age and Kathy's health, it seemed like Sal's offer might turn into a real purchasing opportunity. Our current landlord had been adamant that he never planned to sell his unit at any price.

"I'm not opposed," I hedged. "Another year on the island probably makes sense, and I'd love to keep renting by the water, but why *own* property in Puerto Rico?" I asked. "My teaching job isn't going to stay remote forever."

"I know," Mark said. "At some point you'll return to campus and we'll move back to California. But since that date is indeterminate, I think we should continue to take advantage of the benefits afforded us while living in Puerto Rico."

Sun and oceanfront living topped his articulated list, but the biggest reason was obvious. Mark had saved a bundle in taxes as a member of Act 20 & 22; he was excited by the results of our temporary relocation. Another year in this tax haven meant more movement up the ladder of financial independence and one step closer to Mark leaving his law career. Mark suggested that even if we went back to California sooner rather than later, an oceanfront condo purchase could be a good investment long-term.

"Let's not rush into anything," I said. "I understand that your membership in Act 20 & 22 has economic upsides, but buying property in Puerto Rico is a big decision."

I didn't believe that money was the secret to happiness, but I acknowledged that it helped. Interpersonal relationships, a sense of community, interesting hobbies, professional fulfillment, and one's health all contributed to a sense of well-being, but financial stability contributed to the happiness equation too, so I couldn't ignore my husband's arguments.

I had recently read that for individuals starting out on lower income rungs, happiness accelerated quickly with increased salary and tended to peak at $100,000 of annual yearly income. Resource scarcity was like a prison that strained a person's emotional and physical health. It required its captive to live in chains. When a person fought to meet basic needs like shelter and food, they felt trapped. It's not rocket science; if you offered one of my struggling college students a job that paid $100,000 a year, their happiness meter would soar.

Less was understood about the relationship between high-end earners and happiness. Research on happiness and earners who make at least $500,000 a year was inconclusive, but if Mark was any indication, it helped here as well. Like reading an unexpectedly good book, my husband didn't want our PR relocation story to end. He hoped for a sequel, or at least a few more chapters.

I was still sitting next to Mark on the couch, my feet sandy from my beach visit, when he reached over to gently tuck a strand of windblown hair behind my ear. Then he took my hand in his.

"I wouldn't get too concerned yet," Mark said, taking a breath. "I get the feeling Sal's lonely; this rental offer could just be a ploy for attention."

Compared to the rest of the people we saw unloading groceries or walking dogs in our community, Sal and Kathy stood out. Like old comic book characters, their images belonged to another time and place. Mark was probably right about Sal; they didn't appear to have visitors, and caretaking a wife with dementia must be a lonesome job. I worried for them. What if they had an emergency? The way Sal drank whiskey for breakfast and Kathy got lost in the parking lot, challenge was inevitable and being neighborly, the right choice. I wanted to let them know they could reach out to us in case they needed help, regardless of all the potential rental talk. Kathy reminded me of my dad and the challenges that come with age, disability, and isolation.

Mark told me that Sal had invited us to lunch the following day. Sal wanted to get to know us better and he only talked "business" at the club.

* * *

Mark and I walked over to Sal and Kathy's place at ten thirty the next morning. We thought this would give us time to look around and see if the layout of their place would meet our needs, but Sal had different ideas. He led us straight out to the patio, sat us down, and brought us a drink.

"Nothing is better than this," Sal said, looking out at the view. He had a half-empty drink of his own. The ocean roared each time it hit the rocks below, and the breeze lifted saltwater spray right onto Sal's patio. This condo orientation was different from the one we rented, more elevated and yet even closer to the ocean. The breeze was stronger and palm trees framed the bands of dark blue and turquoise that streaked the Atlantic like a watery quilt. Sitting on Sal and Kathy's patio was like being on a boat.

Mark and Sal talked easily as if they were old friends. I just smiled, happy to be outside. When I first entered Sal and Kathy's, I was struck by the stench, a combination of filthy animal, marijuana, and moldy stuff. The condo was packed with old furniture, stacks of papers, framed family photos, bags of chips, faded pastel-colored abstracts on the wall behind cracked glass, and hundreds of small stuffed animals. It looked like a legion of Beanie Babies had moved in and multiplied. The walls had yellowed from smoke and age. Rusted-out fans hung from the ceiling and the floor tiles were cracked, revealing large chunks of cement foundation. This condo was part Goodwill pile and part hoarder's paradise—with a ten-million-dollar view.

If I had arrived under different circumstances, say to drop off a child for a sleepover, I would have figured out an excuse to take my kid back home. Now I had to figure out a way to redirect my husband's rental dreams. No way was I interested in a "fully furnished" lease. In spite of the early hour, I sipped my drink and thought up rental excuses. Then Kathy joined us and we headed to the club for lunch.

Sal's club was the Ritz-Carlton, where he had been a member since moving to Playa Tortuga. When Mark and I picked the town of Dorado for our relocation, I read articles about the place. The Ritz in Dorado was more than a fancy hotel; it was an upscale community, with hundreds of homes, for the rich and famous. This fifty-acre estate was developed by Laurance Rockefeller, son of philanthropist John D. Rockefeller Jr., in the 1950s. The private grounds hosted homeowners, club members, and hotel guests. It was considered "very exclusive" and touted as a premier location in the Caribbean. The public was not allowed on the grounds, in the restaurants, or on the golf course unless invited as the guest of a member, so this was our first visit, but Sal went there most days for lunch and, of course, cocktails.

Sal gave us more details about the Ritz as Mark drove Sal's car toward the exclusive community. Kathy and I, along with Gidget, who turned out to be blind as well as smelly, were in the back seat.

"Thanks for driving, Mark," Sal said.

A half-empty bottle of whiskey rolled out from under the seat in front of me.

"Drinking and driving is hell when you're my age," Sal confessed with a chuckle.

I looked at the bottle of brown liquid sloshing by my feet and carefully moved it back under the car seat with my toes.

"You're gonna love the Ritz," Sal said. "It used to be the only gig in town for gringos like us. Other places have popped up, but they're second-rate copies. The Ritz is first-class."

I worried I was underdressed. My cotton skirt and tank top came from Old Navy. Everywhere we had been on the island up to this point was casual. Mark and I didn't run with the private club crowd, and if there was a dress code, I didn't know about it.

At the Ritz security gate, Sal ordered a golf cart driver to pick us up and take us to Encanto, a lovely open-air restaurant that bordered a manicured beach. Kite surfers danced in the waves, their bodies carried into acrobatic feats by the wind. Perfect rows of blue umbrellas placed next to white lounge chairs looked like they belonged on a postcard. The restaurant was busy, but that didn't deter Sal. When the hostess told us that pets weren't allowed, Sal waved her off like he was swatting at a fly.

Mark whispered to me and directed my vision to a family sitting at a nearby table.

"That's Peter Schiff," Mark said, his quiet voice filled with admiration.

Schiff was one of the macroeconomists Mark followed. He was best known for predicting the financial crisis in 2008 and preaching the wisdom of gold and silver ownership. According to *TheRichest*, this guy's net worth was $70 million.

"This place reeks of money," I whispered to Mark. I felt like the Walmart shopper who accidently took a wrong turn and ended up at Neiman Marcus.

"Can we get some drinks?" Sal said too loudly from where we stood in the entrance. His demand attracted the attention of nearby tables just as Gidget defecated by my feet.

"I'm so sorry, Mr. Benozzo," the hostess said, taking stock of the dog excrement. "The wait is more than an hour, but I can call someone to take you to the Plantation, where you'll be seated right away."

It wasn't clear if the hostess was just lying to get us out of there, but she never even mentioned Gidget's mess. What kind of place tolerated patrons who let their dog shit on the floor? Sal and Kathy stepped around the feces unfazed. My face flushed with embarrassment as Mark and I followed our hosts to the next golf cart.

The Plantation Restaurant overlooked a golf course. Sal ordered three martinis and a Coke for Kathy. "She can't drink anymore," he said. "Not since she started losing her marbles."

"Wow, Sal, that's a rotten thing to say," I replied.

Sal—who ordered drinks for everyone at the table without asking, insulted his wife, and left his dog's waste for others to clean up—made me squirm in my chair.

"Oh, don't be so uppity," Sal admonished. "This old girl is the love of my life."

Kathy dug in her large purse for Gidget's water bowl, seemingly unaffected by her husband's comment.

"I wish you could have seen her when we first met."

Kathy looked up. Her shirt was on backward today, but her eyes were bright and she smiled at her husband.

"God, she was a knockout," Sal said. "The first time I saw her she was hailing a cab on Fifth Avenue in New York. She had on these boots that came all the way up to her knees and this mane of blonde hair that could stop traffic. She was the most gorgeous woman I'd ever seen. It was love at first sight."

"I told him to go to hell," Kathy chimed in, joining the conversation for the first time. "I told him to stop wasting his money—he kept sending me flowers and chasing me around New York—I didn't want anything to do with him."

Back in those days, Kathy had good reason to be wary of Sal. He was in "The Business," a job from which, Sal informed us, one never retires.

"But when she finally let her guard down, I swooped in," Sal said. "She couldn't get enough of me, and man, did we have a blast. Back in the eighties we were regulars at Studio 54. Those were some good times, some party days. It was probably all the booze and drugs that caused Kathy's dementia, but it was worth it—you only live once."

I doubted that Kathy would agree. She seemed flustered searching for things in her purse that didn't materialize. Kathy was sixteen years younger than Sal, but she appeared older, tiny and sunken. She reminded me of a small child.

"We promised each other we'd die of TMF!" Sal added.

"What's that?" I asked.

"Too Much Fun!"

Sal looked and sounded like someone who should have been cast in *The Godfather*. He wore a large gold crucifix around his neck and had a New York accent. His olive-colored skin, big nose, and head of silver slicked-back hair made him look like Tony Bennett. He was tall, well over six feet, and even though his broad shoulders had started to slump with age, he must have been imposing in his prime. Sal's looks were deceiving, however. He told us that he was born Solomon Benbanski. His people had immigrated from the same part of the globe as Mark's ancestors; Sal was part Polish and part Ukrainian Jew.

"I changed my name to Sal Benozzo as a young man to make it sound more Italian," he said.

This was important, Sal explained, because he used his liquor distribution business to wash money for the mob. His Eastern European heritage meant that he couldn't ever be a "made" man, but that probably saved his life.

"Did Kathy know you were in The Business when she met you?" I asked.

"Hell no," Sal said. "That wasn't something you advertised."

Sal took a drink from his martini glass. Then he picked up the skewered olive, ate it, and threw the toothpick on the ground.

"Now, all my friends are either dead or in prison," Sal continued. "Kathy is all I have left. But life is good. I start each day with a doobie and a Celebrex. I sit in my hot tub and look out at the ocean. My advice to you? Never leave the game if you want to stay young."

The topic of rental agreements never came up, but the conversation was more interesting than I could have imagined. It was the first time I'd met a mobster, and when the salads arrived my interest was piqued.

"How does someone get involved in The Business?" Mark asked Sal.

Sal was silent for a few seconds and then ordered Mark to get out his phone.

"Send me an email that says you're my attorney," Sal said. Then he reached for his wallet, pulled out a dollar bill, and gave it to Mark.

"I've retained you," Sal said. "We have attorney-client privilege, so now I'm gonna tell you some stories."

CHAPTER 13:

LOBSTERS AND MOBSTERS

As Sal devoured a buttery lobster tail, Kathy nibbled on bread, and Mark and I enjoyed our salads, our host made good on his promise. Like turning on a memory faucet, the stories of his life poured out steadily. One story gave me chills. It involved the disappearance of Jimmy Hoffa, the Detroit labor union leader who was involved with the Mafia and disappeared in 1975. Sal told us that Hoffa was well-known for extending the reach of the teamsters in the thirties and forties and for his connections to organized crime. He was indicted for jury tampering in the sixties and went to prison for eight years.

"All the fuckin' rumors? True!" Sal said. "Hoffa was murdered."

Although Hoffa went missing in 1975, he wasn't declared legally dead until 1982.

"It was a cover-up; that's why they waited so long to declare Hoffa dead. Lots of people were dirty," Sal continued. "Hoffa was murdered in '75."

Since the location and circumstances of Hoffa's death were still the subject of public debate the case remained a mystery, but Sal told us that guys in The Business knew exactly what happened to Hoffa, and that he even knew the details. That was just The Business. Sal was so good at The Business, he bragged, that one of the bosses gave him a Tiffany clock. It was engraved with, "We met at the right time."

At the mention of Hoffa, my crossing guard stiffened. I felt her boot tap my shoulder, a reminder that I should pay attention to my surroundings. I could tell that she didn't like me talking to mobsters about people getting murdered.

Sal smiled wide and crossed his arms.

"It felt good, you know, that the bosses valued my contributions," Sal said. "Doesn't seem like this younger generation cares about shit. Makes me miss the good ol' days."

On the one hand, I thought, it was sweet that even tough guys appreciated professional recognition. On the other, the fact that Sal laundered money for the mob meant he was anything but sweet. When I thought about the sorts of crimes that warranted special recognition from a mob boss, my chest felt tight.

As the river of Sal's stories flowed, I realized that he reminded me of my maternal grandfather, Lance Stanford. Grandpa Stanford was a direct descendant of Leland Stanford. Leland Stanford served as a governor and senator of California in the 1800s, helped to build the transcontinental railroad as a member of the "Big Four," and founded Stanford University. Grandpa Stanford was Leland Stanford's nephew. My grandfather passed away when I was in college, but my childhood memories of him were vivid, and he made me feel like being around Sal did. It wasn't just that my grandfather and Sal were hypermasculine, or that they both grew up in a time when sexism and racism were common among white men with power. It was that they both scared the heck out of me.

Like Sal, Grandpa Stanford was a prolific drinker and said offensive things to people he loved. I had heard him call my grandmother "that stupid woman" and worse on many occasions. His outbursts were met with silence from the other adults in the room. I could tell that nobody in my family liked the condescension that surged in cosmic ratio to the cocktails Grandpa Stanford drank, but the unspoken rule was to politely laugh at, or ignore, whatever terrible thing he said.

I didn't yet understand that alcoholic abusers, and sometimes their codependent abusees, vehemently deny any wrongdoing. They fight hard for justifications, and even lies, that legitimize a lifetime of bad behavior. By the time I was ten I was told not to answer the phone until the caller revealed themselves on the answering machine.

"If Grandpa calls and it's after three in the afternoon, don't pick up the phone," my mother instructed on multiple occasions. "He's drunk by then and I don't want to talk to him."

The only strategy she had was to try to stay out of his way. I knew this because I learned the same lesson about my mother when she had too much to drink. The times I had tried to reason, persuade, even joke with my mom when she was drunk, I'd regretted it. Like my Grandpa Stanford, alcohol let loose a tendril of mean in my mother. And when shit-faced drunk, my mother was hell on wheels. Stanford DNA was potent stuff.

It occurred to me at the lunch with Sal, as I thought about these memories of Grandpa Stanford, that my recollections of my grandfather could be imprecise. Grandpa Stanford had been dead for more than thirty years. I wondered if my villainous recollections would seem unfair to my extended family members or if my memories had been tainted by the sands of time.

As a direct descendant of the Stanford family, my grandfather had genetic clout, but that didn't make him a nice person. Like Leland Stanford, who was widely considered a robber baron, my grandpa Lance Stanford was the kind of man who would step on others in dirty boots if it helped him get what he wanted. Unlike Leland Stanford, the ruthless industrialist, my grandpa died penniless, the result of bad financial planning and money mismanagement.

To be fair, Grandpa Stanford liked to tell jokes and his contagious laugh was unusual for its inclusion of a smoker's wheeze. He could entertain a room full of family at the holidays with ease. He was also an excellent cribbage player, and sometimes he'd let me sit next to him and watch as he moved the colored toothpicks around the track. In between cigarette drags he'd bark, "Fifteen-two, fifteen-four, fifteen-six . . ." and I couldn't recall a game he ever lost. Grandpa Stanford was the Cribbage King and he taught me how to play the game. But when I closed my eyes and conjured his image, I felt uneasy. I got the sense that at any moment something bad was going to happen, like the tension I felt in high school as a crowd gathered from nowhere into a giant circle right before a fight broke out. I suspected these feelings were what gave the distressing memories more weight.

My memory of Grandpa Stanford was also affected by the terrible things my mother told me about her childhood. Her earliest memory was of being trapped. She remembered the sounds of her parents laughing (and undoubtedly drinking) in the living room while she wrestled inside a cotton bag she had been zipped inside. It was some contraption that had left her confined to lying on her back, unable to fully stretch her limbs. When my grandparents didn't want to be bothered by their daughter, they zipped her in.

"They used to leave me alone for hours," my mom told me once when I was in high school. "I was zipped into a bag and put into another room so I wouldn't bother them."

Mom walked to the kitchen, opened a bottle of wine, and poured herself a glass.

"That sounds awful," I said, but when I pressed for details, Mom shut down the conversation.

My soul grieved picturing my mother as a baby, crying out for help, comfort, and love. Often, the pain we've endured as children followed us into adulthood. It burrowed deep into our core, distorting our relationships in irrational ways. Unless released, that buried pain could make us sick.

These thoughts flickered in the back of my mind while we sat at the Plantation having lunch with Sal and Kathy.

I understood that Sal was capable of unspeakable things. The Hoffa murder topic was making me queasy, so as we finished our food, I asked Sal a question about growing up in Chicago.

"About the time I started high school," Sal said, "I got a job at the butcher's in the local market. It was run by these two guys, Vinnie and Dominic. One day the big boss walks in and starts busting their balls over costs. I'm just a kid, but I can see they're scared. Profits were down, and that was enough to get a guy whacked in those days."

I put down my fork and took a moment to appreciate the view, aware that Sal's youthful memories did not prevent more murder talk in the context of a perfect setting at the Ritz. We were sitting in an open-air dining room. White billowy clouds moved gracefully above the golf course next to the restaurant. Kathy's dog Gidget had fallen asleep in her lap. Mark and I must have looked like we were having lunch with our sweet, elderly parents.

"I'm a good worker so pretty soon, when I'd show up after school, they would take off and leave me in charge,"

Sal said. "I'd tell the girls behind the counter, 'When you weigh the meat, do it on top of the cardboard,' because even back then, I understood how to play the game."

Sal demonstrated by taking imaginary sliced beef and flipping it onto a scale that didn't exist. Then he downed the rest of his second martini, flashing a fat gold ring on his pinkie finger.

"Well, the big boss comes back a few weeks later and he's happy. He compliments Vinnie and Dominic on getting profits up. But the next day, a government guy shows up and tells me there has been a complaint. I ask the government guy what kind of car he drives and then I tell him, 'Let's meet outside by your car so we can talk away from the customers.' I'm a teenager so he thinks I'm gonna spill the beans on Vinnie and Dominic and he says okay. But first I go into the refrigerator and I take down this big, beautiful side of beef and I ask another guy if I can borrow his overcoat."

"Why would you need an overcoat?" I interrupted, thinking maybe I missed some key element in Sal's story.

"To wrap up the meat," Sal continued. "I wrap up the slab of beef in the overcoat and I take the fucker right out to the guy's car and put it in his trunk. I unwrap the coat and tell him, 'I got one of these for you every month.' The government guy closes the trunk and drives away. Problem solved."

Mark laughed. "That's a great story, Sal."

"It definitely demonstrates creative problem-solving skills," I said. "How did you become such a savvy teenager?"

When I asked Sal about how he knew the inner workings of The Business at such a young age, he told me his father was a shylock, a term I hadn't heard since reading *The Merchant of Venice* in high school.

"When he came to this country, he greased the wheels of business in Chicago. Smart man," Sal said. "And he learned this from his father in the Old Country."

Family histories were like spiderwebs, I thought. They formed strands of connectivity that spread out to create an entire universe. From the proper angle, they were beautiful, comprised of threads that glistened like diamonds in morning sunlight, but they were also sticky and dangerous. The unsuspecting prey who got caught in a web was doomed, zipped in, for the rest of her days. Just like my mother struggled from inside a cotton bag as a baby, and Sal had followed in his father's illicit footsteps, sometimes our birthright was treacherous.

It seemed like Sal and Mark liked each other. They laughed at each other's stories and talked about how much they loved living by the ocean. But Sal was—or at least had been—a dangerous man. Was my husband working the rental angle, or did he genuinely like this old mobster? Mark and Sal shared ancestry in common since their people had emigrated from the same part of the world—Eastern Europe. They also shared an affinity for tax havens, but that didn't explain the chemistry I was seeing.

After lunch, we drove back to our Playa Tortuga community and said goodbye to Sal and Kathy. As we walked up the stairs to our condo, I asked Mark if his connection to Sal felt paternal in some way, but he brushed me off.

"It's more fascination than fatherly admiration," Mark said. "Being with Sal is like digging up a Neanderthal. I don't like the way he treats women or clubs unsuspecting creatures over the head, but I find him fascinating. He is from a different place and time, one of a kind. You're not likely to meet another Sal Benozzo."

I understood Mark's summation, but I didn't think originality made up for his dangerousness. My gut told me to be careful around him. I believed that men like Sal, regardless of age, shouldn't be trusted.

* * *

The first rental deal we verbally negotiated with Sal a week later was a six-month lease that ended with an option to buy.

Mark and I agreed that we could endure anything for six months, and that we could hire cleaners to make the condo livable. When we eventually read the written contract that Sal emailed us, however, the option that it included favored Sal, not us. It allowed Sal to sell us the condo, only if he wanted to do so, after we paid him an inflated lease price for five consecutive years.

After reading the contract, Mark and I walked over to Sal and Kathy's place and asked if we could talk. Sal shook Mark's hand and he gave me a hug. Then he kissed both sides of my face.

"My God you're a beautiful woman," Sal said. "If I was twenty years younger, your husband would have a problem."

I forced a polite laugh and said, "Your wife might have had something to say about that." Then I spun out of his grasp, already wishing we could leave.

Sal directed us to his patio and made us each an unsolicited whiskey on the rocks.

"Sal, we want to begin by telling you how much fun we had at lunch last week. You have lived one hell of a life, my friend." Mark picked his drink up off the table and moved it toward Sal. They toasted to making new friends.

"I appreciate you sending us the rental contract," Mark continued. "Unfortunately, the terms don't quite work for us."

Sal gave Mark an easy smile, as if he had just received a compliment instead of a refusal. Then he tried to soften his bait-and-switch contract negotiation.

"One thing I forgot to include in the contract is that you can use my membership at the Ritz," he said. "Use your own credit card, of course, but just say you're me. When you sign your checks put down my member number."

Given that Sal had been a club member since the early days, when Rockefeller first snatched up the oceanfront property, I doubted Sal's membership offer was possible even if I had been comfortable posing as Mrs. Sal Benozzo. Mark and I were not twentysomethings, but neither of us looked eighty either.

"That's a nice perk, Sal," Mark said. "But we're going to have to pass on renting. However, if you want to talk about selling instead of renting, we are very interested."

"Fucking attorneys," Sal cried when it was clear our minds were made up. "The only reason I'd even let you rent my place is because I like you both so much, but attorneys can't seem to do anything for me, other than bust my balls."

Sal hit the arm of his chair with his fist and then pushed himself back from the table with a loud scrape. Mark and I shifted in our seats, ready to end the conversation. I'd been ready to leave from the start.

Sal stood up. "You know my place in New York?" he asked. His question referenced the real estate link he had shared in his email. Sal owned multiple properties, including a sprawling place in Upstate New York.

"If you saw the video, you know what a beautiful place that is." Sal waved his arms in the air to emphasize the word "beautiful."

"There's mob up in that part of New York too," Sal said. "I bought it off of Pete the Greek, who bought it from the guy who ran the KKK for a while. Anyway, that's where my first real attorney would come visit me. And he would come up all the time. I thought he liked my meatballs, but it turns out he was just fucking my houseboy. Goddamn attorneys."

That was our cue. Mark and I left our unfinished drinks on the table and rushed to the door.

CHAPTER 14:

TELEGRAMS

When we left Sal and Kathy's after declining the rental contract, I was ready for wave therapy at the beach. I needed to contemplate another year on the island, not knowing where we'd live. The lease on our short-term rental in Playa Tortuga would expire soon. After that, we'd go back to River Acres, our California home, where I could settle back into my comfortable routine. However, since it looked like my job would stay remote, we were prepared to return to Puerto Rico for another six months so Mark could complete his second year of Act 20 & 22 residency requirements.

Before heading to the water, I grabbed a book and folding chair, then found Mark and gave him a hug.

"That did *not* go well," I said, referring to our failed rental negotiations with Sal.

I was relieved by the outcome but had the nagging feeling my husband was still interested in pursuing a deal. He loved the physical orientation of Sal's place, the way ocean spray misted the patio like a giant salty spa diffuser, and my husband was a master negotiator.

"I wouldn't be so sure," Mark replied. "It takes at least three moves."

It was the same thing Mark would say about settlement negotiations for his clients.

"Until the other player responds to a gambit, their true motivation remains hidden," he'd told me. "You need to know if they're going to take the gambit and the short-term advantage, or decline in favor of the long game."

I supposed the same logic could be applied to condos owned by mobsters and that more pieces would move around the chessboard before we were finished with Sal and Kathy Benozzo.

"You're sexy when you talk strategy," I whispered in Mark's ear, and kissed him before heading out.

As I approached the beach, I saw Deborah. I hadn't hung out with Deb since leaving her at Julio's crypto party weekend. She was sitting in the shade of a palm tree, a wide-brimmed hat protecting her fair skin, reading a book. We had texted—I wanted to make sure she wasn't stranded—but I still felt a little guilty about leaving her behind. I had broken an unspoken girlfriend rule and I feared this would stifle our nascent friendship. I liked her bubbly personality and hoped for a gal pal here on the island.

The night we'd left the Lake Carite party, I worried out loud to Mark. "What if she can't find a ride home? Or gets hurt? Or drugged?"

"She could have left with us," Mark replied. "She's a grown woman. We told her what was up, and she made the choice to stay. I know she had a work meeting planned, but I think she was on the hunt for more than just a business connection." Mark was a very practical person, but I had other ranges of feelings to deal with.

Deb was single and had told me she wanted a boyfriend. In California I could have introduced her to friends, but aside from a mobster and his wife, I didn't know people in Puerto Rico. And from what I'd seen in Dorado, middle-aged men who looked like stateside transplants tended to be holding hands with much younger partners. Older wealthy men dating younger women was a tired cliché, but the phenomenon was visible in Dorado.

Mark encouraged me to leave well enough alone when we returned from Julio's party that night. "Leaving her there feels like a bigger deal to you than her. Let it go. She won't hold it against you. Deb knows how to get herself out of a jam."

Mark's tone was gentle, but I could tell he did not understand the imperative—the sisterhood rule—of women watching out for women.

I was relieved a few days later when Deb texted to say she was fine. There wasn't a hint of ire in her message. All she wrote was that we had missed one heck of a bash.

The week prior to seeing Deb on the beach that day, after she had returned from the crypto weekend, we were watching the sunset from our balcony when Mark pointed toward the ocean.

"Isn't that Deb?" he asked. "Looks like she made a connection at the crypto weekend after all."

Sitting a few hundred yards below on a grassy knoll was Deb and a much younger man. They were deeply engaged in conversation. They sat close to one another on a small blanket. I couldn't see Deb's face, but the man she was with faced us. He waved his hands in animated conversation. He looked fit and Puerto Rican, his face smooth and tan except for some well-trimmed facial hair. His smile sparkled from a distance and the energy between them buzzed with intimacy.

"Good for her," I said. "And you were right. She's a grown woman. I hope she's enjoying her date."

Tired old clichés be damned. It did my heart good to see the age tables turned. If this was a date, Deb was the older partner.

The day after we saw Deborah and her cute date watching the sunset, Mark and I ran into him at our community beach. I wasn't sure if he had returned to our Playa Tortuga community for a second day, but I suspected he had never left Deb's. Only this time he was pulling a wagon toward the water's edge that contained large brass pots. As we got closer, we realized what he had: healing sound bowls. I thought about Julio's crypto party and the healing sound bowl guy he'd promoted.

"I'm guessing healing sound bowl work doesn't pay all that well. The best-case scenario is that guy thinks he might get a part in Deb's movie. Worst case, she told him that her father is loaded," Mark said.

Sarcasm hung in the air between us like coils of smoke. I knew my husband was joking, but feminist fibers ignited a small jolt in my chest. Why did men think it made sense when they dated younger women, but couldn't imagine that a younger man could be attracted to an older female partner?

"Younger women fall for older men all the time," I said. "Why can't it be the other way around? Deb is lovely. Maybe they just clicked. Regardless, I hope she's having a blast. I get so tired of the middle-aged-cougar stereotype. If men are going to date much younger women, turnabout is fair play. I say: Go Deb!"

My husband wasn't so enthusiastic but his clients were all defrauded. As an attorney who specialized in financial fraud, he had an extra sensitive swindler antenna. I couldn't blame him since he had seen some really terrible stuff: companies who knowingly took advantage of elderly clients; all manner of pyramid schemes; individuals who were scammed out of their entire life savings by unscrupulous realtors, movie producers, and property developers; and sinister family members who drained grandma's bank accounts. When it came to financial fraud, Mark had more stories than there were Beanie Babies at Sal and Kathy's.

Now, I approached Deborah and set up my beach chair next to hers. "How was Julio's crypto weekend?" I asked, kicking off my shoes. The sky was a soft denim blue streaked with cotton candy clouds. Waves lapped onto the sand below, just fifty yards from where we were sitting.

Deborah put her book down and turned her chair to face me.

"So fun. And outrageous," she said. "You weren't wrong. That party was a little over the top. When it got too out of control for my comfort zone, I locked myself in a small bedroom in the main house."

"We saw you at the beach the day after the party with a very attractive man," I confessed. "Did you meet him there?"

"Yes. That's Andre. He gave me a ride back to Dorado, but we're just friends." She brushed her blonde hair from her eyes.

I wanted to ask Deb more about Julio's crypto weekend: Did you take Molly or mushrooms? Was there an orgy? Did you watch the naked fire dancers? But I wasn't comfortable prodding. Deb's lack of detail seemed like a barrier; I sensed that she didn't want to share particulars and that she was being vague on purpose. Like skipping stones across a pond, she only touched the surface of Julio's epic crypto weekend. Vagueness was a strategy with which I was personally familiar.

It wasn't just Deb's euphemistic language that gave me pause; it was also my own history with drugs and parties. I didn't want to explain why I felt triggered when Julio showed me his Thanksgiving platter of magic mushrooms and bulging bag of Molly. I didn't want to decipher the internal code that sent me into evacuation mode, or describe the imaginary crossing guard who lived on my shoulder.

When I married my first husband, I settled down. I became a college professor, and soon after, a mother. By then, the imaginary crossing guard was a permanent fixture in my psyche. She was the part of me that wanted to be more responsible. She was the voice in my ear, the whistle-blowing, stop-sign-waving director that hollered *No!* when old friends invited me to wild parties. With her help, I shoved youthful memories deep into my mind vise and turned the jaws until they were smashed to bits. I didn't talk about drugs and parties and pretended that these parts of me never existed. I was a wife, a mother, and an upstanding member of my college community. I wanted people to respect me and I feared that my past would make that impossible. With each year that passed, I built another wall between who I was and who I used to be.

Memories of crazy parties and exposure to sex workers were something I hadn't thought about in a long time, at least not until Surfer Boy hugged me and Julio showed off his party favors. It wasn't just the lines of cocaine I'd earned babysitting with Danny, my high school boyfriend. There were other incidents from my past I kept hidden, like the time I took a job as a singing-stripping-telegram girl.

Before I graduated from high school, I was spending most nights at my boyfriend Danny's house, a chaotic tract home in a low-rent neighborhood that he shared with his parents and four older siblings. At this house nobody seemed to sleep, loud music was a constant, drugs were plentiful, and people came in and out at all hours of the day and night.

It didn't take long before I decided I needed a different place to live. I couldn't sleep well or do homework at my boyfriend's house, and my mom and I were barely speaking to each other. We had recently gotten into a big fight and she'd slapped me hard across the face. I didn't plan to go back home—my days of tolerating her bad temper were over—but at my boyfriend's house my grades started to suffer and I worried I was about to throw away the academic success I had worked hard to achieve.

As a private school student, I made friends who had grown up in affluent two-parent families. When I went to their houses for sleepovers or birthday parties, I observed how they lived—with parents who seemed relaxed and meals served at dinner tables overflowing with delicious food. I wanted a life that looked like theirs, not mine or my druggie boyfriend's. I believed that a good education was my way out of poverty and my academic decline worried me. I figured it was too late for me to lose my private high school scholarship since graduation was around the corner, but if I failed classes my senior year, that scholarship wasn't going to change the fact that my college admissions prospects would be doomed.

I needed another place to live, but first I needed a better job. My part-time restaurant work wouldn't cover the cost of rent, let alone gas, food, and utilities. When I found an ad in the help wanted pages for a singing telegram performer, I answered it.

"You'll be changing in and out of costumes at your interview," the man on the phone said, "so be sure you wear the appropriate undergarments. And don't forget a bikini."

It was an unsettling request, but the pay was good and I needed the money: seventy-five dollars per performance, plus tips. Coupled with restaurant work, I could get a place of my own. The singing telegram gigs weren't guaranteed and were usually scheduled on the weekends, but most girls, the man on the phone said, booked two to three gigs on Friday and Saturday nights. Performers brought singing telegrams to all sorts of places like bachelor parties held in restaurants, birthday parties at public parks, and retirement parties at office buildings, so the job required employees to manage their own transportation. I had a car and plenty of theater background. Wearing a costume and delivering a singing message sounded like a piece of cake.

When I got to the strip mall office space, a tall man with dark slicked-back hair opened the door in a cloud of Old Spice cologne. He had a thin mustache below a long, sharp nose. The white button-down dress shirt he wore was thin and yellowed at the seams. His black hair had recently been dyed, leaving dirty dark smudges near his sideburns. He was trying to look young by covering his gray hair, but to me he looked old and greasy.

"Welcome," Old Greasy said. "Take a seat."

He closed and locked the office door. Then he took the chair opposite mine. The office was quiet. We were alone in the small entry space, separated by a glass coffee table that held photo albums. He introduced himself and I handed him my typed résumé. He asked me basic questions about my age and recent work experience.

"Do you have a fake ID?" he asked when I told him I was seventeen and about to graduate from high school. "Sometimes gigs are scheduled in bars, so you need a way to get in."

"Yes," I replied self-consciously.

"Let me see it."

I removed the fake ID from the back of my wallet; it was the driver's license of a restaurant coworker who looked similar to me. He asked me for the birth date and address on the license, and when I passed his impromptu test, he said, "Okay. That will work."

"What songs do I sing?" I asked as he handed me back my fake ID.

"Doesn't really matter," he said. "Most girls just sing the happy birthday song. If it's a retirement party, replace 'birthday' with 'retirement.' Hell, you can write new songs for all I care. You're hired to look hot in your underwear. Nobody cares about your voice."

I wanted to believe that I felt surprised in this moment. I liked to imagine that I was shocked by Old Greasy's response and that I'd contemplated a mad dash for the door, but I must have known upon arrival that this job involved delivering singing telegrams while doing a striptease. My mind was a curious place. It could twist vulnerabilities and bad decisions into reconfigured pretzels, braided in different directions. In one part of my brain, self-serving bias transformed regret into a narrative where I played the innocent victim, the naive child who grew up without guardrails. In the other, I knew my seventeen-year-old self made this employment decision consciously even though as a grown woman, I felt embarrassed by that.

"My office is next door," Old Greasy said. "I'm going in there, I'll turn on some music, and when you're ready, I want you to come into my office and pretend it's my birthday."

After he left me alone in the entryway, I shut my eyes and took a deep breath. "You show more skin at the beach," I told myself. "This is not a big deal."

When I heard the music start in Old Greasy's office, I got into character. I wasn't Georgine anymore. I embodied Rene, the naughty, singing telegram girl. She was bold and fearless. Confident and powerful. She could afford her own apartment.

"This is just like a part in a play," I whispered to the empty room. "Nothing more."

I had never done a striptease before and it turned out to be more complicated than I expected. I wiggled my backside and unbuttoned my top, but I felt awkward and nervous. I was too ashamed to look Old Greasy in the eyes so I focused on my surroundings. A stack of magazines on Old Greasy's desk looked like it was about to topple over. A dusty clock on the wall was stuck at the wrong time. Worn-in wall-to-wall carpet that needed to be vacuumed crunched under my black high heels. George Michael's "I Want Your Sex" blared from a silver boom box set on a chair. Then I almost tripped getting out of my pencil skirt and worried the fumble might cost me employment. Finally, when I was down to my black bra and panties, Old Greasy hit stop and I stood in the middle of the dirty, disorganized office and sang "Happy Birthday" with a big fake smile on my face.

"Well, your dancing needs work," Old Greasy said, "but you've got the body of a porn star, so the job is yours. Take a look at the photo albums on the table before you leave. It will give you ideas for costumes."

"Thank you," I managed.

"Make sure you put together a cop outfit," he said. "That's a fan favorite. Guys love to hire someone who will show up at the party and pretend to arrest their friend before the fun starts."

And that was how it worked. Customers came into the office, flipped through the photo albums, evaluated photos of the girls in their bikinis, and then picked out the costume their singing telegram girl would wear to the party. By the time I left that job, I had paraded around in my bra and panties at pizza parlors, in grandparents' living rooms, on car lots, and more. I even got pretty good at it, which decreased my nervousness but not my humiliation. Taking off my clothes for cash felt desperate. It didn't fit with the well-educated, successful life I had imagined for myself. I showed up at gigs each week, but as I put my fake police uniform on over sexy lingerie, I prayed that nobody I knew would be at the party where I was headed. If the Internet had been a thing back then, I doubted I would have been granted tenure as a college professor. "Stripper" did not belong on one's academic vitae! I did this job for a month before I had finally saved up enough for my apartment. Even when my restaurant work improved, when I was promoted from hostess to waitress, I took gigs on the weekends to stretch my finances.

Since moving to Puerto Rico, flashbacks of my wild teenage years had become more frequent. They had started after I visited my high school home on Sierra Gardens, but the island, or the unusual experiences Mark and I had shared since arriving to the island, activated more reminiscences from my incorrigible, dangerous youth. I continued to recollect long-dormant images, old dusty reels from another era. Novelty had opened a secret door in my mind and memories from my adolescence rushed in. At first, the recollections made me anxious. The years of drug use, poverty, family dysfunction, and stripping—the past I'd tried to forget as I became an adult and earned my degrees and professional licenses—made me long for the safety of my life in California. At River Acres, my life was controlled, polished, and respectable. The titles of wife, mother, and college professor made sense.

But as time passed in Puerto Rico, and my identity expanded to include foreigner, Act 20 & 22 member, and eventually, crypto trader, the flashbacks intensified. I had stopped feeling anxious, however, and started feeling curious. Why did these memories keep showing up? Were the flashes of who I had once been, the me I pretended never existed, trying to tell me something?

The old images washed over me sitting next to Deborah on the beach. After chatting about Andre, the man who drove her home from Julio's crypto camping weekend, Deborah and I sat for a while without talking. My mind vise had failed to prevent the unwanted stripping memories from surfacing, so I silently watched the reel unwind and then redirected the conversation to safe territory.

"Did Julio's partygoers talk about cryptocurrency?"

"Absolutely," she said. "The first morning we ate breakfast and shared our thoughts on market directions."

"Mark and I took a deep dive into cryptocurrency literature before the party," I said. "We read a ton about Bitcoin and Ethereum, but we also got interested in XRP."

"I've heard of XRP," Deb said. "But to be honest, my conversations with all those crypto guys is usually about buying more Bitcoin. The consensus is that unless you're a day trader, Bitcoin is really the only place to park money."

Deb sounded like a cross between Julio at our vetting and my dad sharing a big business idea. She was all in on Bitcoin, full of hopeium and excited to use her crypto riches for movie making. I liked Deborah and sincerely hoped a Bitcoin-funded movie project was possible, but I wasn't convinced.

There was a lot about crypto I didn't understand, but I had known what it felt like when there wasn't enough money in my checking account to pay rent. Even with the extra singing telegram work, there were some months I barely squeaked by. I knew about searching the couch cushions and the bottom of old purses for enough change to buy a Cup O' Noodles and a gallon of gas before payday, the sorts of things poor people did as they climbed rungs on the ladder of life. I suspected that struggling actors in 2020 wanted paychecks they could cash at the end of the week, not decentralized electronic currency that wouldn't auto-deposit into their bank accounts. Or would it? I wasn't sure. Even though I'd left Julio's crypto weekend early, I vowed that day on the beach to learn more about how cryptocurrency worked.

CHAPTER 15:

IMPOSTOR SYNDROME

Sunshine streamed across the ocean, past palm trees, and into my office. My desk was littered with handwritten notes on cryptocurrency, and I reordered them. After leaving Deborah that day at the beach, I'd started digging in. I was learning more about decentralized finance, blockchain, and Bitcoin. But now it was time to teach class. I pushed the papers away, adjusted my glasses, and prepared by reviewing my lecture notes. Right on schedule, I started the RES Zoom meeting.

My RES program was growing. A few academic counselors had reached out during the week to let me know they were sending some new students my way. Once my colleagues heard about the Re-Emerging Scholars program, they spread the word and I started getting referrals. As a result, Marcus would join us for the first time.

Formerly incarcerated students had unique challenges, but they were more likely to meet their academic goals as members of a cohort. In RES, students developed a prosocial network, received academic and personal counseling, and had me as their faculty advocate. According to research, education was the best antidote to recidivism.

I welcomed individuals as I admitted them into our Zoom space. Once faces filled my screen, I began.

"It's good to see you all this week. Since we have a new student in our program, I thought we'd start with introductions."

I introduced myself and so did returning students.

"Marcus," I said, "would you mind telling us just a little about yourself?"

Marcus's face, solemn and serious, shifted slightly. "Well, my school counselor helped me get into a construction management class since I'm pretty good at building stuff. The teacher said that sometimes they hire students who do good before the class has even ended."

"Dude, I thought I recognized you," said Big Ed. "I'm in that class too. No lie, I've seen students get construction jobs after one semester. Your counselor is right."

"Thank God," Marcus said with a grin, "because I sure do need a better job."

The class chuckled. We all knew that employment was a challenge when you had a record.

I made a note to contact Big Ed after class about being a student mentor to Marcus. Student-to-student support was a powerful motivator. Then I introduced the day's topic.

"Today we are going to talk about impostor syndrome—what it is and some strategies to manage the experience."

I shared my screen:

"Impostor syndrome is a psychological pattern in which an individual doubts their accomplishments or talents and has a persistent internalized fear of being exposed as a 'fraud.' Despite external evidence of their competence, those experiencing this phenomenon remain convinced that they are frauds and do not deserve all they have achieved. Individuals with this syndrome incorrectly attribute their success to luck, or interpret it as a result of deceiving others into thinking they are more intelligent than they perceive themselves to be."

"Has anyone had this experience?" I asked.

"All the time," Jon said. "Especially when I'm assigned to a group project. I sit there looking at all those eighteen-year-olds who still live with their parents and don't know anything about life, and I feel like a guy pretending to be someone I'm not."

I could relate. When I first started teaching, I felt like I was pretending to be a college professor when I was really a poor kid who had a drug problem and had made a lot of mistakes in her life.

"How do you feel in those situations?"

"Exactly like you said . . . like I'm a fraud. Like I'm not a real college student. Like I don't belong with the other students."

Marcus jumped in. "I'm glad I'm not the only one," he said. "On my first day of class I almost walked out. This is my first time in college and I'm not gonna lie, I'm not college material."

"Look," I said. "I know a college classroom can feel intimidating, but you *are* college material. You're here, right now, because *you* are a college student. All that uncertainty? All that discomfort? It lessens with time. I promise."

No one spoke. My students waited for more so I continued.

"Think back to the first time you set foot on this campus. If you're like me, you probably felt a little overwhelmed. But you figured it out. You found the counseling office. You enrolled. You registered for classes. You did it!"

I smiled at my students.

"You're not college students because you convinced someone you're something you're not . . . you're here because you're smart and deserve this chance. A chance to get an education and to change your life. There will probably be bumps along the way, but I know that everyone on this screen has the power to meet their educational goals. You may feel like an impostor sometimes, but so does *everybody*."

I ended class and closed my laptop. Strange, I thought. Sometimes when I was speaking to my students, I was also speaking to myself. I knew that people were more than their worst mistake, but that those mistakes could haunt us. They caused us to feel insecurity, shame, and self-doubt—even mistakes that were decades old.

I looked at the neatly piled notes on my desk and wondered if I could really figure this crypto stuff out. Talk about feeling like an impostor! When did we stop faking it and actually become the thing for which we strived?

CHAPTER 16:

LA NAVIDAD

In December of 2020, I wrapped up the fall semester of online teaching from my home office in Puerto Rico. Once I submitted students' grades, there was nothing standing in the way of me and the literary world of cryptocurrency. It was like tumbling into an unknown land where everything looked and sounded foreign. Whenever I traveled to a new place, it took me time to acclimate, and Crypto-land was no different. The cryptocurrency crash course information Mark and I had compiled in preparation for Julio's crypto weekend, and the limited research I'd completed during the last few weeks of my semester, were a virtual drop in the bucket. I still had a lot to learn.

If this had been a typical December at my River Acres home in California, I would have been busy with holiday preparations. There would have been parties to host, presents to buy, and a Christmas tree to decorate, but none of the usual holiday traditions applied in Puerto Rico. This was ironic given that Puerto Rico has the longest Christmas season in the world, from mid-November through mid-January. Decorations go up and celebrations commence right after Thanksgiving, but La Navidad doesn't end until Fiestas de la Calle San Sebastián, a multiday party in the streets of San Juan scheduled well after Three Kings Day in January. Still, this was my first Christmas without my daughters or extended family, and I committed to letting it pass as unceremoniously as possible. Every time I walked by the cardboard faces of the Three Kings or a jolly Santa riding a surfboard in my community, I looked away. Instead of decking the halls, I read about cryptocurrency.

I am a tactile learner so I created flash cards to keep track of crypto terminology. I stacked them in piles by subject on the kitchen table where I worked. The new words I learned reminded me that language and culture reflect each other; I have explained to my students that the vocabulary to which we have access impact how we think and what we think about. An example from my lecture on this topic was the comparison between mankind and humankind. When I talked about language and meaning-making in my communication studies classroom, I asked students to shut their eyes and quietly speak each word out loud.

"Mankind," they whispered in unison.

"Okay," I would say. "Now swap 'man' for 'human.'"

Inevitably, my students shared that each word made them feel differently and that the mental images formed as they said each word sat in sharp contrast to one another.

"The meanings of words are in people, not the words themselves," I explained. "Linguistic variation shapes comprehension. Like your grandma probably warned, choose your words wisely."

In my quest to understand cryptocurrency, I encountered wonderful new words. One of my favorites was "hodl," which was used in the sentence "I am hodling." I liked how this word sounded in my mouth when I pronounced it phonetically; it made me think of snuggling up in a big blanket.

Hodlers did snuggle in a metaphorical way; they were people who held on to Bitcoin—now valued at well over $25,000 per coin—for dear life. They were true believers and resisted the urge to sell even during down-market routs. The vocab origination story claimed that in 2013 an inebriated person posted a Bitcoin forum message with a typo. Instead of "I am holding" they wrote "I am hodling," and it stuck. I appreciated that this common crypto vernacular was referred to as a "mantra" by *Bloomberg* magazine. Given that it was written by a drunk, I joked to Mark that my crypto education efforts could reflect budding investment savvy or, just as likely, the intoxicated recklessness of an alcoholic.

Even though my flash card piles of crypto vocabulary words grew, I struggled to fully grasp the information. The meanings weren't in me the way that I had hoped. I surmised that one barrier to an authentic crypto culture connection was my lack of experience trading the virtual tokens. Were those who operated in crypto spaces on the cutting edge, naive, or delusional? I hadn't decided. But if I wanted to deepen my comprehension, I was going to have to jump into the game. Would I become a hodler?

When I shared my intentions to buy Bitcoin with Mark, he offered encouragement and even wanted to participate in what I dubbed "The Experiment."

"Just because people on Main Street don't understand how to buy and sell crypto doesn't mean the practice lacks monetary value," Mark said.

He relocated flash cards to join me at the kitchen table, a cup of coffee in his hand. I was an early riser and had already started my studies for the day.

"Can you imagine what our mothers would say if I told them of my crypto intentions?" I joked. "Probably that I was nuts."

"I think that applies to everyone I know stateside," Mark said. "My friends and colleagues don't operate in this financial space. At least not yet. I asked my stockbroker about buying some crypto last year and he brushed it off as a fad." He took a steaming sip from his cup.

If I figured out how to buy Bitcoin, Mark promised to buy some too. Even though my crypto studies left me with endless questions, I appreciated knowing we were on this educational adventure together.

* * *

On Christmas morning, in our rumpled pajamas, we sat on the couch in front of the few presents we planned to exchange. They were stacked on our coffee table in a modest pile. I reached for what I suspected was a book and carefully separated a taped corner of paper.

"I tried to make sure that they represent diverse perspectives," Mark said. "You can start with *Bitcoin for Dummies* and work your way up to the text on how to read crypto trading charts."

I suspected Mark would read these books alongside me. He seemed quietly pleased that I was finally interested in a topic that he had long claimed was riveting. And I was. In addition to needing a distraction from a holiday when we were distanced from friends and family, I was genuinely interested in the world of cryptocurrency—I thought it had payoff potential and learning about new things excited me.

Still, I didn't feel quite like myself—far from home, separated from family, and talking to my students and colleagues through a computer screen. Was I compensating for relocation angst with increased dependency on my husband?

Was the move to Puerto Rico an adventure with Mark, or a detour away from my own life because of him? These were the questions I filed away like recipes clipped for another day.

"Thank you, sweetheart," I said, opening my Christmas gifts. "These are perfect. I never thought books on crypto would be better than jewelry, but a Christmas pandemic rearranges a girl's priorities!"

I wrapped my arms around my husband and felt the warmth of his face against my cheek. His skin smelled sweet, like pine, and his arms felt strong. Maybe change was always both—part detour and part adventure.

Then I handed Mark a small red box tied with a ribbon. He opened the package and examined the gift.

"I hope you know what to do with this," he said, holding the Ledger crypto wallet. It looked like a fancy flash drive but it was designed to store cryptocurrency instead of Word documents.

"I think I do," I said. "For sure I will in a few days when we start The Experiment. I bought one for each of us so that we can securely store our future crypto."

My research had revealed that Bitcoin worked a lot like cash. In the same way that most people don't want to walk around with thousands of dollars in their wallet, it's not a good idea to have large amounts of money (or rather, keys to your money) sitting in your phone or some other electronic device. Critics of cryptocurrency point to a history of hacks that have resulted in millions of lost dollars. How one stores Bitcoin matters and hodlers must choose between wallet types in addition to a variety of producers. While online hot wallet options struck me as convenient and cost-efficient, cold wallets (like the Ledger drive I gave Mark) were promoted for increased security. Nobody could hack your crypto if it wasn't available in an online account.

After opening gifts and then falling back into bed for my favorite part of the morning's present exchange, we went to the beach. We bobbed around in the water, taking turns classifying the coral chunks by our feet with made-up facts—a game we invented when we first moved to the island to entertain each other.

"This is a bird," I said, doing an impression of an elderly museum docent. "In fact, it is an exact replica of the Dorado bird. Notice its markings and the way its wing tips point just so?" I made it soar above the water like the birds we watched from our balcony in the morning.

"Excellent specimen," Mark said.

"Take a look at this rare find," he countered, pulling a large piece of coral out of the water and examining it from various angles like it was a gemstone. "This unique sample was the nose off the face of Yocahu, the Taíno god of fertility. A priceless relic."

"I see someone has been reading Puerto Rican history books. Well done, sir!"

Mark dropped his coral chunk and pulled me into his arms for a wet kiss.

It wasn't the same as opening Christmas stockings with our daughters, or setting the holiday dinner table, but it wasn't the depressing day I'd anticipated. We had the beach, sunshine, and each other.

On our way back to the condo, our skin coated with salt and arms full of wet towels, we saw a blur of black-and-white fur.

"Isn't that Snowflake?" I asked Mark.

I had recently started feeding a stray cat who slept on our balcony. Mark spotted her early one morning nuzzled into one of our patio chairs. Except for her black ears, she was bright white. Neither of us had been able to pet her yet—she ran at the attempt—but we enjoyed the sight of her at sunrise. Snowflake was feral, yet seeing her around our condo made our space feel homier.

"She's stalking something," Mark whispered. The white of her fur glistened in the sunshine. She was a puff of snow on a grassy mountain, crouched low and focused like a laser beam of intensity. Then in a flash her head shot down into a hole and when it came up, she had a writhing adult iguana in her mouth. The kill. One moment that iguana was living his best life, and the next he was lunch. It happened fast, like the rise and fall of crypto. Was this another nimitta, a sign of things to come? Just like the earthquake in Condado on our first trip to the island, I wondered if the gods were trying to send me a message, only this time, about cryptocurrency.

"I think we got her name wrong," I said. "It should be Snow *Fury*."

CHAPTER 17:

THE EXPERIMENT

I picked December 27, 2020, to start The Experiment. Circling a date on the calendar made it more real, and sometimes a gal has to stop reading and start doing. On that morning I woke up excited, ready to hodl. According to my stack of vocabulary cards, I also felt FUD (fear, uncertainty, and doubt), knew that I'd never be a whale (someone who owns a lot of cryptocurrencies), and worried I'd probably end up a bagholder (an unfortunate soul who wanted to sell at a higher price but was left "holding the bag" since the market moved so fast).

Mark and I sat at the kitchen table sipping Café Rico. A ceiling fan whirred above our heads and tiny specks of dust danced in the morning sunlight that poured through the patio windows.

"Today's the day, right?" he asked.

"Yep. Today I plan to join the crypto community," I said. My right foot tapped underneath the kitchen table in sync with my speedy heartbeat. Then I opened my notebook and told him my plan:

1. Program my crypto hardware wallet (for future transfer of purchased crypto);
2. Download the Coinbase app (there were lots of trading platforms, but this one sounded fairly easy to navigate);
3. Set up an account on Coinbase linked to my bank account;
4. Buy a hundred dollars of Bitcoin to start;
5. Transfer the Bitcoin to my cold wallet and reevaluate holdings.

If I could manage these steps, I'd think about additional purchases based on my crypto research.

"I'm in," Mark said, reaching for his computer. "How do I set up my Ledger wallet?"

In November, when I'd first considered the future purchase price of Bitcoin, it traded well under $19,000 a coin. On the morning of December 27, it had just crossed $27,000 a coin, marking its all-time high. Plus, Bitcoin's market value exceeded $500 billion; its popularity as a currency had grown significantly in little more than a month. If traditional trading principles applied to cryptocurrency—buy low and sell high—the timing of this experiment couldn't be any worse. Snow Fury's iguana kill was a nimitta indeed. I was comforted by the fact that this experiment was educational in nature and our exposure was limited. Still, the crossing guard on my shoulder tensed. She wasn't a fan of reckless behavior so she held her sign high, ready to flash *STOP* if needed. Mark and I agreed that we would only buy a hundred dollars of Bitcoin to start. My goal was to engage in the cryptocurrency purchasing process, evaluate trading platforms, and decode how to navigate a foreign trading environment. In short, The Experiment was about learning.

Economics and investing had always been my husband's forte. I didn't check the Dow Jones or the NASDAQ each morning like he did. I didn't have regular appointments with a stockbroker or keep an eye on VC opportunities. In fact, Mark and I kept our finances separate. We contributed to a joint account each month to pay household bills, but we didn't mix assets. I paid for expenses related to my biological children and Mark did the same. We split utilities and groceries. Our move to Puerto Rico was the first time in our marriage that managing household finances required some careful navigation. With bills from two households piling up, my bank account was getting stretched thin. Even though the goal of The Experiment was primarily educational, I secretly fantasized that learning about crypto, and investing, would eventually add cushion to my dwindling financial reserves.

The first time I got married in my mid-twenties, I was a broke college student and so was he. At that point in my life, there was nothing financial to navigate. My first husband and I lived together for a year and a half before we got married. We were only twenty-two when we cosigned on the lease of our one-bedroom apartment, a reconfigured space in an old Victorian house on Capital Avenue in Sacramento. We both attended school full-time and juggled restaurant jobs. We both had student loans and struggled to pay our share of the bills. Neither of us had financial support from family. We were in the same adulting place: broke, but determined.

This was not the case when I met Mark in my late thirties. Not only did Mark's savings dwarf mine, his average yearly income was significantly higher. When Mark first raised the topic of a prenuptial agreement a few months before our wedding, I was heartbroken. I feared his desire for this legal agreement—financial protection from me in case we got divorced—signaled a lack of commitment.

"I will pay for you to consult with your own attorney," Mark offered. "I don't want you to agree to anything without counsel."

"I don't want a prenup," I said. "I want you to trust me."

"This has nothing to do with trusting you. I love you. I want you to be my wife." He looked into my eyes. "But this is not a first marriage. We don't get the luxury of pretending that marriage always works out."

For weeks I felt twisted up with fear and anxiety. I worried that money—his desire to protect his and my desire to avoid the topic and restore engagement bliss—would wreck the fairy tale I had penned. Mark swept me off my feet during our courtship. His capacity for intimacy was unlike any man I had ever known, and he was generous. He took me on trips to Hawaii and weekend getaways to the coast. He surprised me with jewelry and flowers. He was incredibly handsome, smart as hell, and as mischievous as he was funny.

For the first time in my life, I felt deeply known by a romantic partner. Mark asked me questions, hard questions, like why I believed all the boxes on my daily to-do list had to be completed, when I was most free to be myself, and what happened when I discovered I was in the presence of the divine. Mark wanted to understand why my first meal of the day was always a breakfast salad, and eventually he adopted the same raw vegetable habit. He respected that my yoga practice was sacred and he encouraged me to prioritize it in my life. He told me that he loved the feel of my breath on his skin. And when we relaxed at the end of the day, he automatically took my feet into his strong hands and rubbed on all the spots that decades of waitressing and bartending had left behind.

And he didn't just love me, Mark also worked to form relationships with my daughters. He attended all of their school events and prioritized family adventures to Pier 39 in San

Francisco and skiing in South Lake Tahoe. He wrote secret clues to their well-hidden Easter baskets, took them on bike rides, and told them ridiculous jokes. Mark was the embodiment of Prince Charming for a divorced mom with two kids.

I hadn't seen this financially cynical side of my fiancé and I didn't like it one bit. A few days later, when I cried about my prenup woes to my best friend, she hugged me and listened. We were sitting in the backyard on a blanket, out of earshot from our kids who played Uno at a picnic table. We called these support talks "sessioning," a specific kind of conversation where the supporter listened deeply and gave the supportee their most wise and honest feedback, best friend to best friend.

"What kind of man starts talking about a prenup right before the wedding?" I asked, giving voice to the questions that had kept me up at night. "What kind of man sandbags his bride-to-be with a directive to seek legal counsel? What kind of man asks a woman to get married, only to tell her that he needs financial protection in case they don't make it?"

When I was finished, my friend gave me a serious look and said, "A man who has already been through one ugly divorce."

Her answer felt like being plunged into an ice bath.

"Look, Georgine," she said. "I know that talking about prenups is not sexy or romantic, but it is smart. And frankly, I think it's better to have clarity about money and how it's going to function in your marriage before you get married. You're not kids; you and Mark are grown-ass adults who have both been divorced."

"But I love him," I said, wiping my eyes. "I'm going to be with Mark for the rest of my life. This time I'm not a naive twentysomething. I know what I'm doing."

"Then why not get a prenup?" she asked. "It's not like you're financially dependent on him. You are a tenured professor. You have financial security. A paycheck. A pension.

You worked hard and got to this point in your career so that you didn't have to be taken care of by a man. You know how to take care of yourself."

When my friend saw my puffy face and wet eyes, she softened her tone. "Look," she said. "You are going to have a damn comfortable life because your husband is financially successful, but you don't *need* his money. Stop acting like you do. Besides, I think you'll have a healthier marriage if you are two financially independent individuals."

"So why does the topic freak me out?" I cried. I felt so vulnerable and confused. "Why do I feel so resistant and twisted up about this?"

"Abandonment issues are a real bitch," she said. This woman knew me very well, knew that my childhood had been rough and didn't include a reliable father figure.

I knew she was right. Some instinctive part of me feared that Mark would leave our marriage. In my worst moments, I could see it happening; he would grow bored of me, my neediness pushing him away. The years I spent in therapists' offices talking about my father's absenteeism, and later, my divorce, gave credibility to my friend's summation. Therapy taught me that childhood scripting ran deep. As a young woman, I didn't trust men, especially after I was assaulted by Pat. I believed my romantic partners would lose interest so I clung desperately to the ones I wanted and eliminated those I didn't, knowing that they would leave me eventually anyway. My early romantic life was an internal tsunami, full of hidden turmoil that was just waiting to obliterate the landscape of my love life. I felt unworthy and insecure in relationships for years. Until I committed to some serious therapy, unconscious patterned thinking was the driver of my relational behaviors. My early scripting of loss and loneliness was problematic, and it needed revision. I often thought about this realization when I lectured to my students on the topic of managing difficult emotions.

"Emotions are a lot like children," I explained. "You shouldn't stuff them into the trunk, but you also don't want them driving the car."

After "sessioning" in my backyard, I wondered why I had never heard any of my close friends talk about prenuptial agreements—not even as a thought experiment. I knew lots of professional remarried women and the topic never came up. The backyard conversation I had with my best friend was the first time I had ever discussed the concept. There was something taboo about tethering the topics of love and money, as if the first subject negated the need for the latter. Yet these things lived side by side in our lives and in our marriages. Were my friends embarrassed to talk about their prenups? Were they managing the complicated feelings that these contracts elicited all alone? Or was my experience anomalous within my social network? Maybe people simply avoided what made them uncomfortable, even when it was in their best financial interest, and especially when it wasn't.

I considered my circle of female friends a safe space. We talked about our dreams, our sex lives, our finances, and our disappointments. Love and money mattered to all of us, and yet the contracts by which these forces are sorted before walking down the aisle seemed to be forbidden conversation.

Mark and I talked about the negotiation process of our prenup years later.

"Have you ever talked to your friends about prenuptial agreements?" I asked. "Do your friends, especially your remarried friends, have prenups?"

"We haven't talked about them, and I don't know," he said. "I only knew that I needed one, not just because divorcing my first wife was financially devastating, but because I love being your hero. You make me feel appreciated for what I contribute to our family, and I worried that over time what

I contributed financially would simply become what was expected. I couldn't go through that again—feeling like I didn't matter and that the only thing I brought to the relationship table was financial."

"At least our first marriages taught us some important lessons," I replied.

"I never thought we'd get divorced," Mark added. "You are my person. I just didn't want to stop feeling like you loved me for me." He pulled my body to his and held me close.

I knew that I could never match Mark's financial contributions to our family bucket. With or without economic resources, he would always be the hero of my heart and our family, but I hoped that The Experiment showed him that he wasn't alone in his financial interests or efforts. Neither of us planned to quit our jobs and become crypto day traders, but it seemed to us that adding crypto to one's portfolio made sense. And I wanted to feel like my husband's hero, so I committed to taking the crypto lead and learning how the technology worked.

CHAPTER 18:

XRP

The Experiment started out strong. By the end of the first day, Mark and I learned how to use Coinbase—an app on our phones that housed our electronic crypto wallets. Finally, we owned Bitcoin. Success!

But when I opened my eyes the next morning, my stomach rolled with waves of nausea. What if I had downloaded a fake electronic wallet app? Or what if my bank account, the one that was now linked to my electronic wallet, had been hacked? I had read so many cryptocurrency fraud stories, I knew that a million things could go wrong, especially to a newbie like me who was just starting to play around in the crypto space.

I pushed the sheets off my body with slow-motion focus and rolled to the edge of the bed. By 7 a.m. sunlight framed the outline of our bedroom curtains in bright yellow, but there was only a dim glow. I didn't want to wake Mark, so I tiptoed into the hall and down the stairs to the kitchen in my pj's. I hoped the anxiety-induced nausea that woke me up early would subside if I concentrated on what The

Experiment was teaching me. I sat down at the kitchen table with a notepad and pen. For me, the best way to understand what I was feeling was to write about it.

This phase of The Experiment—Day 2—reminded me of standing at a craps table for the first time. I was eighteen and on my first gambling trip in Las Vegas when I handed the craps dealer dollars for chips. Even on this first adventure, my adrenaline rush was tangled up with a sense of foreboding; I simultaneously loved and hated what was happening when I played craps. The red dice flung down the oblong table, the colored chips stacked by dealers at quick clips, and the shouts by the table crowd all flowed through me like an excitement-anxiety cocktail. I literally felt dopamine surge through my neural network. When I played craps, my pulse raced. I told myself to relax and have fun, but even as I self-soothed, I worried that rolling those dice was the start of a bad habit I'd come to regret, just like cocaine.

Now I asked myself: Did people get addicted to buying cryptocurrency in the same way they craved drugs? Or gambling? Like rolling dice at the craps table or snorting white lines off my coffee table, the Coinbase clicks happened fast, produced adrenaline, and made me want more. I wrote down questions on my yellow legal pad and then transitioned to journaling the feelings I experienced buying Bitcoin the day before.

This realization, that buying crypto felt a lot like gambling in Las Vegas, seemed ominous. It didn't necessarily *mean* anything, but it struck me as something to pay attention to. In the same way I monitored the number of drinks I consumed at a cocktail party or the number of miles I ran, even when I had the energy to run more, I exercised discrimination. People were wired differently, and I knew that my human system, left unattended, could be excessive and indulgent. This was the reason I needed an imaginary crossing guard on my shoulder. I didn't always trust myself to act in my own best interest.

I put down my pen and reached for my laptop; it was sitting next to Mark's on the opposite end of the kitchen table. I opened the cover and clicked my way to the latest cryptocurrency reports. Headlines announced that the price of XRP, a type of cryptocurrency, had tumbled overnight. Ripple, a well-known cryptocurrency company, was about to get sued by the Securities and Exchange Commission (SEC) for selling unlicensed securities in the form of its XRP tokens. During our crash course in crypto, Mark and I had learned that Ripple's XRP token was mostly used by businesses and banks to send payments across borders. It claimed to be an all-in-one digital payment network for transfers of cryptocurrency. This news meant that some forms of crypto had broad-based, international user potential.

Ripple technology was designed to facilitate electronic payments across borders instantaneously and we surmised that the inevitable digitalization of global currencies would add value to the company. Moving money from one country to another was slow; it could take one to five working days for someone in the United States, for example, to wire money to someone else on a Caribbean island. Ripple's XRP tokens facilitated the transfer of money in eight seconds or less.

Another thing that made Ripple interesting was that it functioned like a more traditional company in comparison to other crypto companies. As it turned out, this was also one of the things that got it into trouble with the SEC. Cryptocurrency originators worked in two primary spheres. Some worked with trading platforms like Coinbase, a company that operated in a centralized environment.[2] These

2. Centralized cryptocurrency exchanges are online trading platforms that facilitate cryptocurrency exchanges between customers who prefer a familiar trading environment.

cryptocurrency creators were required to meet a trading platform's criteria—things like security standards and trading volume expectations. Other cryptocurrency creators operated in a financially decentralized environment.[3] In a decentralized environment, trading crypto was like the Wild West except that there was no sheriff to throw the bad guys into the slammer when they broke the law. Either way (centralized or decentralized), to my rookie eyes, it seemed like new coins and tokens simply materialized. New coins and their white paper[4] showed up on trading platforms as if by magic. Anyone who was interested could buy the tokens for their personal portfolio. But Ripple's XRP was tied to currency transfers, not just tokens, which meant it didn't fit neatly into either camp. Was it a service or an investment product?

As I read about Ripple and its XRP token that morning, my fears about The Experiment, and cryptocurrency in general, solidified. Then I read an article in the *Financial Times* about crypto billionaire Sam Bankman-Fried[5], who said, "By number of Ponzi schemes there are way more in crypto, kinda per capita, than in other places."[6] Traversing the crypto landscape was like walking the mirrored corridors of a fun house—nothing looked usual.

---

3. Theoretically, in a decentralized blockchain network, no one has to know or trust anyone else. Each member in the network has a copy of the exact same data in the form of a distributed ledger. If a member's ledger is altered or corrupted in any way, it will be rejected by the majority of the members in the network.
4. According to Bitcoinwiki.org, a white paper is an official document usually issued by new blockchain projects before their ICO informing the reader about the new technology, methodology, product, or service being launched.
5. In 2024 Sam Bankman-Fried was convicted of securities fraud, ordered to pay $11 billion in forfeiture, and sentenced to twenty-five years in prison. See for example: https://www.nytimes.com/2024/03/28/technology/sam-bankman-fried-sentenced.html.
6. Joshua Oliver, "Crypto Billionaire Sam Bankman-Fried: 'I Got Involved with No Clue What a Blockchain Was,'" *The Financial Times*, May 13, 2022, https://www.ft.com/content/83bc681a-a0f9-43bb-b627-c6dacae4a0a3.

If Bankman-Fried was correct, Ponzi schemes lurked on crypto trading platforms like unscrupulous carnies who tricked children into playing unwinnable games. What optimistic child ever won the giant stuffed panda that hung above the ring toss? We all wanted the grand prize—the brass ring, the home run, the winning lottery ticket—but life rarely worked that way. I wondered if it was an addiction to hopeium that drove coin and token values up and down, instead of market trends or financial data.

In contrast to most of the cryptocurrencies I'd learned about since moving to Puerto Rico, Ripple initiated a series of planning steps before it released its token, XRP. Instead of publishing a white paper and unleashing their token on crypto exchanges, they pitched their cross-border money transfer idea to private equity groups, raised money for the Ripple company, and then created their product. When the SEC filed the lawsuit against Ripple in late December 2020, days before I started The Experiment, they argued that the XRP launching process required Ripple to register with the SEC in alignment with the Securities Act of 1933.

Ripple argued that it didn't have to register with the SEC. The company declared that its product was more akin to a "utility" than a "currency" since it provided a monetary transfer service and its digital network was open-source[7] and peer-to-peer.[8] And then a legal battle commenced.

As a rule, investors hate uncertainty. Company valuations on the rise? Good. SEC lawsuit? Bad. But for a billion-dollar company, fines were manageable. What caused investors

---

7. Open-source code is code that is posted publicly online. Anyone is free to use the code for their own purposes, scrutinize it for bugs, or propose new changes or features. Open-source code is the backbone for Bitcoin, Ethereum, and the systems behind many other cryptocurrencies.

8. Peer-to-peer is a term that refers to the direct exchange of an asset, such as a virtual currency, between individual parties without the involvement of a central authority. A strictly peer-to-peer currency exchange was the primary goal driving the creation of Bitcoin, the most widely used cryptocurrency.

sleepless nights was uncertainty. Whatever the outcome of the SEC lawsuit, Ripple was on its way to getting clarity, a point in their favor.

I was clicking back and forth between Ripple and SEC arguments, thinking about a potential XRP purchase alongside the concerns I had over The Experiment, when Mark walked up behind me. He stroked the back of my hair and then kissed my neck.

"Good morning," he said.

"Good morning, sleepyhead," I replied.

"Where's the coffee?" he asked, looking at the empty pot in the kitchen.

"Didn't make any," I said. "I woke up feeling a little sick, but I'd take some now."

Mark filled the pot with water and scooped grounds into the basket.

"You're not going to believe the news this morning," I said. "It looks like Ripple really is going to get sued by the SEC."

"That *is* interesting," Mark said. "What's the basis for the lawsuit?"

"Securities fraud. Take a look."

Mark hit the brew button on the coffee maker and then opened his laptop beside mine. We read Ripple reports and traded observations.

"Do you think they are guilty of fraud?" I asked, trying to manage my anxiety about The Experiment.

Mark knew more about this subject than me. He had shifted his legal practice to a fraud focus the decade before we left California.

"The SEC is famous for huffing and puffing, especially when it comes to large companies," Mark said. "But ultimately the SEC gives most of the companies it targets a cost-of-doing-business slap on the wrist. I have watched plenty of businesses take the fines in stride and then go on to bigger and better things. This is especially true with banks and other financial institutions. It hurts them for a minute, but it's not life-ending."

"It does seem serendipitous," I said. "The Experiment has paved the way to purchase XRP. I saw it listed as a purchase option on Coinbase—one click and we're owners of XRP tokens."

"Compelling," Mark said, and opened the Coinbase app on his phone.

"What do you think of the purchase price?" I asked.

"At its all-time high," Mark said, "XRP traded at $3.84. It dropped by about half when SEC lawsuit rumors started to circulate." Mark looked at me and then back at his phone. "This morning, I see that XRP has dropped even further. It's trading at 29 cents a token."

"If we want some, we'll have to act fast," I said. "I read that US-based cryptocurrency platforms, like Coinbase, have announced plans to delist XRP in light of the pending SEC lawsuit. As soon as that happens, we won't be able to buy or sell the tokens. Anything left in our electronic wallets will get frozen."

"One thing I know from working on fraud cases," Mark said, "is that these SEC prosecutions can take a long time to play out. Ripple would be severely penalized if they have to sit on the sidelines in this dynamic crypto environment for a year or two."

Mark stood up to pour us both a cup of coffee.

"Thanks," I said when he filled my mug. "Even if the lawsuit fines equate to a slap on the wrist, could they survive being delisted?"

I certainly didn't want to buy XRP if Ripple's future was certain death. I'd read multiple articles that described unsophisticated crypto buyers as "exit liquidity." Lots of coins and tokens were headed to zero, and it was most often newbies like me who lost their investment when more sophisticated traders pumped and dumped.[9]

"Potentially," Mark said. "But cryptocurrency is global so trading platforms in other countries won't necessarily delist XRP."

If Mark was correct this mitigated risk, but the thought of learning about new crypto trading platforms that operated outside of the United States scared me. Still, I knew if we transferred our crypto from our electronic wallets on Coinbase to the Ledger wallets I bought us for Christmas, we could sell our crypto someplace else if need be and make a profit when the time was right.

"Do you think the SEC has a good case against Ripple?" I asked, worried about making a mistake.

"I'm not sure, but the analysis I've read this morning is just terrible," Mark said. "It's all by nonlawyers and some of the things argued are ridiculous, at least from a legal perspective."

"Maybe we'll get better reporting after Christmas week," I suggested.

"Maybe," Mark replied. "But it's not just the lawsuit that is going to affect the XRP token price," he added. "Ripple is scheduled to release their next billion tokens on January 1, 2021, just three days from now. And of course, increasing supply generally drives down price."

"I see why XRP is so cheap all of a sudden," I said.

"Exactly. Between the SEC lawsuit, the likelihood of XRP getting delisted from US trading platforms, and the prescheduled release of XRP tokens, Ripple is probably headed for some hard times."

Neither of us spoke. Was this a chance to purchase a valuable crypto token at rock-bottom prices? If so, XRP

---

9. This happens when a targeted cryptocurrency's price is artificially inflated through coordinated buying, followed by a sudden sell-off to unsuspecting investors.

was our giant stuffed panda, a prize within reach. The thought of buying more crypto put me right back at the craps table; my pulse started to race and I was itching to join the game.

"Now I'm scratching my head," Mark continued. "I'm wondering, is this the greatest buying opportunity of all time or is this the last step before XRP goes off the cliff to zero?"

When I watched Mark play chess, I could almost see the wheels of his brain turn. He looked at his opponent, studied the board, and calculated. His eyes would dart around, moving knights and rooks in myriad formations, and right below the focused observation he wore a barely noticeable smile. He called this type of thinking, where a player imagines innumerable outcomes, three-dimensional chess. Given the subtle grin on his face, I suspected he was playing it with XRP possibilities.

"I'm going to buy some," Mark continued. "The price speculation on Ripple before all this bad news broke was phenomenal. Banks need it. If the Internet of Value[10] is a real thing, then I'd be surprised if the US doesn't allow Ripple to move forward. Private companies and all the governments of the world are going to need efficient transaction platforms. Ripple facilitates a solution to this need."

And so, on Day 2 of The Experiment, Mark and I each opened the Coinbase app on our phones and bought Ripple's XRP tokens—thousands of dollars' worth for me and tens of thousands for Mark. We were forty-eight hours into The Experiment and we had completely deviated from The Experiment Plan, which mandated that we only buy a hundred dollars of Bitcoin until I was comfortable managing our Ledger cold wallets. That hadn't happened yet. XRP

---

10. A definition of the IoV is suggested as the "instant transfer of assets that can be expressed in monetary terms over the Internet between peers without the need for intermediaries."

was a crapshoot, and I had no idea if the Coinbase clicks we made to purchase the token were a successful pass line bet or the moment right before crapping out.

* * *

On December 29, 2020, Day 3 of The Experiment, I was reminded of why my youthful gambling experiences were short-lived: I disliked losing more than I liked winning. The value of XRP tokens had dropped from our 29-cent purchase price amount to 20 cents a token. In other words, we had already lost close to a third of our original purchase price. Plus, we accrued fees for making our Coinbase transactions. Things were not going well. I wondered if we would even need the Ledger wallets I bought us for Christmas. By the end of the week, it was possible we would have nothing to put inside them.

I silently berated myself for getting Mark involved in my experiment. I should have waited until I knew what I was doing. Of the two of us, I was the more technologically advanced, but that wasn't saying much in this new world of crypto. I was way out of my depth. The last thing I wanted during this time of pandemic isolation was a husband who felt annoyed with me for the kooky ideas I professed about how best to understand the world of cryptocurrency. I had pulled back the cryptocurrency pool cover and jumped in headfirst, but when I plunged into the cold water I panicked. I had a strong impulse to dog-paddle toward the steps and climb out of the pool.

Just like the day before, I was reading the news when Mark woke up and came downstairs. He sat down in the kitchen chair next to mine, kissed me on the cheek, and looked out at the white-and-gray cumulus clouds. Except for scattered patches of cornflower blue, they filled the sky, their tops like giant puffs of cotton. I got Mark a cup of coffee and asked sheepishly, "Did you see what happened to our Ripple tokens?"

"Oh, yes, I saw," Mark replied. "I woke up and checked Coinbase in the middle of the night."

"I'm sorry," I said. "The Experiment was a dumb idea."

"No, it wasn't," he said. "We missed the absolute bottom purchase price for XRP, but I don't think it's far off. The truth is, I liked Ripple's XRP token at twenty-nine cents, but I *really* like it at twenty cents!"

"Why would an overnight one-third drop in value increase your affinity for Ripple?" I asked.

"I've been thinking more about the timing of the SEC lawsuit. It was literally filed at the last minute. Jay Clayton, chairman of the Securities and Exchange Commission, is stepping down. He was a Trump appointee. If this lawsuit was such a slam dunk, why did he wait until he was walking out the door to file it?"

"Hmm. Good question."

Lots of folks might pass the buck as a professional transition gets closer, but when I read about Clayton in the related SEC press release that day, I was impressed by his long list of accomplishments, including 2,750 enforcement actions since May 2017. He didn't seem like a slouch. Was this last-minute SEC handoff reinforcement that Ripple was destined for a slap on the wrist? If Clayton's legacy was really "an all-out attack on the crypto community," as Ripple asserted, why the suspicious timing of the lawsuit filing?

"Even if the SEC clobbers Ripple with a billion-dollar fine," Mark said, "which I don't think they'll do, the lawsuit still gives investors what they want most—clarity."

"Well, I'm just relieved that you're not upset with me for getting you involved in my crypto experiment nonsense," I said.

"It's not nonsense. Learning about crypto is just another stop along our PR adventure," Mark said. He reached across the table and put his hand on top of mine to give it a flirtatious squeeze.

The early morning clouds had been replaced by clear blue sky.

After we both bought *even more* XRP at the lower price, I asked Mark, "Are you about ready to change into gym clothes?"

Our prework morning routine began with coffee first and exercise second. "What about a run? Or yoga on the beach?"

The weather was gorgeous. It was going to be a beautiful day, and I looked forward to an activity that would take my mind off Ripple, the SEC, and Coinbase.

"I was thinking about my favorite exercise," Mark said, and placed his hand firmly on my thigh. Then he pulled me onto his lap, ran his hands under my nightshirt, and kissed my shoulder.

I have heard it said that the biggest sex organ was right between our ears. That was definitely true for me. I found smart men irresistible. If they also had a good sense of humor, I was a goner.

I have pondered this proclivity, the connection I intuited between intelligence and sex appeal, and believed it was probably a character flaw. Why not be desirous of gentle, sweet men—sympathetic types who specialized in compassion and spent their energy trying to make the world a better place—when it came to feeling hot and bothered? What a person thinks and speaks is often less valuable than what he does, or in the values that drive his life. My closest friends were activists and service-oriented. But not so much for the men I had found sexually attractive.

"Come on," Mark said. "Let's take this upstairs."

After all the crypto analysis and economic intellectualizing since the start of The Experiment, my husband, whose hair was still tousled from sleep, looked damn sexy to me. I supposed that wiring—the sexual kind—was also laid long ago since my favorite way to start a day was with a cerebral man who wanted to go right back to bed.

CHAPTER 19:

THE PENTHOUSE

I set the timeline for my experiment—a self-directed process through which I successfully learned to buy and sell cryptocurrency—at one week. On the last day of The Experiment, Saturday, January 2, 2021, the value of Bitcoin tipped over $33,000, an all-time high. Reports suggested that institutional investors had entered the crypto market and pushed the price upward by legitimizing the coin as an alternative currency. Over the seven days that comprised my attempt to learn how crypto trading worked, we saw many spikes and dips in the crypto market, but on Day 7, Bitcoin literally blew right through the $30,000 price possibility I had wondered aloud about to Mark earlier in the week. Ripple's XRP was holding steady around 22 cents—not much change there—but my crypto portfolio, now much larger than the original hundred dollars I planned to start with, was up 5–20 percent depending on the *second* I checked. Volatility aside, it amazed me that this monetary accumulation was possible in a single week. I felt cautiously excited.

I learned much of this information lying in bed next to my husband. He was facing me, eyes closed, still fast asleep. Sunshine streamed into our bedroom through laser beams that shot between cracks in the heavy curtains covering our windows. Mark looked like a little boy version of himself, sweet and dreamy, his arms wrapped around a pillow as if it were a beloved stuffed animal. My heart felt full.

With a slow, careful motion, I extended my arm, picked up my phone off the nightstand, and started reading the positive cryptocurrency news.

"Good morning," he finally said. His voice was deep and leisurely. Sheets shifted as he stretched his arms.

"Good morning, sexy," I said.

"Watchya reading?" Mark asked.

"The yoozh. Crypto and more crypto since today marks the end of The Experiment and Bitcoin has spiked—again! I'm glad we bought more alongside XRP." I procured my best news anchor voice and said, "CNN cites Nicholas Pelecanos, head of trading at the cryptocurrency firm NEM, who warns that when any asset climbs in price this fast for an extended period of time he becomes cautious, and urges anyone trading BTC [Bitcoin] not to get caught up in the euphoria."

"Always good advice," Mark said.

"It passed $30,000 this morning, but this source predicts Bitcoin could rise to $50,000 by Valentine's Day and that we are at the beginning of what will be an immense bull market,"[11] I added.

---

11. Shannon Liao, "Bitcoin Soars Past $33,000, Its Highest Ever," CNN Business, January 2, 2021, https://edition.cnn.com/2021/01/02/investing/bitcoin-price-30000/index.html.

"That sounds about right." Mark yawned. "Be cautious but buy, buy, buy."

Reports of crypto caution that came coupled with predictions of increased value in the extreme were the norm in crypto news.

"The world of crypto is a tangle of radical contradictions, so we're either brilliant for stuffing our crypto wallets or incredibly foolish—I haven't decided which," I said.

After an intense week where our conversation and reading material focused solely on crypto, Mark and I were keen for a morning walk. There would be future crypto conversations and learning opportunities, but on this morning, we were eager to turn the page.

It felt good to stretch our legs and look for iguanas. It was a warm morning, the kind that brought Dorado residents out early for exercise. In Northern California, we would have been bundled up on a January morning, but in Dorado, our thin T-shirts were wet with perspiration.

On our way home, we bumped into Deborah.

"Did you hear?" Deborah asked, her voice lilting with joy. She was wearing exercise clothes and headphones, and she tapped the electronic device strapped to her bicep to turn off the sound. "Bitcoin is well over thirty!"

I shared her excitement and thought about the increased value of my Coinbase account.

"That number is attention-getting," Mark said. "It's like the crypto market is on steroids."

"Every time Bitcoin jumps by a thousand, I can stay here another year," Deborah said. "Looks like I'll get to live by the beach for a while!"

"Not a bad locale," I agreed.

We were standing under a big banyan tree. Its long branches hung down like an awning that provided shade and its gnarled root system made cozy homes for nesting ducks.

"Are you guys going to Crypto Tuesday?" Deborah asked. "With all the crypto market excitement, it should be an extra fun event."

I imagined a room full of crypto investors high-fiving each other and yelling, "To the moon," a common cheer for crypto to increase in value. It sounded like fun.

"I have a mediation on Tuesday," Mark said.

Since Mark attended legal appointments in California via Zoom, the time change meant he would work late.

"I'm free." I was eager to hang out with Deborah and celebrate in the Bitcoin euphoria. "Can I hitch a ride?"

* * *

On Tuesday, Deborah picked me up just after five in the afternoon as it was starting to cool. She was driving a newly rented, candy-apple-red sedan to take us to Crypto Tuesday. I was looking forward to a night out with others who operated in crypto spaces and thought the color of Deb's car matched my Bitcoin-happy attitude. Once we left Dorado, our sleepy beach town, I volunteered to navigate the way to San Juan.

The Crypto Tuesday event was scheduled at a restaurant named Delavida, but when we arrived, there was a sign on the door saying the restaurant was closed.

"Maybe they closed the restaurant to the public because Crypto Tuesday is a private event?" I offered.

We were peeking through the barred windows, looking for crypto community members inside, when we heard a voice behind us.

"Crypto Tuesdays?" asked a tall man with dark hair.

"Yes," Deborah replied, "but the restaurant is closed."

We introduced ourselves and then Deborah checked for updates on her phone.

"It's been moved," she said. "The group is headed to another restaurant called Wicked Lily. See you there," she told the man. I followed as she turned to leave.

"I'm just happy to be out on this beautiful night," I confessed as we headed back to Deborah's car. The sky turned pink as we walked. I realized on the 22 Este, the highway that led from Dorado to San Juan, that this was the first time I had left my neighborhood with someone other than Mark. Except for the mask on my face, a requirement for people in public spaces, I felt normal, out with a friend to hear a lecture just like so many pre-pandemic nights from my past.

This was my first Crypto Tuesday. When I returned from Julio's crypto camping weekend experience, I wasn't sure I'd be attending any more crypto events. But after conducting my own crypto experiment, I was interested in learning more. Plus, I liked attending lectures. In California, I frequented a local lecture series that gave published authors a chance to talk about their latest books. It was exciting to learn from experts in a face-to-face setting, and I wondered what crypto specialists discussed.

"It's always an adventure with this group," Deborah said. "Misfits and billionaires are wonderful people, but they're not always well organized."

After a few wrong turns, we located Wicked Lily, right off the main strip of Condado, a *subbarrio*, or subdivision, of San Juan. This was the same area where Mark and I stayed when we first got to Puerto Rico and experienced the earthquake that threw us out of bed in the middle of the night. The memory made me a little dizzy.

We parked and started to cross the busy street when a white car pulled up and a man's voice yelled, "Deborah! Get in. We've moved again."

Deborah yelled, "Hi!" over the sound of a horn that was protesting our pickup, quickly opened the back door, and slid across the empty back bench seat. Deborah was my ride and we were blocking traffic, so I adjusted my face mask and followed suit by jumping into the stranger's car right behind her.

We were already in motion when I saw Lana behind the wheel and realized who likely owned the car we were in. The last time I saw Julio, he was showing off his jumbo-sized stash of illegal drugs and I was pretending to sip mezcal from a red Solo cup. Now I was sitting in his car along with Deborah and Lana, Julio's polyamorous partner, and I felt uneasy about our close proximity.

"Wicked Lily was too busy. They couldn't handle our group. But Scott Windsor was there, and he said we could do it at his place. His crib is badass! I fucking love my tribe!" Julio shouted.

We zipped through narrow, unfamiliar streets just as the sun set. I took a deep inhale through the fabric stretched across my nose and put my mind on the waves that graced the shores of Dorado. Then I considered my companions. Did Julio remember me? Was he offended after Mark and I abruptly left his crypto camping weekend at Lake Carite? Would he resent the anti-drug text we sent as explanation for our departure? Was he irritated that I was sitting in the back seat of his car? My mind went into its spinning—as it did when I was in unfamiliar territory and the crossing guard on my shoulder stood at full attention.

When we arrived, the "badass crib" was located in a high-rise called Catina Reef. The building was so close to the beach, it looked as if it must have been built on top of sand. When we entered, the lobby was already full of thirty-something-year-old men dressed in business casual and wearing COVID masks. Deborah and I sat on opposite halves of a suede ottoman and introduced ourselves to the others who sat close by, knee to knee. Besides Lana, we were the only women in the group.

"Give me some money!" Julio announced, halting the polite small talk. "We gotta take care of this doorman. You know he's not supposed to let so many people in this room because of COVID restrictions." A uniformed security guard sat in a small glass-encased room on the far side of the lobby.

I reached into my purse and pulled out ten dollars alongside others, bills in their outstretched hands.

"Yeah, right," Deborah said under her breath, her wallet still clasped tightly between her arm and her rib cage. "Wanna guess how much of that cash the doorman ever sees?"

I came to learn that Julio had lost favor with Deborah. She'd heard him announce at the crypto camping weekend, "My current ladies may not like it, but I'm too much man *not* to get a third, probably even a fourth."

Some men collected baseball cards and others, automobiles, but Julio, it seemed, collected polyamorous women. Deborah warned me of his romantic perspectives in disgusted whispers.

"His constant hustling is getting on my nerves," she said.

I thought about the mixed feelings I had when it came to Julio. I was impressed that he'd built a successful life after ten years of incarceration, but he seemed like a hustler to me too.

Julio collected bills from around the room, folded them into a hefty wad, and slid them into his pants pocket.

Finally, Scott Windsor, a balding man in khaki pants and a white dress shirt with rolled-up sleeves, walked into the lobby to welcome us.

"I know event directions were a little crazy tonight, but I'm glad you all made it," he said. "This evening is going to be special. We have an amazing speaker who I can't wait for you to meet."

After Scott welcomed us, we clustered into small groups, the bellman entered a secret code, and we took turns loading into the building's elevator set for the penthouse on the eighteenth floor.

The elevator stopped inside Scott Windsor's home. When the doors opened, we looked directly into a grand living space instead of a shared hallway, the typical exit point for most building elevators. I had seen penthouses in Hollywood movies, but I'd never been inside one before. The ocean view from this height was spectacular and the feeling of opulence that permeated the space, intoxicating.

Our cluster of elevator riders exited and joined the others. We milled about, admiring the art on Scott Windsor's walls and the enormous chandeliers that hung from his exceptionally high ceilings. A floating glass stairwell, which curved through the center of another grand room, led to additional floors above. Everywhere I looked I saw crystal and glass. It was like being inside a storybook castle made of diamonds where every surface sparkled—just gorgeous.

Instead of wonder, instead of admiration for such beauty or appreciation for the exciting moment, my thoughts turned self-conscious. Something inside me said, *You don't belong.* This level of wealth made a person like me, raised in low-rent neighborhoods, uncomfortable. After a few minutes of walking around, I realized I had felt this same discomfort before. Being in Scott Windsor's penthouse reminded me of being eighteen, the first time I dated someone who came from *real* money.

CHAPTER 20:

FAMILY MONEY

His name was Gary Celestino. I'd met Gary when I was a waitress at a restaurant called Finnigan's. It was right off Interstate 5 in Northern California, and attracted businesspeople who traveled the state. Gary was a sales rep for Xerox. His territory ran from San Jose to Tahoe, and he stopped to eat lunch in my section a few days a week. When he first asked me out, I brushed off his invitation. He was at least ten years older than me, and I was too busy to date; I waited tables Monday through Friday and delivered singing telegrams on the weekend. I was also enrolled at the local community college.

I had been accepted to multiple universities after graduating from my scholarship-sponsored private high school, but I couldn't figure out living expenses. Like my peers (the ones who grew up in affluent families with college-educated parents), I only applied to impressive schools that required relocation. At my private high school, we were encouraged to shoot for the stars! A school counselor had helped me select institutions based on what I wanted to study. She assured me that I would qualify for financial aid, maybe even a scholarship, but I hadn't considered the prohibitive costs associated with moving to a dream college and my counselor failed to mention this fact.

When I finally calculated the money required to move to an unknown town where I did not have friends, a job, or a place to live, I realized I had been foolish not to apply to the local university, but by then it was too late. I thought about student loans but felt overwhelmed by both process and future debt. In the end, I signed up for classes at my local community college and stayed in Sacramento.

After multiple date requests, I gave Gary my phone number and we went out to dinner. He told witty jokes that made us both laugh. His dark brown hair was thick and I liked the way he wore it just a little shaggy. His button-down shirt was always pressed and his oxford shoes shined. Maybe dating someone more mature was a step in the direction of my much-imagined successful life? After the recent breakup with my unemployed cocaine-snorting high school boyfriend, I had to admit, a grown man with a respectable job looked appealing. Plus, Gary lived in San Jose, two and a half hours from Sacramento, so I figured we would see each other infrequently. This, I surmised, left plenty of time for me to manage my busy life.

For Christmas, just three months into our dating relationship, Gary gave me a diamond ring. It was more than a karat in size, and unlike anything my friends had received from their boyfriends. Gary told me it was a promise ring, a sign of where our relationship was headed. I had been surprised when I opened Gary's gift, not yet ready to make promises when it came to love.

That same weekend Gary took me to meet his parents in San Francisco. I had been in plenty of nice homes in

Sacramento, houses where my private school friends lived, but I had never been in a home like this. Gary's family home sat high upon a hill that overlooked the city of San Francisco at a distance and the bay beyond. It had a lavish dining room and chandeliers, just like the ones I would see many years later in Scott Windsor's penthouse. Highly polished antiques and expensive-looking artwork made Mr. and Mrs. Celestino's home feel like a museum. The only modern space was the kitchen, and it included a separate staircase in the back that led to the "servants' quarters."

After the chef served us lunch, Mr. Celestino, Gary's father, informed us that we were all headed to their vacation home. The chauffeur drove us to a small airport where we boarded the Celestino plane and then Mr. Celestino flew us to Palm Springs.

"Why didn't you warn me that your family is loaded?" I asked Gary as the plane took off.

Gary looked at me and smiled, but never gave an answer to my question.

The next day we were sitting poolside at his parents' Palm Springs McMansion. Gary was tugging at the tie of my bikini, a thin yellow string just above my hip bone, with a hungry look in his eyes. A water feature splashed happily into the far end of the pool. I brought the subject of money up for a second time.

"Seriously, why didn't you ever mention that you had wealthy parents?" I asked.

"Because it has nothing to do with me," he said. "I don't take money from my father. I want to make it on my own, and I want to be with someone who respects that choice, not someone who likes me because my family is rich."

I appreciated Gary's determination, but I knew his claim to financial independence wasn't the whole truth. I had puzzled over how he could afford to own a home in San Jose, two cars, and a fancy water ski boat, since he had worked at his Xerox job for less than a year. For most of his twenties, Gary had tried to make it as a musician. He played bass in a rock band. He didn't even start college until he was in his mid-twenties, and now I suspected that he only sought an education after his father had grown tired of supporting a wannabe-rock-star son.

Not long after meeting Gary's parents, I gave him back the diamond ring and explained that geographic distance made it impossible to continue our relationship. The truth was, Gary didn't know me; he had no idea that I delivered singing telegrams in my underwear or that I snorted obscene amounts of cocaine when I was out with friends. He didn't understand that we came from two vastly different worlds, that my successful future was only imagined while his was guaranteed. He made assumptions about me because I had graduated from a private high school and lived in my own apartment. Hell, he didn't even know how old I was since I used a fake ID when we went out for drinks. Gary and I didn't know any of the same people, so it was easy to construct a more polished version of myself, one that wasn't entirely true. Dating Gary was like trying on a new me. But our differences, and the pieces of me that were omitted, made my eighteen-year-old self feel insecure and dishonest. Breaking up was the easiest way out of an uncomfortable circumstance, which was exactly what I did. Just like I gave up on my dream college, I gave up on Gary Celestino. Both, I thought, were out of my league.

* * *

Standing in Scott Windsor's penthouse now, I wondered about the pieces of ourselves we hide and the stories we continue to believe, long after they are no longer true. I was an educated professional. I was happily married. I was standing in a fabulous penthouse in San Juan, Puerto Rico, at an exclusive crypto event. Why did I flash back to a time when I lugged around doubt and uncertainty like a ratty old sweatshirt I couldn't part with, an ugly, unflattering time when I felt alone and life felt daunting? Where did this memory come from and what did it mean?

I stopped thinking about the past and sipped my drink. Scott Windsor was circulating amongst his Crypto Tuesday guests. I watched as he shook hands and gave fist bumps to the crowd of young crypto men that wandered through his home. When he saw Deborah and me admiring the view from behind a vast wall of windows, he walked over to greet us.

"Your home is beautiful," I said. "Thank you for hosting everyone, especially at the last minute."

"You're welcome," he said, "but this is the house that Bitcoin built, so I am happy to share it with my crypto community."

Scott directed us to the penthouse balcony, the location of the speaker interview. On our way, we passed a wall that separated the main foyer from the kitchen; it was home to a fish tank so large it belonged in the Monterey Bay Aquarium.

"It's truly my honor to host tonight's Crypto Tuesday," Scott continued. "Charlie is the speaker and he's the reason I have this amazing life. This evening is the first time I'll meet him in person, but I'm forever in his debt."

I nodded in polite agreement but wondered who Charlie was. I also didn't understand how someone Scott had never met could be responsible for his beachfront penthouse.

"Let us know if there is anything we can do to help," Deborah offered.

"Please, just enjoy," Scott said, and floated away to welcome other guests.

Crypto Tuesday attendees moved additional chairs out to the balcony and helped Julio construct a makeshift set. Video equipment was set up in front of the living plant wall, stage lighting was placed next to the hydroponic towers of fresh leafy greens, and a sound system was erected next to an outdoor couch. The breezy patio was more than enough room for Julio's gear, the thirty-five-member audience, and Rico, Scott's friendly and immaculately groomed standard poodle. I was curious to meet Charlie, the Crypto Tuesday headliner and man who had garnered such adoration from Scott Windsor.

"Take your seats, people. We're about to start," Julio instructed. "Roll camera in three, two . . . Give it up for tonight's Crypto Tuesday guest, Charlie Shrem!"

Charlie Shrem, I soon learned, was an entrepreneur, Bitcoin advocate, and the host of a podcast called *Untold Stories*. His connection to the world of crypto started in 2011 when he was frustrated at the length of time it took to buy and sell Bitcoin. As a result, he and his friend launched BitInstant, a service designed to provide users temporary credit to speed up their Bitcoin transactions. He started his presentation by affirming the attributes of DeFi, shorthand for "decentralized finance," an umbrella term that related to a variety of financial applications. In the crypto community the term originated with blockchain, the technology on which Bitcoin was mined and that held transaction history so that financial middlemen (like banks) could be eliminated. Unlike Visa and PayPal, Bitcoin and other decentralized digital payment methods were bought, traded, and sold without the help (or interference, depending on your politics) of government-sanctioned financial institutions. DeFi was one crypto community answer to complaints by retail investors, and the general public, that governments manipulated money and markets in ways that served Wall Street, not Main Street.

After a short review of DeFi, Charlie moved away from sharing general crypto information and got personal. He told us his story.

"Remember the red phones in CVS?" Charlie asked the audience. "This is how my business worked: People would take their BitInstant codes, probably written on scraps of paper like their grocery shopping lists, and use the red CVS phones to initiate the transaction."

The audience chuckled at his description of such antiquated technology.

"But this was when nobody really knew what they were doing," Charlie continued. "The government didn't even give guidance on convertible currency until 2013."

Charlie explained that he had no intention of circumventing government processes when he started BitInstant. In fact, he claimed that he used to tell his crypto friends who championed Bitcoin's anonymity that their goal should be to "extend the Fed, not end the Fed."

This legal sincerity didn't stop Charlie from going to prison. Prosecutors alleged that Charlie conspired to launder a million dollars in Bitcoin to users of the Silk Road, an online black market and part of the dark web, an intentionally untraceable and anonymous part of the Internet.

"I had no idea that I was obligated to file a suspicious activity report," Charlie explained.

Just like many of the formerly incarcerated students in my Re-Emerging Scholars program, Charlie told us that the lessons he learned in prison were personally transformative. However, unlike my community college students whose incarcerated youth was marked by the effects of poverty and racism, Charlie's personal growth came later. His transformation didn't result from access to education inside prison, but rather by the unlikely act of being incarcerated.

Charlie's life story suggested privilege. He attended a private Jewish school in Brooklyn, New York. He had graduated from Brooklyn College with a degree in economics and finance and launched his first business, a computer repair company, while he was still in high school. Before going to prison, Charlie had a net worth of at least $45 million, according to some sources.

"In prison, I learned how to do things I'd never done before. Like mopping a floor. The first time I ever attempted to mop a floor the other inmates laughed at me."

For Charlie, prison was a great equalizer. It humbled him. He started tutoring other inmates so that they could get their GED and he wrote about his experiences in a blog titled *A Geek in Prison*.

"Once I started the blog," he continued, "people in the crypto community started staking me, and that was the only reason I had access to money. If you don't already know, you need money in prison."

I thought about a security briefing I'd attended for incoming students to my formerly incarcerated student college program. It was held at a correctional facility and we met inside a portable building with thin walls. Bumper sticker decor on the doors asked, "If not me, then who?" and directed passersby to "Open yourself up to new possibilities!" These instructions were listed next to the items inmates could purchase, like travel-sized toothpaste for five dollars.[12]

Julio, who sat opposite Charlie in his interviewer's chair, nodded in agreement. As a formerly incarcerated person himself, he affirmed Charlie's observations.

After the interview with Charlie Shrem was over, Julio walked toward me.

---

12. Autobiographies I've read by formerly incarcerated people like Susan Burton and Albert Woodfox described the inflated prices assigned to goods purchased from "the canteen" and the desperation felt by inmates who didn't have family on the outside who contributed to their accounts. According to these formerly incarcerated citizens, inmate price gouging was commonplace. Sue Burton, a woman whose activism got her appointed to the Sybil Brand Commission, explained that incarceration facilities were not subjected to the kind of public scrutiny that could prevent twelve ounces of Pantene shampoo being sold to inmates for twelve dollars a bottle.

"*Now* I remember you," Julio said as he approached. He spoke sentences that were turned up to max volume. Would he publicly berate me for quietly sneaking away from the Carite Lake party during his crypto camping weekend? Would he chastise me for refusing his "plant medicine" offers? Whatever Julio was about to say, I knew the entire Crypto Tuesday audience was about to hear.

"I hope you tell your husband about tonight, about how we are an inspirational community. I'm guessing this event is much more your speed and I'm sorry your husband couldn't join you for our gathering this evening."

Julio hustled for pocket change, and he procured large quantities of illegal drugs, but he wasn't easily offended. In fact, he was charming.

"Thanks, Julio," I said. "I'll give Mark your best. I look forward to the next Crypto Tuesday event."

The evening reminded me that I had traveled a lot of miles in my life and that my current location looked alien compared to the geography of adolescence. At eighteen, Gary's professional success, maturity, and family wealth filled me with insecurity and ultimately scared me off. But by the time I met Mark, those assets were things I admired and tried to emulate. My own professional accomplishments and personal growth had deepened my ability to appreciate success in the lives of others.

In business, the Law of Reciprocity stated that it was human nature to feel obligated to reciprocate when someone does something for you first. A variation on this line of thinking? You have to spend money to make money. Love worked similarly. Some even believed that the more we loved, the more love we had to give. Unlike business, love wasn't transactional, it was infinite. With both money and love, giving was the key to getting. But I didn't have much to give when I was a young woman. Nor did I have the ability to fully receive. It wasn't until I started accepting myself, adolescent mistakes and all, that my life transformed from a place of struggle to one of new possibility.

CHAPTER 21:

DAUGHTERS

The year we moved to Puerto Rico coincided with our transition to empty nesters, as our youngest daughter left for college to join her three sisters in independent living. With ages spanning a decade—18, 21, 22, and 27—our daughters were scattered across the West Coast in various stages of their journeys. Olivia, our youngest at 18, had just started as a freshman at UC Santa Cruz. Abby, 21, and Raeanne, 22, were continuing their studies at UC Berkeley and CSU Sacramento, respectively. Meanwhile, our oldest, Eden, had recently completed graduate school and begun working as a grant writer in Washington state, where she lived with her husband.

Some sources called this stage of life—when the last of one's children leaves home—a syndrome. According to family science experts, empty nest syndrome was accompanied by a sense of loss, feelings of rejection, and apprehension over the child's welfare. Many parents worried about how well they had prepared their child to live independently, and this worry resulted in parental anxiety and depression.

Until it was time for our youngest daughter to leave for college, I didn't take the symptoms associated with this syndrome seriously. In fact, I had joked that empty nest syndrome should be called "Parent Liberation Day" instead. As the three oldest launched, I felt proud and excited for their success, not depressed or anxious about their absence. Our daughters were capable and self-reliant, and I happily cheered them on as they packed their bags and started college. That changed when Olivia, my youngest, left for Santa Cruz and Mark and I relocated to Puerto Rico.

"It's not like you're never going to see her again," Mark consoled me.

I had just hung up the phone. Olivia was ecstatic when she called to tell me her close friend also got accepted to UC Santa Cruz and planned to rent a two-bedroom bungalow near campus. The friend, Mattie, wanted Olivia to be her roommate.

"I know," I said, wiping away tears, "but I just don't want her to go."

Mark gave me a hug.

"I guess it just hit me that I'm never going to be a mom in the same way again," I confessed. "As long as there was at least one kid at home, I *felt* like a mom."

"You will *always* be their mom."

He squeezed me tighter.

"But it's never going to be like it was," I cried into Mark's chest. "They're never going to need me in the same way, and it's hard to say goodbye to that part of myself."

I wasn't sure which part of my syndrome resulted from our relocation, which part was linked to pandemic isolation, and which part came from waving goodbye to Olivia—the last child to leave home—but our early days in Puerto Rico left me feeling bereft. I transformed from a cheerleader to a worrier. I missed their noise, family dinners, and mother-daughter walks with Lucy the Dog by the river. When my daughters were around, I had the family I'd always wanted. Life was hectic, but I felt complete.

Even though it was Olivia's absence that ignited my syndrome, I had started to fret about all of my daughters. I worried that our three daughters enrolled in college would feel lonely and isolated in their online classes since COVID turned face-to-face class schedules asynchronous. I worried that our daughters would get sick with COVID and that if this health emergency happened, I wouldn't be able to get to them fast enough. I also worried that I was a bad mother for living in Puerto Rico during a pandemic while they lived their lives on the West Coast. In some twisted part of my mind, geographic distance reflected parental commitment. Instead of a scarlet A, I wore a blinking B for Bad Mother on my chest. After decades of devoted parenting, life without my daughters nearby was a shock to my system.

When I read about empty nest syndrome, I learned that treating the symptoms fell into two primary categories. The first was to stay in contact with one's children, and the second was to keep busy with new hobbies. The first was easy enough, albeit managed from afar. I Zoomed regularly with our daughters in addition to calls and texts, but living in Puerto Rico made weekend visits impractical. It was the second piece of advice, new hobbies, that really helped, and my new hobby was learning about cryptocurrency. Learning about crypto took me down rabbit holes of distraction. The potential uses for blockchain, the ledger on which crypto was housed and that allowed for a transparent trading environment, fascinated me. When I studied trading charts, or considered the way blockchain technology was likely to revolutionize financial systems, I wasn't thinking about my daughters' diets, sleep habits, grades, or party attendance. I didn't worry about their commitment to social distancing.

When Abby asked if she and her boyfriend, Sam, could come to Puerto Rico to visit us in mid-January, I was ecstatic. Abby and Sam were both students at UC Berkeley and wanted to spend their semester break at the beach with us. We agreed to COVID safety precautions for traveling and bought them plane tickets the next day. Our first visitors! Finally, I was going to get to hug a daughter, something I needed very badly to do. The emptiness that my mothering heart felt was about to get filled.

On the day my daughter and her boyfriend were scheduled to arrive, I bounced out of bed and drank my coffee while pacing around the kitchen. I imagined the beaches where we would take them snorkeling and the walks around Dorado we would share. I checked their flight information, and the clock on the stove, every few minutes. I tidied up the guest room until it looked like a high-end cabana at a beach resort and organized the refrigerator with all of Abby's favorite snacks.

"I don't want to let you go," I said, hugging Abby on the crowded airport sidewalk. Holding my child in my arms filled my body with joy and relief.

"I'm so happy to be here, Mom!" she said, squeezing me tightly.

"Welcome to Puerto Rico, Sam," Mark said. "We're glad you guys could make it out for a little R & R."

Mark and Sam loaded suitcases into the trunk. The airport security guard had to blow his whistle three times before we piled into our car and drove away from the loading zone.

Abby and Sam had flown all night. They were tired and hungry, but we all shared the giggly pleasure that comes with reunion. As we headed for our Playa Tortuga community,

I turned to look at my daughter in the back seat with Sam. They both had dark circles under their eyes, but they were holding hands and looked happy.

"The beard looks great on you," I said to Sam.

Sam had reddish brown hair and the beard he wore accentuated his warm brown eyes. He looked more mature since the last time I'd seen him.

"Thanks," Sam said. "It will look even better when it hasn't been on a plane for twelve hours."

I was glad to see them snuggled in the back seat of my car, but I knew something wasn't going well for Abby. She was suffering from acne, angry red bumps spread across her cheeks and chin, and her hair was an unnatural shade, the color of blueberry Sour Patch candy. Ever since high school, these were her tells: Stress and anxiety made her skin break out, and a desire to gain control over a difficult problem resulted in a new dramatic hair color.

As we pulled past the security gate that led into our neighborhood, Mark slowed.

"There they are," I said, and pointed to a cluster of iguanas by our favorite duck pond. "I'd officially like to introduce you to our friends, the iguanas. These are the fellas that we have told you so much about."

"They're gorgeous," Abby said. She rolled down her car window to get a better look.

In high school Abby had a pet snake and multiple geckos. She liked reptiles.

"I love the way they hang out together and with ducks—what social creatures," Abby said, admiring the scene. "I promise that before we get back on a plane, I'll have one eating strawberries right from my hand."

The second gate we entered led into our Playa Tortuga community. As we walked up the stairs to our condo, we discussed their flight experience, unusual for the empty seats.

Air travel during the time of COVID had declined. Sam told us that the airlines were suffering and that the reduction in global passengers was estimated to be in the billions.

"Oh my God, Mom," Abby said when she walked through the front door of our home and saw the Atlantic Ocean spread out before her. "You're never going to want to come back to Sacramento when you have this view."

"We love it," I said. "Living by the ocean is pretty cool, but we miss you and your sisters. I'm looking forward to being back in California this summer."

"Well, get over it," Abby said. "I think visiting you guys in Puerto Rico is going to work for all of us. Do you know it's pouring rain in Berkeley right now? It's definitely better if we just come to you!"

"I'm glad you like it," I said. "Why don't you take some time to get settled, and then we'll walk down to the beach before dinner."

"Not before gifts!" Sam said.

I liked Sam. He and Abby had been dating for a year, and it seemed like they were getting serious. Sam was a nurturer; he had an impulse to make sure others were comfortable. I suspected this came from having a mother with MS; Sam's mother had suffered with the disease for many years and was confined to a wheelchair. Sam participated in her care and it was obvious he admired her when he described her positive attitude and courage. Sam was a few years older than Abby. He only had one more semester before he graduated, and I wondered if their disparate academic tracks—a pending graduation versus a long academic road ahead—was causing my daughter's stress.

Abby grabbed her backpack and pulled out some boxes tied with rumpled string.

"Let's sit on the patio," Mark said, and we all moved outside.

"We didn't mail gifts for Christmas because we wanted to hand-deliver them," Abby said. She handed me a gift the size of a cigar box. I pulled the red string and lifted the lid.

"It's from The Xocolate Bar, one of my favorite chocolatiers in Berkeley," Sam said. "Abby told me that you love chocolate."

"Guilty! These look amazing. Thank you."

The box was handsome and filled with pieces of chocolate that looked like artwork. One was shaped like a butterfly and others like hearts and shells.

"And this is for you." Sam smiled and handed another gift to Mark.

Inside the package that Mark unwrapped was a box filled with exotic spices.

"I know that you appreciate good food, so I'm guessing you love to cook," Sam said.

"Not exactly," Mark replied. "But I *do* love to eat."

"Well, I wanted to share some of my favorite flavors with you both, and I hope you'll let me cook for you while we're visiting," Sam said.

Abby smiled wide and put her hand on Sam's knee. I could tell by my daughter's grin that she appreciated the kindness Sam showed us. I could also tell, by the adoring way Abby looked at Sam, that my daughter was in love.

Abby had met Sam when she moved into UC Berkeley's sober housing. Unlike her past school-housing units at the university, this one restricted parties and substances. Anxiety, coupled with drugs and alcohol, gave Abby a rocky start to collegiate life. In year two, she took a semester off, came back home, enrolled in an outpatient program designed to treat substance dependency and mental health challenges, and regrouped. I wasn't convinced that returning to UC Berkeley was the right choice for her and had hoped she might consider transferring to a university closer to home. But my daughter was determined to go back. She was feeling healthy after a semester of focused self-care, and she pleaded for another chance. When she returned, she met Sam. Like Abby, he was a sober undergrad. This fact gave Mark and me hope that her second attempt at college would go better.

Abby was academically gifted. In high school she debated on a nationally recognized team, took all AP classes, and earned straight A's. She graduated high school with one of those GPAs that exceeded 4.0. Before this trip, she told me that she had finished the semester at UC Berkeley strong and that she was looking forward to some time off after surviving a grueling round of final exams, but her blue hair made me wonder if I knew the whole story.

I was sitting across from Mark on the balcony when he unwrapped the box of spices from Sam. Mark loved ethnic food, and Sam's gift was perfect for a man who had grown tired of mofongo and cassava root, typical Puerto Rican dishes. Mark handed me the box. Inside, Sam had included wild asafetida, and a variety of fragrant curries.

"Thank you for these," I said to Abby and Sam. "I can't wait to try them, but the best gift is just having you both here."

Sam smiled and yawned.

"Why don't you two take some time to rest? You've had a long flight."

"Thanks, Mom," Abby said. "I wouldn't mind a short nap. See you in an hour?"

Abby gave me another hug before Mark escorted the kids upstairs to the guest room, and I lingered just a moment in her arms. It was hard to believe she was twenty-two. I remembered the stages of her life as if they were being played on a movie reel: the way she wanted to sleep with her head tucked tight into the crook of my arm as a baby, the day she fell at the park and knocked her front tooth loose, the way her long blonde hair glowed in the sunshine when she made daisy chains in the grass, and mostly, how she loved stories. She was insatiable. As a child, Abby was her happiest when someone was reading her a story. By the time she was a toddler, we had read the Peter Rabbit series so many times that she knew the text by heart, and by second grade it was difficult to get her nose out of a book.

* * *

During the week that Sam and Abby visited, we had wonderful adventures. We went to the beach with paddleboards, hiked, and fed bread to the ducks, turtles, and iguanas that lived near our home. Sam cooked us shakshuka on one day and curried pumpkin another. We rented a boat and took a trip to the shores of Culebra, an island off Puerto Rico proper known for its amazing underwater life. We snorkeled with giant sea turtles, stingrays, and fish of every variety.

Sam also helped me with cryptocurrency. When Mark and I shared what we were learning with the kids, and explained we needed to move XRP into our cold wallets before Coinbase delisted the token in response to the SEC lawsuit, Sam offered to help.

"There is a big blockchain community at UC Berkeley," Sam said. "They have one of the best blockchain technology programs in the world, so lots of guys there trade crypto. I have a sense of how it works from discussions in my business classes. I'm sure I could watch a YouTube video and help you move crypto from Coinbase to a cold wallet."

"All you need to do is watch a YouTube video?" I asked.

My feelings about Sam's offer were mixed. I was grateful for the help. I felt nervous about moving our XRP tokens from Coinbase to our cold wallets and the thought of having another pair of tech-savvy eyes to watch me conduct the transaction was calming. However, it also annoyed me. My crypto studies had started in November, two months prior to my daughter's visit. I had listened to interviews, made flash cards, watched videos, read books, analyzed financial articles, and browsed numerous news reports. Yet my daughter's twenty-five-year-old boyfriend, who had never traded a single crypto token in his life, thought watching a three-minute YouTube video was more than enough preparation.

There are quantifiable moments when I have realized that the younger generations see a different world than I do. Sam's belief that a YouTube video sufficed for adequate cryptocurrency trading preparation was one of those times. Was I overly cautious or was he overly confident? Was the world of cryptocurrency better suited to the recklessness of youth or was I simply disadvantaged because of my age? After all, when I started college, I typed class papers on an IBM Selectric, cell phones didn't exist, and the Internet was not a thing. Age, I supposed, was both gift and detriment.

"I would appreciate that, Sam," I said. "I'd feel more confident with your help."

"Great. I'll watch a video and then we can move your tokens to your cold wallet. No problem."

* * *

The day before Abby and Sam were scheduled to fly back to California, I asked my daughter to join me upstairs for a talk. Mark and Sam were headed to the beach for one last snorkeling adventure, and I had yet to uncover the reason for her candy-colored hair.

We retreated to my bedroom. Abby sat on a chair next to my dresser and I sat at the foot of my bed. My legs were crisscrossed and I leaned back on my arms for support. I felt relaxed and happy to have some alone time with her.

"I'm glad that you and Sam spent your holiday with us," I said. "I have missed you so much, and it does my heart good to share space with family."

"Thanks for having us out, Mom," Abby said. "Sam and I have had a blast. And I can tell he really likes you guys, especially Mark."

Abby sank into the chair and threw one leg lazily over the armrest.

"Having you in Puerto Rico made my holiday feel special and I have really enjoyed watching you and Sam together. You make an adorable couple. Are you two getting serious?" I asked.

"I think so. Things are going really well," Abby said. "We are so much alike. We love to cook and travel. We're both super nerdy and we laugh at each other's jokes. This is definitely the most serious relationship I've ever been in. I don't have much to compare it to, but Sam and I just work, you know?"

I did know. Sometimes people just clicked. I had watched Abby with Sam all week, and agreed that they seemed like a good fit. Mark and I had joked when we first dated that it's hard to find a match if you're a square peg and everyone else was shaped like a cylinder; we were both square. It seemed this way for Abby and Sam too.

"How's school going?" I asked.

Abby was quiet. Then she moved both feet to the floor and sat up straight. Her left sandal bounced at high speed against the tile like a rabbit's foot. The blue hair question was finally being answered.

"Not as well as I had hoped," she said.

"Organic Chemistry?" I asked.

This was Abby's second attempt at the notoriously difficult class.

"I failed the final," she said, tears welling in her big, round, beautiful eyes.

Organic Chemistry had taken on legendary characteristics in Abby's life. She told me that she had nightmares about her professor and felt nauseous each time she joined the class Zoom. Like a nagging toothache, she thought about the pain with every bite.

"I'm sorry, honey," I said. "I know how much you want a science degree, and I know how hard you are working in chemistry, but maybe it's time to think about changing your major."

"Absolutely not," she said. "I am going to get a degree in chemistry."

Abby had a wide streak of stubborn inside when it came to her academic success. While this had served her well as a child, I worried it resulted in misdirection as an adult.

"Why did you pick chemistry as a major in the first place?" I asked. "Reading was the thing you loved as a kid. I always imagined you would be an English major."

"I do love English," Abby said. "But AP Chemistry was the hardest class I ever took in high school, and my chemistry classes have continued to be the most difficult classes I've taken in college. I want to graduate knowing that I conquered my toughest challenges."

"You have overcome plenty of challenges," I said. "You did not have an easy start to college, but you came home, got sober, and started again. Anxiety and depression have been challenging enough. Why torture yourself with coursework?"

"It's not the same thing," she said. "I need to overcome intellectual challenges. I can make my mind do this. I just need to work harder."

"But you love English," I pleaded. "You're a gifted writer and were practically born with a book in your hand. Getting a college degree doesn't have to be like dragging your body through broken glass. Why not study what you love? What you excel at naturally? Imagine taking upper-division classes that you actually enjoyed."

"I want a degree in chemistry from UC Berkeley, and I can still do it—I've got one more chance to take O Chem before I have to switch majors. The policy allows for three attempts." Her breath caught in her throat. "Please believe in me."

Abby started to cry. I looked at her crumpled face and felt my heart seize. Seeing Abby's torment, her struggle and determination, caused me physical pain. I wanted nothing more than to support my daughter. But what kind of support was best? Do I push harder for change? Do I remind her that paying for the classes she continues to fail was expensive? Do I lecture her about the serious consequences of academic probation? Do I share my concerns about O Chem on her mental health?

As a college professor, I had counseled many teary students over the years. I reminded them that education is a journey and that sometimes along the way people hit a roadblock. The best thing to do was take out one's educational map and consider possible variations to the path originally charted. Detours were not inherently bad and oftentimes they were necessary.

If I had been talking to a different twenty-two-year-old student who failed O Chem for a second time, I wouldn't have felt racked with pain. I would have given clear direction. My advice: Find a path to graduation that doesn't require O Chem. Followed by a warning: If you don't change directions now, you are likely to fail out of college.

But I didn't say any of those things. Instead, I fought back the tears I wanted to cry for my daughter.

When I didn't respond, Abby slid from the chair and onto the tile floor of my bedroom. Her head bent forward to meet her hands, and her body shook with each sob. I lowered myself to the floor and sat next to my daughter. Then I wrapped my arms around her and pulled her into me; her head rested on my shoulder, just like when she was upset as a small child.

"I do believe in you," I said into blue hair. "You have a brilliant mind and a generous heart. You have your whole life in front of you. You are more than the degree you earn or the work you do. College is challenging, but it should also be fun. I'm worried that chemistry can't give you that balance."

"I promise to have fun once it's over," she said. "But right now I need your help."

I saw myself in my daughter. She had inherited my fair skin, my love of baked goods, and when it came to academic pursuits, incredible determination. But why didn't she understand that learning could be joyous? A safe haven? An unending source of entertainment?

"All right," I said, pulling away from our long embrace. I looked at my daughter with confidence.

"We'll figure this out," I said. "We'll find another O Chem class and we'll get you the support you need to pass. Third time is the charm, right?"

Sam left Puerto Rico as scheduled, but Abby extended her stay by a few days so that I could help her devise an O Chem plan of attack. She enrolled in an O Chem online class at a different institution (one that was likely to be easier than the UC Berkeley class), requested outside-of-institution approval from her UC Berkeley counselor, researched chemistry tutors, and set up a semester's worth of support. Abby and I also planned weekly Zoom meetings so we could check in and talk about her assignments each week. This time was going to be different.

There is a deformity in a parent's heart that makes them believe in *next times* for their child at an alarmingly high rate. This irregular beat floods them with hope and sometimes prevents them from seeing clearly. Next time their child will come home by curfew, next time their child will complete their chores before they go out with friends, and next time they will study harder in school. Next time is a version of second chances, a conviction that led me to work with formerly incarcerated students, so my heart beat irregularly most of the time. I believed in second chances and next times. These allowances were lucky bridges in my own troubled youth, and my next time beliefs intensified where my daughters were concerned. Fortunately, I most often watched as they learned from their mistakes. Over the years they self-corrected without much interference—next time they did better.

And yet my strong adherence to next time hasn't always served my daughters well. Helping Abby enroll in O Chem at another college struck me like that, as a misguided effort grounded in magical thinking. A few years later, when Abby was finally dismissed from Berkeley permanently, I categorized my O Chem problem-solving support as one of the worst parenting decisions I ever made. I wished I had helped her chart a new path. She was driven to study chemistry by an allegiance to perfectionism, an emotional fallacy I knew well and one I often saw in my female students. So many women I knew, young and old, held themselves to impossible standards. I wished I would have helped her slay *that* dragon instead of sending her out to battle carbon-containing compounds in a compromised state. Like penny stocks or meme-worthy crypto, Abby's O Chem efforts were practically worthless. My actions demonstrated that I loved my daughter, but they failed to clarify the economics of her excessively risky academic investment. Love, I thought, is never enough when it comes to raising our daughters.

CHAPTER 22:

FIGHTS

The week after Abby left, Deborah picked me up for the regularly scheduled Crypto Tuesday event in San Juan. This time Mark joined us. Deborah had attended these events religiously since our initial vetting with Julio, but this was only my second Crypto Tuesday, and Mark's first.

"What can I expect?" Mark asked, settling into the back seat of Deborah's rental car. Unlike California, lots of people I met in Dorado rented cars because their time on the island was punctuated with extended trips back home, where they lived before relocating to Puerto Rico.

"You never know with this crew," Deborah replied. "I saw that tonight's speaker is Michael Terpin. I don't know much about him except that my crypto connections respect him for his shrewd investing, and the rumor is he hosts wild parties at his mansion in San Juan."

We drove to Delavida restaurant, the usual locale for Crypto Tuesday events. A hostess directed us to a large back patio reserved for the crypto attendees. The generous space included a stage pre-set with video equipment, picnic tables, and an outdoor bar. Waitresses wearing black shorts and white polo shirts walked around taking orders and delivering food. The crowd, predominantly thirty-something-year-old men, talked and clinked their beer glasses together, making indecipherable toasts. It looked like a fraternity scene from a movie—brothers enthusiastically drinking and laughing as if the Sigma Chi characters had been aged by a decade. This was a tight-knit group of men.

Mark, Deborah, and I found our way to the empty side of a picnic table close to the stage. Opposite us sat a heavyset man and a fine-boned woman. The man's face was red and his shirt was wet from perspiration; he looked uncomfortable even though the sun was setting and the cool breeze had tempered the day's humidity.

"Hi, I'm Georgine," I said, extending a hand. Mark and Deborah followed suit.

"Hi," said the man, "I'm Robert and this is my wife, LeAnne. We just moved to the island last week." Robert blotted his face with the cocktail napkin from underneath his drink.

It wasn't just their presence at Crypto Tuesday that gave clues about their attraction to the island. Robert wore a rocket ship emblem on his dark blue button-down shirt. I knew this to be a Bitcoin-inspired insignia. It meant that Bitcoin was headed "to the moon!" Robert was clearly a crypto enthusiast.

"Where did you move from?" Mark asked, leaning toward them with interest.

"The East Coast," Robert said. "I recently finished my PhD in mathematics at MIT. I was working in analytics, but I decided to make crypto my full-time job. No place better for crypto than PR."

"What do you think of Puerto Rico so far?" I directed the question to LeAnne.

She wore a large diamond ring on her left hand that matched the sparkly bracelets on her wrist. Women were the minority at crypto-related events, so I gave LeAnne a big warm smile to let her know I was glad she came and that she could be friends with me and Deborah. I leaned toward her to communicate I was interested in her response.

"I suppose it's going to take some getting used to," she said, and smiled weakly at her husband.

She was silent after that so I relaxed my attentive posture and observed. LeAnne had pale creamy skin and dark brown hair, which gave her the look of a porcelain doll. Her eyes were a watery blue and her rose-colored lips, full. Her expensive Gucci bag sat on the table between us. She looked like Snow White, except that she would have been better suited for boutique shopping or fancy day spas, not marching around the forest with dwarfs.

Just then, Julio and another man, who had a serious look on his face, approached our table and addressed all five of us.

"Welcome, everyone!" Julio said. "I would like to introduce you to tonight's Crypto Tuesday guest speaker, Michael Terpin." Julio turned toward us. "Michael, this is Deborah, Mark, and Georgine."

Julio pivoted toward our new friends. "And this is Dr. Sayer and his wife, LeAnne. Everyone, this is Michael. I'm hoping you will entertain him while I get my equipment crew going."

Julio had questionable ethics and a stable of girlfriends, but he was great with names. His ability to make people feel welcome impressed me.

I nodded at Michael, our new table addition, and scooted closer to Mark to make room for him to sit next to me.

"I'm so glad to meet you," Robert said after Michael sat down at our picnic table. "I think what you're doing for our community is truly admirable. Thank you for fighting. A lot of people in your position would have given up by now, but you're making the world safer for all of us in the crypto space."

Michael Terpin was a short man who wore round spectacles atop a prominent nose. The curly auburn hair that framed his face was streaked with gray. I imagined he was close to seventy, even though his fashion choices—a black Pink Floyd T-shirt, cargo shorts, and open-toe sandals—suggested a younger, more carefree age.

"Thank you, Dr. Sayer," Michael said. "I appreciate that."

Before I could admit that I didn't know Michael's story, he launched into a spontaneous explanation. Michael told us that in 2017, he lost $24 million in cryptocurrency because AT&T had been careless with his security.

"I went into an AT&T store in an affluent Connecticut suburb," he said. "I wanted to buy a new iPhone. The employee who helped me switched my SIM card for a different SIM card."

"Oh no," I gasped. I thought about my mobile phone store history through the lens of Michael's experience. I had heard of jewelry being reset with fake gemstones during cleaning or repairs—but my SIM card? For years I'd waltzed into stores and handed over my phone without a second thought. I banked, and purchased Bitcoin, right from my mobile phone. At that moment, I promised myself to be more careful in the future.

"I'm so sorry, Michael," Deborah said.

"This happened despite the fact that I registered myself with AT&T as a high-security customer. Once my SIM card was swapped, the scammers were able to hack my account and steal my crypto," he said. "AT&T alleged that my hack was unfortunate but committed by sophisticated criminals, not the result of negligence on their part."

"That is total bullshit!" Robert said. "AT&T should have stepped up and taken responsibility for their lack of security and process oversight. That scam was executed with the help of *their* employee!"

Everyone chimed in about the lack of security. It was something on all our minds.

Michael sued. He won his case against the primary suspect convicted of orchestrating the crime, but was not able to recoup losses. I knew from Mark's legal cases that this was typical. Even if the fraudster got caught and criminally prosecuted, it was unlikely the money (or crypto) they stole was sitting in some bank account. The bad guys didn't make monetary recovery easy.

Michael was determined to keep fighting. He told us that he wasn't going to let AT&T off the hook.

"Every time we amend our complaint to the court, every time we file evidence that points out the flaws in AT&T's counterarguments, we have prevailed," Michael explained. "I don't plan to give up. I'm on the right side of this."

"I admire your tenacity," Mark said. "I know firsthand how a long court battle takes a toll on a person and his family. The pursuit of justice is exhausting."

"Are you an attorney?" Michael asked my husband.

"Yes," Mark said. "I'm a fraud attorney."

"Then you know that what happened to me is more common than people think."

Mark nodded. I'd heard a lot about fraud cases through the years.

"Crime rings—essentially gangs—target these minimum-wage employees and pay them for the SIM cards," Michael continued. "The AT&T employee who switched mine probably made 150 bucks. The craziest part is that when we caught the ringleader of this operation, we found out it was a fifteen-year-old kid. He'd been targeting mobile phone employees and hacking accounts since he was thirteen."

A smiling Julio walked back to our table and clapped his hands. "Okay, Mr. Terpin," he said. "We're ready to get started."

Michael excused himself and walked to the stage with Julio. They sat down on two carefully positioned chairs, behind microphones. The crowd quieted and turned toward them. Julio looked at a man standing behind a video camera and held up his fingers for a countdown.

"Rolling in one . . . two . . . Welcome, my friends, to Crypto Tuesday! It is my honor to introduce tonight's guest. He is a serial entrepreneur and the guy who now owns Mike Tyson's Las Vegas house in the *Hangover* movie, Mr. Michael Terpin!"

The audience clapped and then Michael shared his story about getting scammed by the AT&T employee. He said he felt a responsibility to fight on behalf of all the people who didn't have the money to take on a giant like AT&T. Michael was soft-spoken, his voice measured compared to the booming commands of Julio, but he seemed sincere and articulate. Even though he had been swindled out of millions of dollars, he focused on legal facts, not personal outrage.

"I really admire Michael," Robert said, his voice low from across the table. "He doesn't have to keep fighting. When you have billions, $24 million is the cost of doing business, but he wants the government to take crypto seriously; he wants the same protections under the law that traditional investors enjoy. He really is fighting for all of us."

Like Robert, I was impressed with Michael's decision to keep fighting. Standing up for what you believed in was only easy in theory. It came with costs. I had never funded a long arduous lawsuit, but I knew that the Davids who fought the Goliaths usually paid a price.

At age sixteen, I had learned this lesson when I told my mother I wanted to be a vegetarian. I had just finished reading *Animal Liberation*, a 1975 book that argued for the ethical treatment of animals and advocated for vegetarianism. I decided that eating animals was wrong and announced my decision to stop eating meat.

"Good for you," my mom said, looking up from her book. I was standing in the doorway to my mom's bedroom while she relaxed on her bed with a Danielle Steel novel.

"As soon as you no longer live in my house, I think that's a fine decision, but for now, you eat chickens, pigs, and cows."

Her feet were propped up on a pillow to keep them elevated on the days she worked double shifts at the restaurant. This rest time helped her manage the swelling that came with long hours serving hungry customers stacks of pancakes in the morning and taco platters at night. I had interrupted her rest to share my new food plan.

"If you read this book by Peter Singer, I think you'd understand," I suggested. "There are obviously differences between humans and animals, but eating them is speciesism."

I'd read that animals felt intense fear before they were killed, and of course they felt pain when they were slaughtered. Meat processing was a horrendous business, and it would all stop if we just ate a vegetarian diet. Demand drove the brutality.

She slammed her book shut and smacked it down on the bed. I could see the pink burn scars, little frown shapes, that ran down the inside of her forearm from carrying hot plates. Then she looked at me with annoyance. My breathing got shallow and my shoulders tensed. If I continued to push her, it wouldn't go well for me. I knew this for certain. My mom did not tolerate disobedience. I wanted to tell her about the inhumane conditions that animals faced in CAFOs. I wanted to share information about animal testing by cosmetics companies. I wanted her to understand that this new dietary choice was a chance to do something right, maybe even something noble. But I looked down at my feet and let her think my silence was contrition.

"I don't know what speciesism is," my mom said. "But I don't care either. The answer is no."

Then she picked up her book, flipped back to the right spot, and started reading. After a few minutes of standing in her doorway, of being ignored while I stared at my feet, I quietly left, feeling powerless, just like those poor animals at processing plants.

Since Mom worked as a waitress most evenings, the topic lay dormant between us for more than a week. I made dinner for my brother and myself, and packed my own lunch for school. It was easy to excise the meat products from my meals. At least it was easy until Mom had the night off work and decided to cook dinner.

"Tonight, I thought we would eat dinner as a family," she said. "I'm cooking." Her voice was sweet and gentle, nothing like the voice of my no-nonsense mother.

Before we sat down to eat, I knew it was a test. I had smelled the hamburger grease from my bedroom. Besides, my mom hated cooking dinner. I had been wrong to relax, foolish to think she had forgotten about our earlier conversation.

Stay calm but firm, I told myself. Maybe once she understood I was serious about my new diet, she would accept my decision. I forced my feet to move toward the kitchen and sat down at the wooden table.

"How was your day?" she asked in the same phony voice that had announced "family dinner."

"Fine," I replied. I looked down at my plate. Sloppy joes. Rust-colored glop sloshed atop an open-faced hamburger bun. Small pools of fat formed along the edge of my plate. My body felt like a statue, made of plaster, not flesh.

"Eat your dinner." Her voice returned to its familiar tone.

"Mom," I said calmly, my hands clasped and frozen in my lap. "I really appreciate that you cooked us dinner. It was very thoughtful. But I don't eat meat anymore. I'm sorry."

The energy around my mom radiated heat. She seemed to grow larger as she pushed her chair back hard and stood tall. She screamed, "Oh yes you do, or you will eat nothing at all!"

Then my mom reached across the table, grabbed my plate, and threw it into the kitchen wall. My eyes were squeezed tight as I heard glass shatter and fall onto the linoleum floor. When I opened my eyes, sloppy joe was splattered across the room like the remnants of a cafeteria food fight. Brown sludge trickled down the eggshell-colored wall, the oak cupboards, and the dirty table legs.

"We'll be eating in our bedrooms tonight," Mom said to my brother. He stood up but didn't say a word. His cheeks flushed pink and his eyes were wide with shock. We both knew that nobody was allowed to talk.

Mom's icy blue stare had the power to cast spells and boil children. "You clean up this mess," she said, emphasizing each word individually. Then she picked up her own plate and glided down the hall to her room as if nothing had happened.

Sitting at the Crypto Tuesday picnic table, I realized that I had thought a lot about my past failures since moving to the island—things that filled me with shame like drug use and stripping. But this memory was different. It suggested that there was also power in the difficult moments of my adolescence. Some fights were worth it, especially when I exercised my will to align with my values. This incident with my mother had added fiber to my bones and helped me grow into the adult I became.

Vegetarianism didn't cost me the dollars that Michael Terpin's fight cost him, but it added another layer of complication to my life. My mother didn't back down from a fight; no one born of Leland Stanford's DNA embraced quick surrender. Just like her father, Lance Stanford, my mom was uncompromising. Her rules were the law and they demanded respect and obedience. End of discussion.

For the next year that I lived with my mother, my diet, among other things, was a searing source of conflict. But unlike most things we fought about, vegetarianism strengthened me. It was something I believed in and my mother's opposition only galvanized my resolve. I was still a plant-based eater all these years later. For that, I have my mom to thank. Stanford blood flowed in my veins too.

I looked up at the stage where Julio and Michael Terpin sat. Michael took a breath and leaned closer to his microphone. "I am just sick and tired of the hypocrisy. Government and financial systems work one way for the rich and another way for regular people. Take, for example, the SEC accredited investor regulation. It's just another instance of how the middle-class investor has it much tougher than the wealthy investor."

Mark had explained this regulation to me. It was a rule that simplified things for hedge fund managers. In order to get hedge fund access, a person had to be an "accredited investor," and in order to become an accredited investor, a person needed a net worth of a million dollars or to have earned at least $200,000 a year for two consecutive years. Perhaps it was reasonable to require retail investors, operating in complex financial spaces, to obtain some designated level of knowledge, but how did a certain income level sustained over multiple years prove investment preparedness?

"The accredited investor regulation protects the rich from the middle class," Michael said. "We're told that these regulations are designed to protect people from making uninformed investment decisions—from doing something stupid and losing all their money. But that seems disingenuous when people walk into Vegas casinos every day, drunk, and are allowed to put their life savings on red." Michael shook his head in disgust.

Michael had become a permanent resident of Puerto Rico in the mid-2000s. Just like my husband, he was lured to the island because of Act 20 & 22. He was well-known for angel investing—he supported a host of crypto-funded projects on the island and encouraged the Crypto Tuesday audience to do the same.

"Look. I know we are all here because of the tax incentives," Michael said. "But don't forget that we have a responsibility to put some of that bounty back into the island. We have the ability to improve infrastructure, governance, and the lives of the Puerto Rican people. It's the right thing to do."

"Speaking of investing in Puerto Rico," Mark whispered to me as the audience clapped at the conclusion of Michael's talk, "I saw Sal today and he invited us to lunch tomorrow. He's accepted that the rental deal is off the table and now he is willing to discuss selling his condo to us."

I smiled and nodded at my husband, but my shoulders tensed and my clasped hands froze. I had complicated feelings about buying Sal the mobster's condo. I thought about the clarity of Michael's closing words: "It's the right thing to do." When it came to Puerto Rican real estate, I wondered what that meant for me.

CHAPTER 23:

ANXIETY

Before our scheduled lunch with Sal and Kathy, I needed to clear my head. I wanted to get my ongoing Puerto Rican residency stress under control so that I could consider a potential real estate purchase and communicate those thoughts to my husband with clarity. As a general rule, change caused me anxiety. So did spending large amounts of money. I liked control, financial cautiousness, and daily predictability—vocabulary words missing from my adolescence. That part of me, the one personified by the tiny crossing guard holding a stop sign, had a hard time wrapping her head around owning a condo in Puerto Rico.

I decided to go for a run.

"I'll be back in an hour," I said to Mark, and pulled my ponytail through the back of a baseball cap. "I need some exercise."

"Have a good run," he said, heading upstairs. "See you when you get back. We should head over to Sal and Kathy's at noon."

I had long used exercise as a way to prepare myself for difficult experiences. Contentious work meeting? Better outcomes after yoga. Disagreement with one of my daughters about boyfriends or curfews? Perfect time for weight training. Conversation about the purchase of a mobster's run-down, filthy condo on a Caribbean island far from home? Not before a long, hard run.

As I tightened the laces on my shoes, I thought about the path that got us to this decision point. Mark and I had agreed that a second year on the island as a member of Act 20 & 22 made good economic sense. My college campus planned to continue remote operations due to COVID; I could teach in Dorado, Puerto Rico, just as easily as I could teach in Sacramento, California. And once the lease ended on the current rental, we would need another place to live. However, renting a place and buying a place were two very different approaches. The first suggested a temporary residence while the latter, something more permanent, made me feel uneasy.

I knew from my divorce that feelings of resentment in a marriage were like slow-release poison. Little by little they weakened the betrothed until the hosts were so sick with disappointment that survival no longer mattered. Instead, freedom from pain emerged as the couple's singular desire. Whatever Mark and I decided about the parameters of our continued residence in Puerto Rico, it had to be collaborative or else we'd be risking venomous results. Unspoken betrayals and unfinished conflicts could damage the love in one's heart.

If Puerto Rico was to be a more permanent kind of home, I had to face that there would be difficult conversations ahead regarding my job, proximity to family, and about River Acres, the house we owned in California. I wasn't ready to print my name on the title of a second home. It meant stretching my financial resources too tightly if I did.

I grabbed a gate key from the kitchen drawer and headed out the door to start my run by the beach. As I stretched my legs to warm up, I looked out at the ocean and took a long deep breath. There was nothing like an expansive space to remind a person that their individual presence occupies a tiny spot on the globe. Earth is the fifth-largest planet in the solar system, I thought, almost 4,000 miles in radius, and home to approximately 7.8 billion people. The space I inhabited in Puerto Rico underscored my diminutiveness, a speck on a small island, in a vast ocean, on a large planet hanging in an infinite sky. I felt swallowed up by the forces of nature when I ran the trails in Dorado, and this speck needed nature to help relax her.

After running the first mile, the anxiety I felt subsided. I left the shoreline path and headed toward a defunct golf course that bordered my Playa Tortuga community. Its green slopes were strangled by crabgrasses of all varieties. The course was mowed regularly, but the hairy grasses wound their tendrils around the smooth, tight blades left from days when these ranges were still pristine. The unused cart path doubled as my private running trail. I entered the course on the back nine, which was marked by a weathered cement headstone announcing the tenth hole and its 525-yard distance. Bit by bit, my stress turned into gratitude. I felt lucky to run alongside this tropical beauty.

A low-hung metal railing, twisted and broken from Hurricane Maria, guided my ascent toward the hole's shaggy green. After a steep incline that slowed my running pace, I stopped. The view from where I stood was breathtaking. It revealed endless miles of ocean to the east and tropical island to the west and south. The entirety of the front nine was also visible from the top of this bluff. Finger lakes, sewn into the course for increased water play, were edged with palm trees and tall reeds. Each lake teemed with life, home to ducks, turtles, and iguanas. In its heyday, this course would have been as elegant as it was difficult.

After my ragged breath slowed, I began a 360-degree rotation ritual. My arms and eyes spread wide and the aperture of my memory clicked at high speed. From this golf course perch, I rotated clockwise until vast rolling hills of emerald filled my view. The lush landscape was of Toa Alta, a great location for hikes, and beyond that, the town of Bayamon, where we went shopping for groceries. While the clouds above the ocean were gentle and white, gray and purple ribbons constructed the inland sky. This foretold of heavy rains above the island's interior. I wondered which sky was the nimitta, the prediction, for our pending lunch with Sal and Kathy: gentle or fierce?

Finally, my easy breath returned, and I was ready for the next leg of my run. *Pace yourself*, I whispered, trying to organize the jumbled real estate configurations that floated through my mind. Then I ran on.

* * *

"I'm home," I yelled, walking through the front door. I took off my running shoes and headed to the kitchen for a glass of water.

"Good," Mark said, descending the stairs to greet me. He carried a pad of paper. "I've been doing some research to prepare for our meeting with Sal and Kathy. Can I talk to you for a minute before you jump in the shower?"

"What makes you think I plan on taking a shower?" I smiled.

Mark looked at me and crinkled his nose. Then he sat on the couch and I sat down next to him, hoping my stench was tolerable.

"I've spent some time looking at real estate prices in Dorado," he said. "If we can agree on a number, I don't think we can lose. Given the cost of rent, condo ownership makes sense."

Mark handed me his notepad. It included the prices of condos in our neighborhood plus an owning-versus-renting cost comparison.

"But what happens in year three when I have to be back on campus for work?" I asked. A droplet of sweat fell from my hairline, rolled down my face, and plunked on the couch.

"That's a problem for year three," he said. "We can always rent it, or do some rehab and turn around and sell. There are literally no other places for sale in this price range with ocean views in Dorado."

The ink on Mark's notepad started to blur where my fingers had touched the paper, so I set the pad down on the coffee table in front of us. I could hear excitement in Mark's voice, but I pressed on with my concerns.

"Wouldn't our inevitable location problem be easier to manage if we rented next year instead of purchasing a place?" I asked.

"Sure," Mark said. "But in the long run, buying Sal's place—for the right price—puts us in a position to make money instead of paying somebody else's mortgage with our rent checks."

Mark looked into my sweaty face and smiled. The tone of his voice was soft, but certain.

"Sal's condo with that ocean view isn't just any old place," he continued. "It's special. You're right, buying it presents potential challenges, but I think they're problems we can handle."

He gave me a light kiss on the lips, careful not to come in contact with the rest of my perspiring face.

I wasn't convinced. Flashing concerns popped into my mind like squares on a *Jeopardy!* board: A real estate market crash, changes to the Act 20 & 22 laws, elderly parents who need our help on the West Coast, and hurricanes, to name a few, blinked in bright lights. Plus, rehabbing Sal's condo into a livable state would require demolishing and remodeling. How do you purify a space that's been occupied by a mobster for more than thirty years? What gruesome mementos might we find if we dismantled walls and cupboards? I had heard that burning sage supports space purification, but does that apply in a home where the former occupant had probably murdered people? Was there enough sage in all of Puerto Rico?

And finally, money! I didn't have enough for my half of the purchase price. Even if Mark financed my half at a reasonable interest rate and let me pay him back in monthly installments like he did when we bought River Acres, I doubted I could afford a second mortgage. The cost of my dad's health care needs had recently increased and I also helped out two daughters in college. My paychecks were stretched thin and my recent crypto success didn't come with future guarantees. Mark was a member of Act 20 & 22, but I wasn't. He saved a bundle on taxes, but I didn't. His tax savings opportunity, what we referred to as *our* tax savings opportunity, was quickly becoming a giant financial anchor around my neck.

Instead of sharing these thoughts, I took a few deep breaths. Sal was unpredictable. Why start negotiating with my husband when the old mobster was unlikely to cooperate? We had heard from neighbors that Sal had previously started discussions with others living in Playa Tortuga about selling his condo and the deals always flopped.

"That guy changes his mind constantly," one neighbor told us. "There was a time when I was going to buy his place. It fell through. With him it always does. I'm not the only one in Playa Tortuga that's happened to, either. He's been here thirty years and he's always been crazy."

"Schmoops," Mark said, using my pet name. "Today is just about having a conversation." Then he took my wet hand into his and smiled tenderly into my overheated face.

"There is no decision to make this afternoon," he said. "I understand that buying property in Puerto Rico makes you uncomfortable, but at this stage we are only considering possibilities. Just talking. Today should be about having fun with a mobster and his wife. How many times in your life will you get to dine with the Benozzos at the Ritz-Carlton?"

I silently hoped that today was the last. My tolerance for Sal, with his sexist language and innuendo, was waning. Not so for my husband. He made his intentions crystal clear when he called me Schmoops—an endearing sweetness that usually accompanied pillow talk. Now I was certain his property interests were serious.

CHAPTER 24:

DEALS

After I cleaned up from my run, Mark and I walked over to Sal and Kathy's. Kathy wasn't around but Sal welcomed us into a familiar scene: awkward hugs in the doorway, a smell that permeated the air like haze from a grocery store dumpster, and finally, whiskeys on the porch.

Wind blew my freshly washed hair in a million directions and palm trees that lined the coast hunched in unison like tropical flags of warning. The dark interior skies I'd watched during my run had made their way to Dorado, a nimitta for sure.

"You both know I only talk business at the club," Sal began, "so I don't want to get into details here, but I do want to start by thanking you for hearing my offer. Our kids are really putting pressure on us to move to Florida and live by our grandkids. They also think it's time that they help out with Kathy. She's going downhill. She doesn't want to take her medication and this week she decided to hide my teeth! It's not her fault. It's this fuckin' brutal Alzheimer's disease. But my goddamn teeth? Some days I want to kill her. Literally."

"Is Kathy joining us for lunch?" I asked, thinking it was strange I hadn't seen her.

"Oh yeah," Sal said. "She's fine today. She's just upstairs watching the Hallmark Channel. She loves that shit."

"Well, we appreciate the conversation too," Mark said. "We are interested in buying your condo and would love to land on a deal that's advantageous to both of us."

"To making friends *and* deals," Sal said, raising his glass for a toast.

Sal called for Kathy and the four of us headed to Sal's car. On the way, Sal handed Mark the keys.

"It's better if you drive," Sal said. "I got pretty high this morning and now I'm a little drunk."

"You have an impressive constitution, Sal," Mark said as he took the keys and walked to the driver's side of the car.

"Nothing new about that," Kathy said to me with a tilt of her head, a girlfriend sharing secrets. "Sal is a big fat lush."

She was right. There was nothing to add to Kathy's observation so I asked, "How are you feeling today?"

I climbed into the back seat, helped Kathy with her seat belt, and lifted Kathy's dog, Gidget, onto her lap.

"Just terrific," she said, "except I gotta live with that jerk."

Kathy used both hands to point at Sal's head, the back of which was visible over the passenger seat headrest. Then she made a face and stuck her tongue out at him like an angry five-year-old on the playground.

As Mark backed the car out of its parking space, Sal said, "I got one for ya: Why are women's feet smaller than men's feet?"

"I have no idea," I said and pushed Gidget back toward Kathy to stop her from crawling onto me. Gidget smelled like a dirty barn. I rolled down my window.

"So they can get closer to the sink to do the dishes!" Sal laughed at his own joke.

"Good Lord, Sal. That's awful," I said.

"Here's another one," he continued. "Why do men never get hemorrhoids?"

"I can't imagine," I said.

"Because they're already perfect assholes."

This time, Kathy laughed with Sal.

I groaned. I wasn't sure I could endure a lunch with these people.

"See," Sal said, pleased with himself. "I may be a bastard, but I believe in equal opportunity joke telling."

Once we pulled through the security gates of the Ritz-Carlton, Sal directed Mark toward Coa, another of the exclusive restaurants on the sprawling resort property. We parked and walked slowly to the entrance.

"I'm sorry, Mr. Benozzo, we don't allow dogs in the restaurant," the hostess said after greeting us.

"Nonsense," Sal said. "Go talk to your manager. You're gonna make an exception for me."

When the waitress turned to go find her manager, Sal grabbed four menus from the hostess stand and headed inside.

"Come on," he said. "Follow me."

We sat at the table Sal picked for us and accepted the menus offered by his meaty hands. From Wagyu rib eye with truffle mashed potatoes to local greens and fresh fruit, the options were plentiful, but I wondered if we were actually staying for lunch. The hostess who greeted us was obviously annoyed that Gidget had joined our reservation.

"Mr. Benozzo! Welcome to Coa!" said a tall man in a gray suit who walked over to our table five minutes later. "It's wonderful to see you. Enjoy your lunch."

Mark and I exchanged an inquisitive look. I shook my head and went back to reading the menu.

"Thanks," Sal said to the man in the suit. "Would you do me a favor and start us out with three martinis, dry, and a Coke for Kathy?"

"Of course, Mr. Benozzo," the man said, and headed in the direction of the bar.

It wasn't until Sal had ordered us a second round of drinks that he finally announced, "Here's the deal. I don't want to sell my place and move to Florida, but it's time."

Sal looked at us and then at Kathy. For all his faults, I believed he loved his wife.

"My son wants me to keep the condo so the family can use it for vacations," Sal continued, "but I said, 'Fuck that.' I want someone in my place who is going to appreciate it. Someone who is actually going to live in it. Not my son who works too much to use it, or one of these other Act assholes who just pretend to live in Puerto Rico but take their G7s to other islands or wherever. Besides, the IRS hired a team of cocksuckers whose sole purpose it is to catch these idiots."

I'd heard about the G7 jet rumor at a Crypto Tuesday event. It detailed the ways in which some of the Act 20 & 22 members tried to sidestep their Puerto Rican residency requirements with the help of private jets.

"When it comes to selling my place, I want you guys to have it," Sal said. "I like you both. That's the truth."

Our waiter set down three fresh martinis. Then he brought out our lunch plates.

"We think the world of you and Kathy," Mark said. "And we appreciate this opportunity. We know what a special spot you have."

"But you gotta meet my terms," Sal said, leaning forward with bloodshot eyes. "First, no real estate agents. I'm not paying some dimwit a commission to sell my place to people I handpicked. Second, I'm selling the place as is; the price is nonnegotiable and it needs to be paid in cash. Third, you need to bring the cash to my lawyer in Panama. He handles all my business transactions and that's where I do my banking."

Was this guy for real? Did he really expect us to fly to Panama with a duffel bag full of cash?

"I hope you know that I would never offer anyone a deal that I wouldn't take myself," Sal added. "I'm not saying I'm perfect, but I believe a deal like this should be a win for everyone. For me, it's not about the money, it's about selling to the right people."

I doubted Sal's intentions were so altruistic. It was hard to imagine that mobsters didn't care about money. Especially Sal, someone who used his liquor distribution company to wash mob money.

"When I was just a little boy, around seven," Sal said, "my grandfather put me on his knee and said, 'Solly, you are going to make a lot of money. A lot. But never keep it in your own name.' That's one of the reasons I was able to play the game for so long. It's also why you have to go to Panama. The other reason?"

Sal brought his hand to his mouth and pretended to zip shut his lips. Then he threw away the imaginary key. "I know how to keep my fucking mouth shut."

Watching Sal was like watching a movie starring Al Pacino.

Sal proceeded to tell us other stories about his grandfather, Alexander Benbanski, who emigrated from Eastern Europe. According to Sal, his grandfather was a bootlegger and the reason his family got started in the liquor distribution business in the first place.

I excused myself and headed to the bathroom. Buying a condo from Sal was full of risk, the kind that exceeded fluctuating property values. I stood in the empty bathroom and let the cold water from the sink rush over my hands and then splashed the water on my face. I didn't usually drink whiskey, followed by vodka martinis, after a morning run. The effect had me feeling woozy. In addition to the alcohol, Sal's purchasing terms unnerved me. I stared into the bathroom mirror and blinked at my reflection. Maybe Kathy wasn't the only person living in that condo with mental health challenges; Sal had to be out of his mind if he seriously thought Mark and I would hop on a plane to Central America with undeclared cash in a suitcase.

When I finally dried my hands and left, there was Sal, standing in the small corridor that led to the bathrooms. He took me by both shoulders, pressed me into the wall, and moved his body so close to mine that the crucifix he wore around his neck almost touched my chin.

"What are you doing?" I asked, feeling disoriented.

My head spun. I felt the cool cement wall through the back of my thin cotton sundress and the force of Sal's fingers pressing into my flesh. The smell of vodka hung in the air between us.

"If I wasn't eighty-six years old, I'd take you back to my place right now and fuck the hell out of you," he said. Then he laughed like he was telling a joke, let go of me, and walked into the men's room.

The alcohol and spinach salad in my stomach churned, and for a moment I thought I might throw up in the hallway. When I walked back to the table, I found Mark and Kathy laughing about an orange dog toy that they handed back and forth between them. Gidget sat below their quick-paced exchange, mesmerized, her head following the toy like the arm on a swinging metronome.

Just as I was about to tell Mark what had happened in the hallway, Sal sat down at the table and asked, "Anyone want dessert?"

"No, thank you," I said. "We've had enough."

Sal ignored my sharp tone and asked, "Did I ever tell you about how I used to come home from school to find my father's car up on cement blocks, engine on, big rock on the gas pedal to make the wheels turn?"

I could hear Sal talking, but I was unable to concentrate on what he said. I felt a breeze float through the restaurant and brush my skin, but I drifted from the moment and my thoughts turned inward.

The exchange I had with Sal by the bathrooms sent me back to a time when I was eighteen, the last night I had ever delivered a singing telegram.

I was hired to show up as a cop to a bachelor party. The address took me to a tract home, yellow with white trim, in an average-looking neighborhood. It was the kind of place where elementary school teachers and dental hygienists lived; the lawn was freshly mowed and a bike with training wheels was leaning against the garage. I pulled into the driveway, parked, and clicked on the interior car light. My contract directions said, "Bachelor party for Ron. Pretend noise complaint."

The Aggressive Cop was a performance I had given before. I would drive to an address, knock on the door, and tell whoever opened it that I worked for the Sacramento PD. Then I would flash a fake badge with swirling bluster, put my hands squarely on my hips, and puff out my uniformed chest. Rattling off fake ordinances, I announced that I was responding to a noise complaint and I'd ask to come inside to take a look around.

Once I made contact with the person of interest named in my contract notes, I pulled out my handcuffs and ordered him into the nearest chair. By this point, the partygoers were standing around, trying their best not to bust out laughing.

Most often, everyone at the party was in on the gag except the person being celebrated.

I knocked on the front door of the yellow-and-white house. The man who opened it looked surprised to see a police officer standing on the other side.

"Good evening, sir. I'm Officer Smith," I said, and started in on my usual badge-flashing shtick. "We've had a complaint about the excessive noise coming from your house."

The man looked confused.

"We've been playing music, but not too loud," he said.

"Sir, in Sacramento County, noise levels are not to exceed fifty-five decibels. You are in obvious violation of the law." My voice was steel. "I'm going to need to take a look around."

That's when a small group of men in the background started to giggle and a moment of recognition put a smile on the confused man's face.

"You must be Ron," I said.

I walked confidently into the house with my chin held high. I looked around like I was surveying the premises.

"I am indeed," said the man, "and I've been a bad, bad boy." Ron said this to me while holding out his hands—he was ready to be cuffed. Unlike most of my clients who were embarrassed by the attention, Ron was emboldened. He looked me up and down and then licked his lips. I looked away and wished the gig had been scheduled at a public place like a pizza parlor.

Ron was wearing a white T-shirt, Wrangler jeans, and cowboy boots. He was tall, at least six feet. His eyes were too close together, his brown mustache needed a trim, and just like Sal Benozzo in the bathroom hallway, his breath smelled of vodka.

"Oh yes, you have been a bad, bad boy, Ron," I said, playing along. I clicked my play cuffs around his wrists. "You are in very big trouble."

Ron's friends laughed on cue. Then we all shifted from the entryway to the living room. One of his friends grabbed a chair from the kitchen while the others navigated to the couches. The men got comfortable. One of Ron's friends hooted loudly and then high-fived the person sitting next to him.

Ron's party was small; only five twentysomething men in addition to Ron occupied the living room space. This was the fourth time I had been hired for an in-home male-only party—all bachelor parties—and I hadn't liked the vibe at any of them. Most of my gigs were birthday parties, coed extravaganzas where someone most often turned fifty. At the bachelor parties, some guests were surprised to learn I wasn't a sex worker; it made me wonder if the bride-to-be influenced the entertainment selection process. Singing telegram girls were a scoop of vanilla, even in the eighties.

I walked over to the duffel bag dropped earlier in the entryway, unzipped it, and pulled out my boom box. Then I hit play.

"Pour Some Sugar on Me" blasted as I walked in a circle around Ron. I smacked the barrel of a toy gun into the palm of my hand and pretended to contemplate how best to levy Ron's punishment. Suggestively, I ran my finger up one of his arms, across his strong shoulders, and down the length of his other arm.

Ron sat in a wooden kitchen chair placed in the middle of the sunken living room. A large pile of children's toys had been shoved into one corner and an oak coffee table, littered with bottles and rolled-up bills used to snort cocaine, into another. Ron's friends sat on hideous gray couches, eager to watch the show, fresh drinks in their hands.

I learned early that a good striptease happened slowly. Each button, each untucked corner of clothing, each inch of newly revealed skin, took time. Before I sang, "Happy bachelor party, dear Ro-on . . ." my job was to entertain.

To captivate. To make the party memorable. To get people laughing with a dramatic party entrance and then make them feel just a little bit naughty, a little bit uncomfortable. The more I embarrassed the party boy, the more fun the audience had and the easier it was to play my role.

Before unbuckling my officer's belt, I felt the fingers of Ron's cuffed hands on my ass.

"Oh, no, no, no, Ron my boy," I admonished. "This is not *that* kind of a dance. No touching, my friend."

"Take it off!" one of Ron's friends yelled from the couch. "I wanna see your tits."

"Hey," I said to my audience with a warm smile and a firm voice, "watch it. This show is PG-rated."

They laughed.

Once I started to move my hips to the rhythm of the music, the energy in the room buzzed with electricity. I slowly turned, taking small practiced steps while releasing one side of my belt from its steel buckle and gliding the leather strip back and forth provocatively through the belt loops of my pants. I looked at Ron. Instead of discomfort, the emotion most often detected on the face of the guy handcuffed and sitting alone in the middle of the room, I saw eagerness, same with the faces of Ron's friends.

When I turned back toward the men sitting on couches, I felt Ron grab me a second time. Again, I pushed his cuffed hands back down toward his lap and shook my head no. Then I repositioned myself in the center of the room, a small triangle of space between Ron's chair and the couches of leering men. The air was thick with their impatience.

I dropped my belt on the floor to more shouts of approval and began my striptease routine. *You can do this*, I thought. *Dance. Sing. Get the fuck out of here.*

Very slowly, I unfastened one button at the top of my police shirt. The heels of my black stilettos twisted in the living room's knotted brown carpet strings, making it difficult to balance and sway at the same time, but I corrected by shifting weight higher onto my toes.

"Damn, girl," one of the men said. "I knew you were the one I wanted at this party the moment I saw your bikini picture. That is one fine ass."

"We're willing to pay to play!" another man yelled.

Shouts of agreement echoed like home run cheers in a baseball stadium. The hair on my arms prickled. This was all wrong.

Sticky sweet Def Leppard lyrics poured from my boom box like syrup that coated everything in its path.

The men on the couches looked possessed, their unblinking eyes tearing me apart. I felt my legs start to tremble. I wasn't in control of the room, or these men, and all I could think was that I had to get out of there. Now.

Instead of ripping my fake police pants off at their Velcro-secured sides, I yelled, "Sorry, guys. You hired the wrong girl!"

I took the handcuff key from my pocket, threw it toward the toy pile, and bolted for the front door. I grabbed the duffel bag with my car keys on the way. I didn't pick up my belt. I didn't stop the music. I didn't breathe. I was in flight, desperate to escape the danger that was closing in around me. It wasn't a question I considered, or a fear that gnawed my nerves; it was a complete knowing. To survive I had to run.

The night air carried me from the door to my car and filled my lungs with fresh oxygen, enough to start my ignition with shaking fingers.

"What the fuck!" one of the men yelled from the doorway as my car started. "Get back in here, you bitch."

"Contact my company to get your money back!" I screamed at him from inside my car, and pulled out of the driveway as fast as I could manage.

The neighborhood sky was pitch-black but streetlights blinked in rapid succession through my windshield, stars guiding me out of the wilderness, until I pulled onto the freeway and headed for home. That's when the tears came, salty rivers that streamed down my face and fell onto my cheap polyester costume.

Sitting at the restaurant table, I realized Sal was still telling Mark his childhood story about finding his dad's car raised by blocks. I looked over and watched Kathy dig around in her purse. She was searching, lost in her own thoughts, just like me. Sometimes, memories were elusive. They hid from us like mementos buried deep at the bottom of an overstuffed bag. Other times, things we'd rather forget were flung into wide-open spaces by happenstance. That's when our past rushed in like an unexpected gust of wind through a window, knocking over neatly framed photos and shattering their glass.

The waiter approached our table and asked, "Can I get you anything else today?" Sal just kept on talking, so the waiter set the check down and left.

"That's right," Sal said, his words slurred from weed and booze. "Once my father learned that he got paid by the mile, that's what he did each week, put the car up on blocks and ran the odometer like crazy while he sat in the house drinking beer."

"You've got to be kidding me," Mark said with a laugh. "What a crazy childhood."

A crazy childhood might have been the one thing that Sal and I had in common.

CHAPTER 25:

GIFTS

Mark drove us back from the Ritz-Carlton to the Playa Tortuga community. It seemed like we were spent after a three-hour lunch and nobody spoke on the drive home. When we parked, I helped Kathy gather her things—random plastic bags, two purses, a chipped dog bowl, a leash—and followed her up the stairs with Gidget. The Benozzos' front door was unlocked, so I opened it and scooted Gidget inside the foul-smelling house. Then I helped Kathy settle on the couch in front of a flat-screen TV, said goodbye, and headed for home. I waved to Mark from the sidewalk. He and Sal were standing next to Sal's car. They were deep in conversation, heads nodding, serious looks on their faces, but I was done with Sal Benozzo so I kept on walking.

When Mark finally got home, I was upstairs lying down. I had changed into shorts and a T-shirt and rested under the cool stream of air that blew from an inverter above our bed. A large glass of water, my third since getting home, was on the nightstand next to me.

Mark walked into our bedroom, sat down by my bare feet, and shook his head from side to side as if he was about to say something inconceivable. He brushed his dark hair back into place with his fingers.

"You are not going to believe the conversation I just had with Sal in the parking lot," he said.

"Try me."

After our drunken lunch, punctuated with sexual harassment in a restaurant hallway, I didn't think there was much Mark could say about Sal Benozzo that would surprise me.

"I've done my research. I have a pretty good idea of what the fair market value is for Sal's condo, including the added cost associated with a remodel," Mark said. "But I was blown away when he finally told me what he'd like us to pay. It's at least a hundred thousand less than the place is worth, maybe even one-fifty. The sales contract he plans to propose will look a little screwy—about 30 percent of the price will be tied to his furnishings—but in the end, this chance to buy Sal's condo is a big win."

"Why would Sal give us his place at a discount? And why in the world would we pay for furnishings that have to be hauled straight to the dump?" I asked, worn out from the exasperation I felt toward Sal Benozzo.

Everything about the man was screwy. Sal lived in a world where people smoked weed and drank whiskey before lunch, spit out sexist jokes like gumballs from a penny machine, and sexually harassed their neighbors. I didn't plan to visit the land of Sal Benozzo anymore.

"It's because he wants to avoid capital gains," Mark said, answering my second question first. "And I think he's telling the truth; he's offering us a deal that he knows will make us happy. He wants to sell his home, a place he has loved for more than thirty years, to people he genuinely likes. He's eighty-six. Money is not his motivator. What Sal values is the feeling that we're friends and that it's his friends who live in his beloved home by the ocean."

"Well, *you* may feel like his friend," I said. "But friendship is not the feeling I get from that dirty old man."

I told Mark what had happened between Sal and me outside the restaurant bathrooms.

"That asshole cornered me. He told me that if he was younger, he'd 'fuck the hell out of me.'" Saying the words out loud made me feel sick to my stomach. I stared at the ceiling. "The nerve of that guy. He's unbelievable."

"No fucking way!" Mark stood up from the bed and paced with his arms crossed. Heat filled the room, and I thought he might hit something. Then he took a breath and sat back down on the bed. "Jesus, George, I'm sorry. Are you okay?"

"I am. It rattled me, but I'm all right now," I said.

Mark was quiet. I reached for the glass next to the bed and took a long drink of water.

"To be honest," I continued, "the hard part was that Sal's behavior triggered me. The exchange reminded me of being a teenager, a time when I thought I was going to be attacked."

I couldn't stand Sal. He emanated the energy of men who saw women as sex objects first, and people second. Misogyny sweated off his words like the condensation of water molecules on our martini glasses at lunch. Sal's sexism was slimy, and his intentions, slippery to the touch.

"Do you want to talk about it?" Mark asked. He moved from a sitting position, climbed fully onto the bed, and lay down next to me. He took my right hand into his left and then moved his leg closer to mine so that our corresponding feet touched too.

"Not really. It was a long time ago."

Mark knew I had worked as a singing-stripping telegram girl to pay the rent when I was young. He knew that my adolescent life was chock-full of drugs, parties, and boys, but instead of making me feel ashamed when I told him stories from that era, he made me feel understood. Mark told me I was a survivor. He reminded me that none of us are the same people today that we were at eighteen. Or nineteen. Or twenty.

It wasn't that I didn't appreciate Mark's offer to explore my feelings—feelings that had turned into painful brain hooks when Sal cornered me—I just didn't want to talk about it. I hadn't told anyone about my last gig, the reason I quit the party entertainment business. The panic that erupted when I thought the men at that bachelor party were going to rape me warranted concern, but I had relived enough singing telegram girl adventures for one afternoon. I would tell Mark what happened, but I needed some time.

"What I do want is your understanding," I said, my voice firm. "I don't plan on joining any more multi-martini lunches with Sal and Kathy."

"I get it and I don't blame you for wanting to keep your distance. I'll make it clear to Sal that his behavior was unacceptable." I felt Mark's foot press against mine.

"I appreciate that, but don't go to too much trouble," I said, a combination of disgust and defeat in my voice. "Whatever you say, I doubt it will make any difference."

This was a lie. What I really wanted was for my husband to march over to Sal's house and punch him in the stomach for laying his hands on me and for not keeping his pornographic octogenarian thoughts to himself. Just one hard punch. Not the kind of sock in the gut that does any real damage, just enough to knock the air out of him. But I didn't say this. I'd spent my adult life learning to act reasonable, not violent. The crossing guard on my shoulder had been training me to avoid danger for decades.

"That old mobster is unlikely to change his wicked ways. I just don't want to be around him," I said instead.

"Understood."

I wasn't looking at Mark's face, but his clipped response told me he was angry with Sal.

"Besides, my spring semester is about to start," I continued, my voice lighter. "Even if I wanted to join future day-drinking social events with the Benozzos, which I don't, it's not possible. Next week, I'm back to teaching classes on Zoom."

Teaching classes for college students was a million times more appealing than tolerating Sal Benozzo or washing down my salad with vodka martinis. I was glad for the schedule change.

"No wonder Kathy can't stand him," Mark said.

"He must have been a terrible husband," I agreed.

I had imagined that Kathy's behavior toward Sal—the prickly things she said to him, the mean faces she made behind his back, the urge to hide his teeth—was attributable to advanced cognitive decline. Healthy wives liked their husbands, right? Dementia could rewire people, leaving them with personalities other than their own. In Kathy's case, however, it might have been the simple loss of filters. Perhaps the aggravation she felt as a woman married to a womanizing, drug-using, alcoholic mobster finally flowed without inhibition. Maybe a whole lot of the original Kathy was still in there.

"I'm sure you're right," Mark said. "Being married to a man like Sal can't be easy."

"In contrast," I said, switching gears, "I actually like my husband and prefer him alive. I'm glad the price point for the condo is good, but I'm not sure buying a condo from a mobster is a smart idea and I'm certain that flying a bag of cash to Panama is insane."

I let go of Mark's hand and sat up on the bed so he could see my face. I wanted him to know I had serious concerns.

His dark brown eyes, shaped like almonds, made him look soulful, even a little sad, but there was a gentle smile on his lips.

"I agree with you on the Panama part, but George, I really think that we should buy Sal's condo. Or at least try to buy it. I'm under no illusion; executing a deal with Sal won't be an easy process. That guy is a real piece of work."

I looked away. Outside our bedroom window long channels of whitecaps blew for miles across the Atlantic Ocean. In between the tight waves, the afternoon sun kicked off bright sparks of shimmering glare like miniature angels that danced across a watery floor. Living at the ocean's edge was magical.

I turned back toward Mark.

"You really want to buy that condo even if you're only an Act 20 & 22 member for another twelve months? Even if we only live in the condo for a single year? Even if I am cash poor and you have to finance the whole thing?"

"Yes. Even if," Mark said.

He took a breath and then the tone of his voice shifted; it projected solemnity, as if he were speaking inside a church.

"Buying Sal's condo is part of a larger conversation," Mark said. "Are you up for it now?"

Here it comes, I thought. Mark wanted to sell River Acres, our family home, despite my stipulations when he applied for Act membership. Despite the years I had left teaching in a California classroom before I could retire or the fact that our family lived on the West Coast. Even despite the fact that our dog sitter kept raising her prices. My pulse quickened in anticipation of broken promises.

"I am," I said. "We can't keep talking about the purchase of PR real estate in the abstract. If you are serious about this, we need to hammer out the details—the first of which is that I don't want to sell our home in California, but unless

I take equity out of that house, I can't afford my half of anything we buy here."

Instead of taking a deep breath, like I had trained myself to do when anxiety started to strangle my synapses, objections burst from my mouth. Mark knew I didn't have the funds to buy Sal's condo. I didn't want to say it out loud. The admission pricked self-consciousness around the gap in our income levels. Would I need to defend my professional choices, the ones that produced far less revenue than his?

My husband had access to money that I didn't, and that was fine with me. I had accepted the income disparity when I signed our prenup the month before we exchanged vows on a beach in Lake Tahoe. Even though our prenup had a sunset date—our tenth wedding anniversary two years ago—we had continued to maintain financial independence after that date passed. But now, did Mark really accept that my financial ceiling was lower than his? Did he expect my indebtedness to match his rich person's spending decisions? A trickle of sweat appeared on my brow.

Over the years, I had come to believe in the wisdom of our prenuptial agreement. The once bemoaned request had served me well and I valued my financial independence. I still got excited on the first of the month when my paycheck auto-deposited into my account and I enjoyed the satisfaction that came with good pay for good work. I felt proud to add my half of living expenses into our joint account and contribute financially to the life we shared. Admittedly, I had it better than most Americans who earned a middle-class salary. The interest Mark charged me on my mortgage payments was below average bank rates. Plus, if I had needed money, Mark would have given it, no questions asked. While I wasn't the asking type, conveniently I never found myself in need during the time we had been married.

The seventeen-year-old girl I used to be, the one who barely scraped by when she first moved out of her mother's house, was living the kind of cushy life she hardly believed possible. She didn't worry about bills. She didn't take a calculator to the grocery store. She didn't hustle for tips. She was free from the financial desperation that drove her to escape in drugs or parties, or take high-risk jobs. That younger me didn't want to make a mistake by overextending her monthly resources now.

"I know you don't have the money for a second mortgage," Mark said, looking serious. "That's what I want to talk to you about. But before you come to any conclusions, I need you to hear me out."

"I'm listening," I said, reluctantly meeting his eyes, then looking away.

"I'm going to start with the thing you don't want to hear: selling River Acres."

This time I took a deep breath and stayed silent. I looked at the pictures on the wall opposite our bed. Three 12x12 matching beach scenes in cheap black frames, typical of seaside rental properties, helped me resist the urge to scream. I focused on the square in the middle, the one that contained a bright red umbrella.

"I know you love that house," Mark continued, "but when we head back to California in a few months, I think it will be obvious that River Acres is way more house than we need without any of the daughters living at home, not to mention it will sit empty next year when we come back to Puerto Rico."

He paused to look at me.

"However, I don't want to sell River Acres so that you have the money to pay for Sal's condo. I want to sell so that you can take equity out of River Acres and sign up for the workload reduction program we talked about. You could supplement your reduced income with earnings from selling our Sacramento home."

Oh, I thought, he remembered that?

Before moving to Puerto Rico, Mark and I had attended a pre-retirement workshop for my teaching job. I planned to keep working for another decade, but I wanted to make sure we knew what to expect once I was fully retired. Our medical insurance, for example, was paid for through my job and wouldn't continue in retirement.

The pre-retirement workshop was packed with chubby, sight-impaired, gray-haired professors. I looked around the room and wondered if this was what I was destined to look like after thirty years in a classroom. It was a sobering scene, but Mark and I learned important information about my retirement process. Tenured professors at my college had the option to drop down to 50 percent of their teaching load during the last five years of employment. Of course, this dropped their yearly pay by 50 percent during the reduction time period, but their benefits stayed the same and they continued to accrue full years of service credit.

On the way home from the workshop, I told Mark that the workload reduction program sounded dreamy. I fantasized about being a full-time writer, but teaching paid the bills. If my workload reduced to 50 percent, I could teach one semester and write during the other.

"I'd give anything to start that program at fifty-five and slow roll into retirement, but I can't imagine only getting half my paycheck for five years," I said on the drive home from the workshop.

"You never know," had been Mark's response, but that was as far as the conversation went.

Now, as Mark turned the conversation in a direction I was barely able to endure, I looked at the red umbrella, struggling to stay calm and listen. The water glass on the nightstand was empty. Was selling my family home worth an early retirement?

"And just to be clear," he continued earnestly, "the money you still owe me on River Acres? That loan is forgiven." He turned my head so I would look at him. "I don't want you to make house payments to me anymore—I want you to know how much I appreciate your willingness to take a chance on Puerto Rico. And Sal's condo? If we actually do buy it, I'll pay for it. I can afford to cover the cost without your help."

I shook my head, shock waves rolling over me. Nothing Mark just said made sense. We always split purchases and costs down the middle. We were a couple who had consciously embraced economic autonomy for the last twelve years. The red umbrella looked blurry. I felt like I did after running too hard, dizzy and a little breathless.

"If you only have to teach one semester a year in California," Mark went on, "and if you're willing to live in Puerto Rico the other seven months, I can continue my Act 20 & 22 status. The tax savings literally pays for our life here, and more."

Mark took my hand again and waited until our eyes locked. "Does it really matter where we live—California, Puerto Rico, someplace else—as long as we're together?" he asked. "To me, home is wherever you are."

I looked at my husband, at his sad eyes and beautiful mouth. At his broad shoulders and smooth olive-colored skin. Tangled-up feelings swirled around my insides like ribbons at a maypole dance. Did Mark really just encourage me to start a pre-retirement program, forgive my River Acres mortgage payments, and propose *he* buy *us* Sal's condo?

I just sat there unable to respond, my eyes burning.

After more than a decade of unraveling money from love, after navigating prenuptial agreements and splitting utility bills, I was overwhelmed. I felt like the girl who rubbed a lamp, had a genie pop out, and was granted three wishes.

For a second, all her problems were solved, but then what was the catch? Was it good fortune or a trick?

It was a lot to process, this level of revision to our life's plan, and I struggled to find the right words. How does one say thank you for houses? For early retirement? For financial ease? For a moment when her life takes a spectacular turn?

"I don't know what to say. I'm stunned," I said. "Your offer is more than generous. Thank you . . . this sort of changes everything."

"I see you," Mark said, lightly brushing hair from my face. "I see all the ways you help your dad with his medical needs, and I have watched you teach summer school and take on extra classes so that you can afford to help your daughters in college. You are a good person, George. You are my person. I love you and I want PR to work for both of us. We're in this *together*."

My eyes felt moist and my nose started to run. Mark smiled and handed me a tissue.

Most people wanted to help their family but couldn't afford that luxury. I was lucky, not better. I understood the way that privilege worked, but his words soothed the adolescent girl inside me whose consciousness was scarred by scarcity and whose heart craved love and protection.

I lay down on my side and tucked into a ball. *Hold on to this moment*, I told myself. I wanted to harness the warm swells in my body that came when I saw my worthiness reflected in my husband's eyes. I wanted to see myself the way he saw me. I felt exhausted and loved in equal measure.

Mark gave me a lot to think about. If I accepted his gifts, what would that mean for my self-sufficiency and sense of independence? How would it impact our relationship? Would my husband grow to resent me if the economics in our marriage shifted? My mother's parenting mantra lurked in a dark corner of my mind: *Never find yourself financially dependent on a man*. And yet, I trusted my husband. We had seen each other through plenty of challenging times, and only grown closer. The love we shared was not bound by a ledger; it was a force that continued to evolve, fortified by support and acceptance.

Mark lay down next to me, pushing pillows out of his way and rotating my hips so that he could pull the balled-up me close. His embrace felt comforting and his torso pressed into my back, our bodies forming united curves, like spoons in a silverware drawer.

"If you hadn't agreed to this crazy Puerto Rico adventure, none of this would be possible," Mark said into my hair. "But I see things differently now. I'm not just focused on our retirements. Act 20 & 22 has changed our lives. If we continue Act status for another five or ten years, we'll be able to create a legacy, and we're going to be dead a lot longer than we're going to be alive."

I listened as Mark's breathing slowed and turned rhythmic. I closed my eyes and my mind started to wander. I saw Mark, stooped with age and a shock of white hair, the beautifully lined faces of my daughters as grown women, and tiny grandbabies not yet born. They were images trapped in clouds, pictures of the legacies we leave behind.

CHAPTER 26:

LEGACY

I felt completely relaxed. My breathing had slowed, my body was wet with perspiration, and the sounds of crashing waves filled my ears. I opened my eyes and let my head roll to the side. Mark lay next to me, face up, on his yoga mat.

"That felt great," I said, sitting up. "Now I need to get ready for class."

Mark smiled but stayed silent and kept his eyes shut, enjoying his final Savasana. I rolled my mat into a tube and bent down to kiss my husband's sweaty forehead.

I loved these yoga mornings. We started by placing our mats side by side on the living room floor, then breathed and twisted in unison. Familiarity added comfort, a slow-motion dance we'd completed a thousand times before. With each new asana we looked out across the ocean, felt the breeze rush in through the sliding glass doors, and exhaled into the places our aging bodies resisted.

After an emotional night, followed by a romantic morning in bed, my mind reeled with thoughts about the way life might change. I was on the brink of another new phase, one in which a permanent Puerto Rico address equaled an increased level of financial support, an early retirement, and a happy husband. It was a lot to consider and the morning's yoga helped ground me before meeting with my RES students on Zoom.

I showered and changed quickly so I had time to review my lecture notes. Then I opened Zoom on my computer and started class.

"Thanks for being here," I said to the screen full of faces. Instead of our usual icebreaker, I had planned something different.

"To start us off today, I'd like you each to share something you learned about yourself during the break."

Silence.

"C'mon," I encouraged, looking at the faces of ten somber men. "Was your break really that bad? Surely you learned *something*?"

Today was our first meeting of the spring semester. I hadn't seen my Re-Emerging Scholars since right before Christmas and I knew that the holidays could be challenging. Some of my students were estranged from their immediate family. Others were living in Sacramento because it was their county of release and their parole conditions didn't allow out-of-state travel, even if they had been invited to long-distance family gatherings. For students lucky enough to have family nearby, they needed to be careful about exposure to environments that might "violate." If they had family members who used drugs, for example, the smart choice was to skip the festivities. All of this added to their holiday stress.

"Well, my holiday wasn't too good," said Big Ed. "My family is sort of messed up. This was the first Christmas I've been home in a long time. I was really looking forward to it, but my dad and my uncle got into a huge fight. What I learned is that I'm not the only one in my family with a bad temper."

A few students offered knowing smiles.

"I feel you, man," said Jon. "You think going home is going to be one thing, a good thing, but I'm still waiting for that to happen. My mom's using again. On Christmas I carried her to bed and left. It sucked."

Holiday experiences varied, but mostly, my students were disappointed. I had planned to give a lecture on student support services, things like tutoring and new student club opportunities, but I switched gears after our warm-up exercise. My students needed emotional support more than campus updates. The thought of legacy was fresh on my mind from the night before, so that's where I went.

"It sounds like some of you faced family challenges, but here you are, ready to start a new semester. By pursuing an education, you are taking steps to change the legacy you leave behind for your children . . . Are you familiar with the idea of legacy?"

We considered varied definitions of the word. We debated the relationship between a college education and the legacy of one's reputation. We described the values that would influence our own legacies. We imagined the faith, ethics, and assets that we would like to pass on to future generations.

"How do you want to be remembered by your family? Your community?" I asked my students. "What do you want to leave behind?"

My students were smart and worldly. Some loved attending college and others thought it was mostly bullshit—classrooms full of bougie kids taught by out-of-touch professors. But they were united on one thing: the legacy they *didn't* want to leave. They didn't want poverty, racism, addiction, and violence—the legacies they had inherited—to be their final story. They wanted something better for their children, families, and communities. We all did.

"Thanks for such a thought-provoking class," I said. "I look forward to seeing you all next week."

I closed my laptop and thought about legacy, what I hoped to leave behind for my family. Mark was right. If we extended his Act 20 & 22 residency, it would likely help our children, and our future grandchildren. Doesn't every family want to leave something for the generation that follows them? I could never understand how my Grandpa Stanford, a descendant of one of the wealthiest and most powerful families in California history books, died penniless. Or how he didn't encourage my mom—with her sharp mind and wit—to attend college. I wanted my children to have better breaks than I received, or than my mother received, for that matter.

But caring exclusively about our own family wasn't enough. Without the people who helped me when I was younger, without the scholarships and grants that gave me access to higher education, I could have easily ended up like one of my Re-Emerging Scholars—incarcerated for drug-related crimes. If Mark and I were going to stay in Puerto Rico under Act 20 & 22, if we continued to improve our financial situation, helping our kids was just the beginning. We also had to find ways to help people in our community. I didn't know exactly what that would look like yet, but I believed that wealth was both a blessing and a responsibility.

I zipped my laptop into its case and thought of that memorable line from the musical *Hello, Dolly!* where Dolly Levi compares money to manure—worthless unless spread around to help young things grow. Anyone fortunate enough to have financial freedom also had an obligation to help others who weren't so lucky.

CHAPTER 27:

UNFATHOMABLE HURRICANE

The next day I stood in the shower, shampoo lathered into my hair, after a run along the cart path through my out-of-service neighborhood golf course. I was eager to clean up and start my Christmas present from Mark: a book about the future of cryptocurrency. The crypto markets had been volatile the past few days, and I hoped to learn more about the impact of stablecoins and historical trends.

Mid-wash, as I was daydreaming about reading on my shaded balcony, the stream of water dwindled to a few drops and then disappeared completely. This was not the first time I had experienced the cessation of water in our condo. Without warning it just stopped. The water, it seemed, was turned on and off by a mysterious force for unknown reasons.

I stomped my foot in disbelief, squeezed my eyes tight, and felt the sudsy mass piled on the top of my head start to topple. I twisted knobs back and forth hoping to end what seemed like a prank, but finally grabbed a towel and wiped soap from my face. Defeated and dripping, I headed downstairs to the kitchen sink and stuck my head between the faucet and unwashed breakfast dishes. Relief was my goal, but I found none. My eyes stung and my skin felt sticky. *Joke's on me*, I thought, as the smell of stale coffee filled my nose.

I patted myself dry with kitchen towels, wiped the soap foam from my hair, and walked back upstairs to find clothes. Mark had left early to meet with Sal, so he missed my exasperated kitchen nudie show. After our big talk about finances two days earlier, we'd agreed to move forward on the potential purchase of Sal's condo and talk to a California realtor about putting River Acres on the market. If selling the house meant participating in the workload reduction program at my college, I was in favor.

Once we'd popped the champagne to celebrate our big decision, Mark texted Sal and scheduled a meeting to discuss contract language for a sale-by-owner purchase and, I suspected, drink whiskey. I took a pass on both activities. I had woken up feeling content, bursting with all the sweet things my husband had recently shared, and happy to keep my distance from Sal. I'd planned on an easy morning after I finished my run—not the waterless kind. The uncooperative shower jarred me from my faraway state of mind.

When I called the condo administration office they sent Rafi, the Playa Tortuga maintenance manager, to my door. He checked the main water line to my unit and declared, "No water."

"That much I already know, Rafi," I said.

"It's worse for you," he explained in broken English. "You live up high and the water has to work hard to get here."

Similar to Sal's place, the condo we were renting offered amazing views. It displayed coastline that ran from San Juan eastward, and tracked all the way through Dorado to the Ritz-Carlton beaches that bordered the town of Vega

Alta. From the balcony, we watched magnificent sunsets of orange, red, pink, and purple while pelicans plunged head-first for dinner along the shores of our community. Who knew the price for such visual fortune would be problems with running water?

"But this keeps happening," I complained. "Is there a water agency or some other municipality I can call to figure out what's going on and how to get it fixed?"

Rafi made a sour face and waved his hand in front of his nose as if to push away a bad smell.

"No," he said. "Just wait. Better tomorrow."

I believed Rafi was trying to be helpful, not dismissive, but his answer frustrated me. He was probably just trying to keep me from wasting my time, I thought. A citizen water complaint (that landed on a giant pile of other water complaints) was likely to evaporate, unanswered, from the desk of an overworked civil servant, but I still wanted action.

I put on a baseball cap to cover my soapy locks and walked next door. I hoped that Alberto and Ana, our neighbors, would direct me toward a solution.

Alberto and his girlfriend Ana were both born and raised on the island, and when I had a question, they often had an answer. It was Alberto who had explained to me that iguanas were an island pest when I saw their corpses piled next to a dumpster and gasped. Alberto also showed me how to open a coconut with a machete, pop in a straw, and enjoy the hydrating treat whenever I was so moved.

Alberto's father was a well-known medical doctor on the island and Alberto was working on his PhD in psychology. I knew that his condo was his parents' vacation home and that he worried about our climbing property values.

"I don't have anything against all of you here for Act 20 & 22," Alberto told me one day. We had started up a conversation after bumping into each other while taking our trash to the sunken community stormproof bins. "But if the prices of our condos keep rising, I'm afraid my parents will want to sell and I'll have to move."

"Where would you go?" I asked, hearing the concern in his voice.

"I'm not sure, but I can't stay in Dorado," he said. "This place has turned into a rich person's bubble. It's gotten more beautiful every year, but only gringos can afford to live here."

I looked away. It made me uncomfortable to know that Mark and I were part of the reason Alberto fretted.

I thought about what he'd said for a moment before responding. The gentrification of Dorado, our sleepy little beach town, was undeniable. Original owners who sold their homes to the stateside transplants moving to the island under Act 20 & 22 had made impressive profits. Sometimes they doubled or even tripled their money, but the increased Dorado home values decreased housing options for local buyers. Dorado had excellent schools, beautiful beaches, a new hospital, and fine restaurants. It was considered one of the best places to live on the island, but only people who saved a bundle on their taxes could afford to pay the inflated real estate prices, which did not include most natives to the island.

"It's not just Dorado," I said in a quiet voice.

Act 20 & 22 didn't reward locals with the same fiscal advantages as transplants. I thought of Scott Windsor's penthouse, the mansions I'd seen in the Ritz-Carlton community with Sal and Kathy, and the ultra-expensive sports cars parked outside of Crypto Tuesday events. Bubbles of wealth had formed in other coastal communities too, and where Act members clustered, gentrification followed.

"I know," he said. "But Dorado is my home. It's the bubble I wish would pop."

"I hope your parents don't sell anytime soon," I said. "Mark and I would miss being neighbors with you."

When I knocked on Alberto's door, my skin and hair coated with soap, I felt thoroughly annoyed. The island was beautiful but not efficient. Living in Puerto Rico equated to unreliable utilities, swerving around massive potholes on the way to the grocery store, and ongoing supply challenges. I felt like a human seesaw. Last night I had celebrated making Puerto Rico a permanent part of my life, but today I saw obstacles.

"Hi," I said. "Do you guys have water?"

"Yes, but we've switched to our cistern, so I know it's gone off for everyone," Alberto said. "Come on in."

"Thanks," I said as I walked inside Alberto's home. My previous conversations with Alberto and Ana had always taken place outside and were linked to random moments of proximity, like when we pulled up with a carload full of groceries at the same time.

Their place was the mirror image of mine. I could see the wall that separated their unit from the one I shared with Mark and the way our kitchens were shaped like horseshoes facing different directions.

"Have a seat," Alberto said, waving to a kitchen table where Ana sat. "Can I get you a cup of coffee?"

"Sure," I said, taking an empty chair.

Textbooks, a laptop, pens, and pads of paper covered most of the table's glass surface. A beautiful picture of a sea turtle hung on the wall and made me think about how the ocean steered life on an island. It also reminded me of the times I'd seen these same sea turtles snorkeling with Mark.

"Good morning," Ana said. "Please excuse the mess, we're studying. Alberto has exams tomorrow and I'm writing a paper for my poli-sci class."

Alberto was probably thirty, but Ana wasn't a day over twenty-five. She was lovely—thick black hair cascading in curls, her smile bright and infectious. Next to Alberto, with his gruff voice, stocky build, and shaggy beard, Ana looked exceptionally feminine.

"Thanks for letting me interrupt your morning," I said. "I was hoping you might help me figure out what to do about the water. Ours keeps turning off. It's driving me a little crazy. Are there shut-off notifications that I am missing? It keeps happening when I least expect it."

"No. You're not missing anything," Alberto said. "Nothing unusual is going on with the plumbing. It's the electricity—they're related."

Mark and I had also experienced long stretches of time without electricity so we kept a small generator in the closet. When the lights went off, we started up the generator and plugged in our refrigerator and our Wi-Fi. It was hot without AC, but at least we could work and our food didn't spoil.

"The electrical grid is much worse on other parts of the island. We have it good in Dorado," Alberto continued. "But when the electricity goes off at the water plant, nothing flows. The only thing to do is get a cistern. We installed one on the roof after Hurricane Maria."

"It's really bad where I'm from," Ana said. "I was born in the mountains. Even though Hurricane Maria happened years ago, our part of the electrical grid is still a mess. We lose water and electricity all the time. That's why I try to do my work here; when my computer dies at my parents' house, sometimes days go by before I can charge it back up."

I took a sip of the coffee that Alberto had set down in front of me.

Rafi probably thought my incredulity over a temporary stoppage was ridiculous. Listening to Ana compare Dorado's water access to other island towns offered me a larger perspective, and I wondered if I was exuding the expectations of the privileged though I knew what it was like to have nothing.

I set the mug down and leaned back in my chair.

"Were you on the island when Hurricane Maria hit?" I asked.

"Of course," Ana said. "We both were."

I knew that Hurricane Maria reached Category 5 intensity and hit Puerto Rico just two weeks after Hurricane Irma pummeled the US Virgin Islands. At its peak strength, Maria's winds blew at 175 miles per hour. FEMA's Caribbean Distribution Center warehouse, the only emergency stockpile in the islands, was located in Puerto Rico, but the majority of its supplies had been deployed to support Irma relief and had not been replenished before Maria arrived. Residents who stayed on the island during Maria encountered apocalyptic results with little access to aid or provisions.

"I was in the mountains with my family. We have experienced tropical storms all my life, but nothing like Maria," Ana said. "We got gas for the generator, bottles of water, and extra canned goods like we always do before a big storm, but nobody was prepared for the size of that hurricane."

"The hurricane lasted for three days." Ana's voice lingered on the number three, like she couldn't believe it had gone on for so long. Then she started unconsciously winding a long strand of hair around her finger, something I'd seen students do when they were delivering a speech to the class and felt anxiety.

"We stayed inside my house all that time," she continued. "Even before Maria hit, it had been raining like crazy. We couldn't drive in those conditions and had already used up some of our backup food. My house is at the end of a one-lane road. It's difficult to drive in and out during regular rain, so when heavy rain comes, we try not to go anywhere."

"Ana's house is in a sort of pocket," Alberto said. "It's much cooler where she lives, but her home sits on the side of a mountain. They're trapped there in bad weather."

Ana closed her laptop. She tapped the handle of her coffee mug and then looked at me.

"After three days, when the winds finally stopped, I walked outside. I couldn't believe it. It was . . ." Ana paused, searching for the right word. "Scorched," she finally said. "Everything was gone."

"What do you mean?" I was confused about her choice of words. Flames would scorch the earth, but I did not understand how that was possible during a hurricane.

"The winds had stripped all the leaves off the trees and ripped all the flowers and plants out of the ground." She shut her eyes for a moment and then took a slow drink from her coffee cup. "Where I live, everything is very green. The landscape is thick, like a tropical forest. But when I walked outside, the green was all gone and the world was brown. It looked like there had been a fire. My mom came outside with me. The first thing she said was, 'There are no more birds,' and then she started to cry. She was right. It was silent. And then I realized that the world didn't just look dead—it sounded dead too."

"I'm so sorry, Ana. What a harrowing experience. It must have been a shocking thing to see." I tried to imagine such devastation, but I could hear in her voice how terrible it was to live through it.

Ana looked down for a minute and then tucked the long black curl she had been twisting behind her ear.

"It was shocking," she said. "There was so much death, and not just birds. A few days later, we noticed the bees were going crazy, flying around in big swarms looking for flowers to pollinate, or maybe looking for their hives, but it was all gone. Where there used to be so many plants, now there was only dead animals left."

We were quiet for a moment.

"My dad was a diesel mechanic at the biggest poultry farm in Puerto Rico. It's near my house. Most of the chickens there got killed by the hurricane," Ana said. "The smell where we live got really bad. One of my dad's coworkers walked to our house and asked my dad to come help. They walked to the poultry farm together, but it was hard because they had to climb over all the broken trees and downed power lines. When they got there, they dug giant holes with tractors so that they could bury the rotting birds."

"Oh my God," I said, imagining the scene.

"My dad didn't really talk much after that." Ana's voice was full with sadness.

It was hard to imagine the island scorched and silent. The Puerto Rico I knew was lush and flourished with life. Ana's description of her mountain home reminded me of El Yunque, Puerto Rico's rainforest, the only one in the United States forest system. The tropical climate in Puerto Rico produced immense biodiversity. The hummingbirds, parrots, coqui, lizards, and bats that lived in the rainforest attracted visitors from around the globe. Ana's description of the island post-Maria clashed with all the beauty I had seen.

"What we saw was awful, but what we didn't see, and what we didn't know, was just as bad," Ana continued.

Communication blackouts happened across the island after the hurricane. In the most remote locations, it took up to eleven months to restore electricity. People literally lived in the dark and suffered the feelings of isolation that accompanied the not knowing—not knowing when they would have access to water and electricity, if gasoline to run chainsaws and generators would arrive, or if food supplies would be replenished on market shelves. After Maria, many residents were forced to live in the not-knowing for months. How would I fare under such conditions?

I wondered. And how did other Act 20 & 22 members on the island react?

"We walked to the houses in our neighborhood to check on the old people, but nobody knew anything," Ana said. "Was help coming? Was there water and electricity in other places on the island? Would the government bring us supplies? There was no communication—no Internet, cell service, TV—and we couldn't drive because the roads were blocked for miles. More days passed, but nobody came. We finally organized ourselves. My mom and I went door to door and asked all the people to come together. The men started clearing trees off the road with chainsaws and the women combined food supplies. We cooked community meals and walked food to the old people who couldn't leave their houses. Eventually we could drive trucks down the mountain and get supplies and information, but it took three months before we had electricity and running water. Even when we drove into town, food and other supplies were rationed. We were only allowed to buy one pallet of water at a time. Nobody had enough of anything."

I asked Ana how they got information, or guidance, during these months without access to electricity and she told me that once a week they went to Caguas. For her family, this was the nearest location with cell service. Ana's aunt was in Miami for work when the hurricane landed and they called her each week for updates. For three months, her relative living in Miami had more access to information on hurricane rescue and recovery efforts than she did.

"We lived in the dark for a long time," Ana said. "We felt angry and helpless. Many people were sick. Old people couldn't get their medicine. It was really bad."

Ana told me that access to medication was the biggest challenge for her community. Her neighbors had purchased extra supplies and stored extra gasoline for generators before the hurricane. They shared food with each other. But when it came to medication, people didn't have what they needed. Some of her neighbors had diabetes, she said, and the insulin ran out quickly.

"Did help ever come to you, to your neighborhood?" I asked.

"Once," Ana said. "About two months after the hurricane I saw a big government truck at the bottom of the hill from where we lived. I yelled to my mom and my neighbors and we all ran to the truck. They gave us each one small box of supplies. That was it. One box. If I hadn't been outside when the truck came through our town, I would have missed it."

"What is your neighborhood like now?" I asked, feeling quite sheepish about my previous water complaints. "Does it feel like people in your town have recovered from Maria?"

"Definitely not," Alberto jumped in. "I'm completing my residency hours now and practically all I do is counsel people with PTSD from Maria. We suffered a collective trauma. The entire island of Puerto Rico is still healing."

Speakers at the Crypto Tuesday events often pitched island charities, and encouraged audience members to donate money, but I doubted that any of them had lived for months without electricity or medication. It was clear that the gap between Puerto Ricans and Act transplants had widened; opportunity, access, and support didn't favor local Puerto Ricans.

"And recovery is complicated because of the corruption that exists here," Ana said. "Everybody knows that there is corruption in the Puerto Rican government, but it's not just at the top, it trickles down to every level. The only reason my town got electricity back after three months is because my dad bribed the electricians with chickens he got from the poultry farm. It was like that everywhere after the hurricane—people asking for cash to do the jobs they were hired to do."

"I guess sometimes tragedy brings out the best in people, and other times, it's our lower natures that dominate," I offered.

"That's true," Ana said. "Some people were definitely taking advantage, but most of us tried to help others and we got strong. We learned that we needed each other. We came together in my community and those people will be my family forever. Maria taught us about what really matters in life: our family, the people we love, helping others, and caring for the sick . . . All the material things are meaningless when you are focused on survival."

As Ana shared her story, I thought of *la brega*, a term I learned about when Mark and I first moved to the island. There was no direct translation for la brega in English, but for Puerto Ricans it meant to struggle and to find a way to get around the imbalance of power that permeated their lived experience. La brega was sometimes referred to as "a way of life" for the Puerto Rican people. I thought of this word when Ana described her dad bribing city workers with chicken. And I heard it in Rafi's response to my water frustrations: "Just wait. Better tomorrow."

La brega is layered; it functions as a noun and a verb. It is an approach to living that helped my neighbors survive everything from the residue of colonialism and government corruption to history-making hurricanes.

Sometimes la brega was defined as "trabajo," or work, but it suggested determination, endurance, and even hustle. The word highlighted that thing inside of people that makes them scrappy, the part that keeps trying even when the cards were stacked against them. I understood this definition; hustle and determination were prominent themes in my adolescence.

La brega also acknowledged systematic inequity. It implied that sometimes grappling with forces beyond one's control was inevitable, and that existential perseverance was a requirement for being a successful human. I made a mental note to share this concept with my RES students in a future Zoom class.

"Thank you for sharing your story with me, Ana. I've never experienced anything like Hurricane Maria," I said. "I'm glad you and your family survived. Your courage inspires me." I sat up straighter, adjusted my baseball cap, and felt connected to the endurance that fueled the human spirit.

I spent most days grading papers and making lesson plans. Or learning about cryptocurrency. While Alberto was completing his residency and helping his community, I was stuck in my head and quick to complain about the things that annoyed me.

"Thank you for the hospitality," I said before leaving. "I'm grateful we are neighbors."

I gave Alberto and Ana a hug goodbye.

"We feel the same," Alberto said. "I'm sorry there isn't a better solution to the water problem."

The water was still off when I returned home, but it didn't matter much anymore. I went out to the balcony, sat down, looked at the ocean, and considered Ana's story.

I had watched Hurricane Maria pummel Puerto Rico on a television set from the safety of my living room at River Acres. News coverage live-streamed reporters pelted by rain and palm trees bent into right angles, while satellite images of a giant cyclone played on repeat. I thought about the disgust I felt watching a US President toss paper towels at a crowd of displaced people. But during that time, I only understood the devastation in the abstract. Ana's story changed that and gave context for la brega, a word I'd been chewing on since moving to the island.

Time with Alberto and Ana made my morning water troubles insignificant, and my determination to march into the water company with complaints seem silly. Perspective was humbling. It made me more aware of my expectations—not just related to water and electricity, but of my need to control my surroundings, to execute agreed-upon plans, to live a life where surprises were minimized at worst and eliminated at best.

Moving to Puerto Rico had challenged me. The stipulations for the Act 20 & 22 relocation plan I had negotiated with Mark applied to a version of my life that no longer existed and a version of me that was changing. Thirty years of careful professional planning had also been dramatically revised; my blueprint for retirement was obsolete. I had compensated for an unstable childhood by wielding certainty and control in adulthood, but living in Puerto Rico was starting to make me think certainty and control belonged to the delusional. Life was full of surprises, some horrendous and others quite glorious.

If Puerto Rico was a teacher, she was adamant. In place of expectation, she insisted on patience. Instead of certainty, she supplied chaos. Living in Puerto Rico was like managing the dial on an old radio. When I looked at the ocean, the radio dial was set to a classical station. Slow was fast enough and I could count waves in time with the magic of a string quartet. Other times, the dial moved to acid rock and entropy ensued; the system spun with inefficiencies, volatilities, and natural disasters.

I looked at the ocean from my balcony and heard Mozart's Requiem. The space between the shore and horizon was vast with shades of cobalt blue. Hurricanes had swirled through my life, I thought, filling my childhood with a series of near misses, but I always landed on my feet. In contrast, most of my adulthood was safe, careful, and sanitized. Did either approach to living fit me anymore? Middle age made one thing clear: A Category 5 life disaster could change everything in a second. Puerto Rico started teaching me this lesson the moment I landed on her beautiful, complicated shores and encountered an earthquake. That was the moment my midlife adventure had started to unfold.

CHAPTER 28:

SUPER BOWL SUNDAY

"Are you excited to watch the Super Bowl?" I asked Mark. It was February 7, 2021, almost a month after our last meeting with Sal, and the Tampa Bay Buccaneers were set to play the Kansas City Chiefs at Raymond James Stadium in Tampa, Florida. Mark and I had just laced up our tennis shoes and were headed outside for a morning walk.

"I am," he said with a big smile. "Today will be the first time I've watched a live sporting event since we moved to Puerto Rico."

We had decided not to pay for television when we moved to the island since all the local stations were in Spanish. Our Spanish comprehension required face-to-face patience as opposed to announcer-speed fluency, but life without local television was hard on Mark since he loved sports. Mark had played baseball growing up and had even been offered a chance to play baseball at Wake Forest University in North Carolina. The posters that covered the walls of his boyhood room paid homage to the LA Dodgers; however, a championship sports game of any variety filled him with joyful anticipation.

"How about you?" he asked.

"I hope it's a good game, but mostly I'm looking forward to spending time with Kevin and Tricia. They seem like an interesting couple, and I think it would be good if we made some more friends."

We had met Kevin and Tricia at a Crypto Tuesday event where Kevin was the featured speaker. In his interview with Julio, he shared his perspective on the future growth of the crypto markets, and we were intrigued. Kevin and Tricia were originally attorneys from Chicago but had moved to Puerto Rico in the mid-2010s. They were both semi-retired now and Kevin had shifted his professional energies toward finance. He worked in traditional markets as well as crypto. Since it looked like Puerto Rico was going to be our permanent home, I wanted to expand our social circle and an interesting couple from Chicago was a good start. Deborah, Mark, and I, having attended the Crypto Tuesday event together, happily accepted their Super Bowl party invitation.

A morning walk, or run, was one of the things I enjoyed about living in a warm climate. I locked the front door and followed Mark down the stairs to the parking lot. In front of our condo a man was climbing a palm tree, metal spikes attached to the bottom of his work boots. He cut down coconuts and dropped them onto an old mattress below.

We waved at Juan, the guard on duty that morning, and let ourselves out of the front gate. It wasn't long before we arrived at the neighborhood pond and I pulled out bread slices from the bag slung over my shoulder. Excited by our arrival, ducks danced and wiggled their tail feathers, iguanas scurried away, and turtles popped their heads up near the pond's edge. I handed Mark a few slices of bread.

"Good morning, my friends!" I greeted.

I slowly walked through the duck crowd, careful not to step on webbed feet as I dropped bits of crust. The pond was home to flocks of Muscovy, a type of duck with black and white feathers who grew warty red bumps on their heads. It made them look like they were born with lumpy party masks or royal crowns, depending on the patterns of their growths.

"These ducks make me want to attend a masquerade ball," I joked with Mark.

"You'll have competition for tickets if the turtles are invited," Mark said. "Look at this group." He stood at the water's edge in front of a tangled mass of bobbing heads and shells. "I'm not sure I've ever seen so many turtles bunched together."

Mark leaned toward the pond, his large fingers tearing delicate bits of bread and throwing them into the water.

"Okay," I finally said. "Breakfast is over."

Mark and I dusted crumbs from our hands and continued toward our neighborhood park.

"How are things going with Sal?" I asked.

It had been a month since I'd seen Sal, but the day before, when I had gone over to Alberto and Ana's looking for water answers, Mark had been over at Sal and Kathy's to work out final contract details. Since we agreed not to use real estate agents to broker the deal, Sal and Mark had to agree to the terms of the sale on their own. Mark had my blessing to move forward with the condo purchase, but the thought of being sexually harassed by Sal at the restaurant left a grime on my skin I couldn't scrub off. I'd be glad when the negotiating was over and the deal was done.

"That guy doesn't make anything easy," Mark said. "Yesterday he informed me that in order to purchase his condo I needed to buy his car—in addition to his furnishings."

Mark looked down at the sidewalk and sighed.

"Do we really want his car?" I asked. "It smells almost as bad as the condo."

"I don't know," Mark said. "Probably not. But if that's what it takes to make this deal work, it's an option on the table. My bigger concern is that adding his car to the deal creates one more reason that this whole negotiation could go sideways."

"Can you just tell him that it needs to be a separate deal, that we can talk about buying his car after you complete the purchase of his condo?" I asked.

"I know that sounds like a reasonable request," he said, "but Sal *needs* stuff to negotiate. He's looking for reasons to stretch out this process. Every time we get close to agreeing on the details, he starts to change his mind. He knows he has to move to Florida, but he doesn't want to, and he definitely doesn't want to be that old person whose kids are calling the shots on his life. I think he's terrified of losing his independence."

There were lots of charming quotes about aging, uplifting sentences about gaining wisdom alongside wrinkles, but the increased dependency and physical frailty challenged even grisly mobsters.

"Do you know what kind of relationship he has with his kids?" I asked.

"Okay, I think. But this process is complicated for him."

"I get that. At eighty-six, I'm guessing mortality seems like more than a hypothetical construct."

"That's a big part of it. Plus, he doesn't want to leave the game," Mark said. "When he's negotiating with me, he's making deals and doing business. He feels alive. He's dragging his feet on purpose."

We took a large synchronized step over a muddy strip of grass leading into the park. Then I opened a low gate and we started walking around the dirt track. The morning sun bounced off nearby bleachers, creating a wall of glare, so I pulled a pair of sunglasses out of my bag and secured them on my face.

"On a happier house note," Mark said, "the real estate prices in Sacramento are sky-high. This really is a perfect time to put River Acres on the market."

A sigh slipped through my lips and I hoped my husband hadn't noticed. I was committed to selling River Acres, but when Mark spoke of our home, it felt like saying goodbye to an old friend.

The Sacramento Bee, our hometown newspaper, reported that the housing market was heating up because of the pandemic. People who lived in urban areas were moving back to the suburbs, and people from the Bay Area who now worked remotely wanted to trade in their shoebox-sized flats in Silicon Valley for much larger homes two hours east. Our River Acres property fit the needs of both demographic groups. Some reports in early 2021 claimed that Sacramento was the hottest housing market in the entire country.

"What do you think we could sell it for?" I asked.

"A lot more than we paid for it," Mark said. "I've scheduled a phone call with the realtor tomorrow."

My eyes never left the dirt track, but my breath caught in my throat.

"We're doing the right thing, George," Mark said, and reached for my hand.

"I know. And I'm grateful for the chance to expedite my retirement. It's just . . ."

I searched for a word that combined gratitude with reluctance, but my self-reflexive mind rerouted to the terms *selfish* and *bullheaded*.

"It's still hard," Mark said, finishing my sentence, which endeared him to me.

Could a house act like a security blanket? Did scarcity in my youth make me unnaturally attached to a structure? Letting go of River Acres poked at some old psychological wound, a need for stability born of unparented childlike fears.

"Exactly. Let's pick up the pace," I said, and I started to run.

* * *

Unlike California, Super Bowl Sunday in Puerto Rico was a low-key sporting event. There were no guacamole and chip displays at the end of grocery store aisles or team gear on sale at local sporting goods stores. During a pandemic on a Caribbean island, the game was superfluous. We hadn't considered watching until Kevin invited us to the socially distanced Super Bowl party in his community.

Last week, Deborah had offered to drive since we were all heading to the same place.

"Jump in!" she said when she picked us up on Sunday afternoon. Even though COVID mask wearing was still required in Puerto Rico, we had stopped wearing ours around Deb. "This is going to be a blast!"

Deborah was one of those people who I imagined bounced out of bed in the morning, threw back the curtains, and sang, "Rise and shine!" at full volume. She was effervescent, the kind of person who made a mundane car ride festive, and I was pleased our friendship had grown.

"Thanks for driving, Deb," I said, as Mark and I got into her car.

We headed to the Ritz-Carlton gated community a few miles from Playa Tortuga, the same place we'd had lunch with Sal and Kathy. After passing through multiple security gates and navigating our way through winding mansion-lined streets, we arrived at Kevin and Tricia's home.

"Wow," Deb said, pulling into the driveway. "This place is something else. What a gorgeous property. I have a feeling we're in for a fun party!"

If my past crypto party experiences in Puerto Rico were any indication, "fun" was only part of what we were in for.

CHAPTER 29:

HEDGING BETS

"It looks like the front of a fancy state capitol building," I said to Mark and Deborah before ringing the doorbell. "Maybe a giant lives here."

When the door opened, we were greeted by a blond angelic-looking child.

"Hi," I said. "Are your mom and dad home?"

"My mom is upstairs and my daddy is on the phone, but you may come in," said the child.

Walking into Kevin and Tricia's home was like entering a cathedral; the ceilings were unusually high and stamped with ecologically themed renderings in molded frames. Like the Sistine Chapel, this home had art painted onto the foyer ceiling.

"What's your name?" I asked the little boy. I forced myself to look at the child instead of the beautiful art above my head.

"Lucas," he said. "It's very nice to meet you."

The boy couldn't have been more than five. In addition to a practiced greeting, he had big green eyes and bouncy curls that landed on pale shoulders. He was wearing swim trunks and his feet were bare.

"Isn't he adorable," Deborah said.

"Welcome," Tricia called from the top of the stairwell. "I see you have already met Lucas."

The little boy ran to meet his mother at the base of the stairs. He squeezed her legs and then ran in another direction yelling, "Byeeee!"

Tricia invited us into the living room. "Kevin will be out in just a moment. As usual, he's on a call."

We followed Tricia into a space that looked like a hotel lobby. I imagined Lucas flying kites inside this room—with open windows, tropical breezes could lift a bright silk triangle tied to a string more than three stories high. Everything here was oversized: ceilings, archways, couches, tables, rugs, paintings. It wasn't just the front doors that implied fairytale proportions. Sitting in the exaggerated space made us look like we had climbed Jack's beanstalk and landed in the giant's entertainment chamber. I thought of the large art installations I'd seen by Robert Therrien. The inside of Kevin and Tricia's home didn't look like a place where real people actually lived and I felt transported to a make-believe location, a scene curated from one of Aesop's fables.

Tricia was second-wife young and beautiful, with thick blonde hair that fell to the middle of her back. She had the little boy's pale jade eyes and a wide smile that communicated warmth. She told us that she still practiced law part-time and worked full-time raising Lucas, the couple's five-year-old son. Kevin also practiced law part-time, she told us, but had cut back his practice a decade prior so that he could shift his attention to interests like race car driving, cryptocurrency, and options trading.

"Sorry to make you wait," Kevin said, walking into the room. As soon as he entered, Tricia stood up and left without a word. The energy between them felt strained. It seemed as if they had been fighting before we showed up and my high hopes for starting a friendship with this couple were downgraded to an ambivalent maybe.

Kevin was older than his wife by fifteen, maybe twenty years, but he wore linen clothes and sandals that would have looked cool on a twentysomething man. "It's been crazy for a Sunday. I needed to clock time in my barometric chamber and crypto is cooking in anticipation of Super Bowl ads. The day got away from me. Anyway, I'm happy you could all make it. Let's have some wine and then we'll head to the Plantation. Follow me."

Like an orchestra conductor, Kevin waved his hand and we all stood and walked through a formal dining area that contained a shiny black table with seating for twenty-four. It glistened against the bright white marble floors. On the far wall, a life-sized picture of Kevin inside a red-and-gold racing car, his hands glued to the wheel, a look of concentration on his face as he sped around a track, made the room pulsate.

"Dining room," Kevin announced as he led us onward. He had a mercurial face and moved from one topic to the next with NASCAR-like energy.

"I want you to pick something you like," he said, leading us past the enormous kitchen and into a refrigerated room. It was lined with expensive bottles of wine and large enough for all four of us to stand inside. Kevin obviously liked California reds.

"This is a beautiful collection," Deborah said.

"We have it flown in from all over. Wine is one of my many hobbies," Kevin admitted. "Being from California, you probably recognize some of these labels."

"Wow," I said, admiring the impressive options. "PlumpJack is one of my favorites."

I had worked in plenty of restaurants when I was a college student, none of which had a wine cellar this large or well stocked. Bottles of Caymus, Opus One, Stag's Leap, and Darius II, plus hundreds of others that I was unfamiliar with, lined his cellar walls.

"If you like PlumpJack," Kevin responded, "you'll really like this."

Kevin pulled a bottle of Cade from the chilly cellar wall, uncorked it, and poured each person a small taste to start. Then he decanted the ruby liquid so it could breathe.

"Delicious," I said. "Thank you."

The scene was a ground-level, less populated version of Crypto Tuesday at Scott Windsor's penthouse. Julio and his crypto crew were missing, but I felt equally out of place. Sipping expensive wine around a table built inside a wine cellar, built inside a mansion, was vastly different from the regular days in my life. It was like waking up on a movie set, and I tried to cover up my discomfort with a smile.

"How is your law practice these days?" Mark asked Kevin.

The coolness of the wine cellar calmed me.

"Fine, but my latest development is the start of my own hedge fund," Kevin said.

"Congratulations," I offered, wondering how an individual would begin such a massive undertaking.

"Don't congratulate me yet," Kevin laughed. "I need to make my clients some money first."

Kevin was a successful attorney; I learned that he had argued a large class action against Big Pharma all the way to the Supreme Court—and won. This translated into justice for thousands of citizens (and millions of dollars for Kevin). He had also gained Formula 1 fame, given the glass-encased memorabilia, pictures, and trophies exhibited throughout the house. But how did someone go from attorney to race car driver to hedge fund manager? The latter job title was synonymous with well-coiffed men in Manhattan high-rises whose résumés boasted a lifetime of money management.

"Oh, sorry, I don't want to jinx you," I said. The group laughed politely. "I meant congratulations on such an interesting professional transition."

I admired people who reinvented themselves professionally and personally. It takes courage to reimagine one's life with dramatic flair. I knew from experience it also took luck, and in Kevin's case, access to wealth. Hedge fund managers made millions, even billions, in a good year, but rounding up rich clients required connections. Kevin's notoriety—in the law and the worlds of racing and crypto—provided exactly that.

"It's impressive you're adding hedge fund manager to your legal résumé," Mark said.

"If banks can do it, so can I. After all, banks are just hedge funds," Kevin said. "People think banks hold on to their deposits, but they only have to keep 10 percent to meet fractional reserve limits. They repackage our money and generate loans. Borrowing is forever. Just think of all the derivatives that are created off that repackaged 90 percent."

Kevin described the fiscal start of 2021 with the acronym TINA, which stood for "There is no alternative." He explained that timing was key to his hedge fund start-up. In a TINA environment, wealthy people used hedge funds to protect their assets, even if they had doubts about the long-term strength of the stock market. When interest rates fell to zero, things like CDs and money market accounts—fixed income products—couldn't attract serious investors. In 2021, interest rates were shockingly low and TINA made hedge funds an important piece of a wealthy person's financial portfolio. In spite of global instability, a pandemic, a historic US deficit, and an inflated stock market, the financial industry remained strong. Perhaps whatever genius enabled Kevin to argue Supreme Court cases and win car races could also manifest hedge fund returns.

"Let's sit and I'll open another bottle," Kevin said.

We followed him out of the wine cellar and sat down on tall stools placed around a hulking kitchen island. A glass centerpiece, taller than Lucas, held exotic flowers with red and gold blooms framed by palm fronds. Industrial-sized appliances were built into the kitchen walls.

"Part of my approach," Kevin continued, "is to offer my clients something other than the 2 and 20. I am proposing a 0 and 30 model to my clients, and only asking for a million-dollar buy-in."

The formula 2 and 20 was how hedge fund managers got paid; they earned 2 percent on their client's investment (regardless of what happened with the initial investment) and 20 percent of all profits. Some argued that this incentivized hedge fund managers to take risky positions. Not only were they guaranteed 2 percent of the capital, risk held the potential for exciting financial reward. Why not shoot for wild profitability? Technically, hedge fund managers were playing with the house's money. Even if the investment was a loser, the hedge fund manager still made a profit, and if the investment paid off, they cleaned up with an additional 20 percent. Kevin's model—0 and 30—meant he didn't make a dime unless his clients made money. Presumably, this would give his clients confidence.

The typical financial advisor, in contrast to a hedge fund manager, only made 1–2 percent off of their client's portfolio gains; successful management of a $10 million portfolio (or ten $1 million portfolios) equated to a yearly salary of $100,000–$200,000. It took exceptional self-assurance for someone new to the hedge fund management game to skip the financial advisor step, learn how to navigate compliance laws, register with the SEC, expect 30 percent of clients' gains, and start with a million-dollar ask.

"This last year has given economists a lot to think about," Mark said. "Given the pandemic job losses and quantitative easing, how would your fund perform in a down market?"

Kevin took a sip of wine and then set down his glass before looking directly at Mark.

"I want to preface my answer by admitting that I think a downturn is inevitable. But even if the market turns by 70 percent, I anticipate my strategy will pay off," Kevin said. He was purposefully elusive; his money-making ideas came with a million-dollar price tag.

Watching the exchange between Kevin and Mark reminded me of movies about Wall Street if the setting—usually a boardroom or an exclusive golf course—was a luxury kitchen. While I didn't have anything to add to the conversation, I was fascinated. How many former singing telegram girls got invited to sip wine with the 1 percent? Listening to Kevin talk about the world of hedge fund management was akin to eavesdropping, like hearing a message that wasn't meant for me. Was this typical? Did wealthy men share the secret rules for how to win the money game while sipping wine in giant-sized kitchens?

"I agree," Mark said, "I think that we're due for a market correction.[13] Any predication on when that is?"

Kevin wouldn't bite. "Nobody knows which snowflake will cause the avalanche," he said. "But since the snowpack is layered with the instability of massive debt, there is no doubt it will be cataclysmic."

"How will that affect Bitcoin?" Deborah asked.

"In the long run, good," Kevin said.

---

13. A stock market correction is generally considered to be a decline that is at least 10 percent but no more than 20 percent.

Kevin believed like others in the crypto community that Bitcoin was the best future store of value that regular citizens could acquire.

"But the weak hands shake out, so it may be best to hold off on buying Bitcoin right now," he added.

Deborah nodded agreement. Tricia wandered into the kitchen, poured herself a glass of wine, and sat down. She listened to the conversation for a minute but looked bored and started scrolling on her phone.

If a major market correction was inevitable, Kevin explained, some people with Bitcoin would be forced to sell their holdings to cover financial obligations impacted by a market crash. Even if Bitcoin was an excellent store of value, a sell-off would bring down its price. Our host's point was that we should be patient but prepared to move on a Bitcoin price drop. Just eleven months before our Super Bowl conversation, Bitcoin had dropped down to $3,596 before its value soared.[14]

We finished our wine while Kevin grabbed a few more bottles from the cellar and loaded them into a pressed-leather satchel. Then we climbed into his six-seater golf cart for the drive to where his community's Super Bowl party was scheduled.

"I don't think I've ridden in an electric Porsche golf cart before," Mark said. "Nice stripes."

"I wanted the emblems to match my race car, so I had this customized. Makes it more fun to drive," Kevin said.

We drove through a neighborhood of impressive homes with sprawling lawns and curated tropical foliage before hitting a pristine stretch of private beach. Modern-day Norman Rockwell families sat under umbrellas in white

---

14. The day after the Super Bowl, Bitcoin hit another all-time high of $44,795.20. Some analysts linked this spike to the fact that Tesla disclosed via an SEC filing that it purchased 1.5 billion Bitcoin and announced that it would accept Bitcoin as a form of payment.

sand. We moved along the golf cart path past couples on bikes, chatting as they pedaled, and others in fashionable running gear out to get their daily exercise. The light pink sky was stretched wide over the Atlantic Ocean and told of the breathtaking sunset yet to come while the voice of Robin Leach, narrating an episode of *Lifestyles of the Rich and Famous*, droned on in my head. It felt dreamlike to be in this place, where my surroundings didn't align with what I knew to be real life.

Kevin's community Super Bowl party was set up like a drive-in movie, but for golf carts instead of cars. As we approached the large open-air space, we were greeted by pretty party staff dressed as cheerleaders. They waved their pom-poms in excitement at our arrival and directed us to our designated drive-in stall. I thought of all the fake smiles I had plastered on my face from behind a bar, the other end of a cocktail tray, or while singing "Happy Birthday" in my underwear. Then I closed my eyes and reminded myself I was a guest, not a worker.

The party was located at the Plantation Lawn, a place named after the sugarcane and cotton plantations that symbolized colonial rule in the Caribbean. I wondered who could have possibly thought this name was a good idea, but the only people of color—Puerto Rican cheerleaders in skimpy skirts—didn't have time to complain. Instead, colonialist structures of race and class were reinforced by golf cart drivers who arrived in a steady stream, barking orders at the costumed waitresses and squabbling over Super Bowl facts. We were served buckets of ice-cold Medalla just as announcers began their pregame hype on the drive-in-sized movie screen.

Kevin and Tricia introduced us to their COVID-masked friends in neighboring golf carts—people with jobs in technical fields, science fields, pharmaceuticals, and banking. We greeted each other with the customary pandemic wave and made small talk about our experiences relocating to the Caribbean.

They were all here for the same reason Mark and I were: Act 20 & 22. These tax laws gave the Puerto Rican government a chance to compete with other Caribbean islands for residents that brought their businesses, entrepreneurship, and wealth to the community in exchange for tax relief. If states like Florida and Nevada were winning retirees who relocated to take advantage of favorable state income tax laws, Puerto Rico was winning wealth managers, software designers, and Bitcoin billionaires with federal tax discounts. Companies like Google, Apple, and Twitter reaped organizational tax benefits by relocating their headquarters to countries like Ireland, but for individuals who preferred to keep their US citizenship, Puerto Rico was their Ireland. Still, I knew from my time with Alberto and Ana talking about the impacts of Hurricane Maria that Act 20 & 22 didn't serve most Puerto Ricans the same way it did stateside transplants. It created wealth bubbles and gentrification. It was true that Act members helped to stimulate the local economy, but their glamorous lives were lived behind security gates and on private beaches. Their children went to elite private schools and they could travel to Miami for improved medical care. Local Puerto Ricans cleaned their houses and cooked their meals. What were the cultural and systematic impacts of Act membership? What did it mean for the Indigenous people of the island? I wrestled with the ethical conflicts while admiring the manicured surroundings.

"Hey," said a man in a red golf shirt over the din of friendly conversation. Ten of us stood in a circle discussing football plays. "My dad just landed in the hospital. Does anyone have a plane I can use tomorrow?"

"Sure," "Yes," and "No problem," were the simultaneous responses.

No joke. Red Shirt's dad was scheduled for surgery the next day and not one but *three* of his neighbors offered him the use of their personal aircraft so he could get to Palm Springs.

The term "capital mobility" was banking vocabulary for the efficient movement of money. It's sometimes applied to customers who cash in their money market account at one bank and move it to another with higher annual yields. The lesson taught that money goes where it is treated best and given the conversation spread across the Plantation Lawn, there was no doubt that Dorado, Puerto Rico, treated money well. Perhaps it was my hardscrabble youth, or the fact that I was a community college professor and not a Bitcoin billionaire, but bearing witness to capital mobility of this magnitude caused me grief.

Economic inequality was often defined as the unequal distribution of wealth and opportunity between different groups in society. My formerly incarcerated students, all of whom grew up in poverty, were particularly sensitive to this reality. When you started with very little, and were released from prison with nothing, life was daunting. The men and women in my college program felt the effects of barely scraping by every single day. I considered what my students would say if they knew I was on the Plantation Lawn having conversations about borrowing private jets. Would it change how they felt about me? Would they continue to come to class if they knew I attended a party at a place that celebrated colonialism, a place where wealthy white people ordered fancy dinners from inside golf carts made by Porsche? Would they see me as part of the solution or part of the problem?

As I watched the Tampa Bay Buccaneers stomp on the Kansas City Chiefs with Dorado's well-to-do, I experienced a wide range of emotions. I was fascinated by this glimpse into a moneyed lifestyle, and inspired by the interesting work and professional reinvention discussed amongst the men. And I was an awkward, middle-class fish swimming in a gilded sea. But mostly, I was acutely aware of the income inequality on display in the Ritz-Carlton community, and that made me feel like a traitor to my students and others who were more like I had been—struggling to survive.

CHAPTER 30:

FOR SALE

Mark's phone rang exactly at noon. We were sitting next to each other on the living room couch, note-pads and pens in our hands, as we readied ourselves for a conversation with Kim, our realtor. Mark answered the call, announced that I was by his side, and switched his phone to speaker mode.

"Hi, Georgine!" Kim said. "Long time no talk to."

"Hi, Kim," I answered.

"I'm so glad you reached out." I heard clapping hands on the other end of the line. "I'm excited to work with you again!"

Kim was the realtor I used when I got divorced from my first husband and had to sell my home as part of a marriage settlement agreement. Once she sold the house, I was able to wrap up my divorce and move on with my life.

"I've been to your property on River Acres and I'm impressed. I think it's very close to market ready."

Mark had arranged for Kim to pick up a house key from a neighbor so she could look around before our phone meeting.

"Since you two are in Puerto Rico," she continued, "I can have my assistant set up services—things like window washing and yard detail. Your River Acres residence is gorgeous and I think we can handle all the preparations for a sale in your absence."

I felt a bubble of grief rise in the pit of my stomach. There was so much I would miss about my Sacramento home, like sitting on the porch with a morning cup of coffee to watch red foxes rustle in the riverside bushes, or the sight of squirrels and birds tussling for tree branch access from my kitchen window. And at dusk, my favorite time of day on the river, I'd miss seeing the barn owls that Mark had named Thornton and Willamena. They'd swoop down from a towering palm tree in our front yard before flying across the river to feast on the field mice along the riverbank. We'd hear their screeches of success a few hours later, their silky feathers gleaming underneath a darkened sapphire sky.

"Thanks for making the trip out to our house," Mark said, playfully tapping my bottom lip like he was teasing a pouting child.

"We understand that the real estate market in Sacramento is currently strong; we'd like to find a buyer before that changes," he added.

"I think you're smart to take advantage of timing. Interest rates are at all-time lows, and I have a number of affluent clients who want to relocate from the Bay Area. Between the low inventory, reduced interest rates, and COVID, I am confident you'll do well. This is definitely a sellers' market."

After trying to take a pretend bite of his finger, I offered Mark a smile.

When the time came to discuss the listing price, we haggled with Kim, but just a little. Mark had three prices listed on his notepad: a dream price, a realistic option, and a rock-bottom consideration. Kim deferred to Mark before we had to relinquish our starting number.

"Okay. I'm willing to give that number a shot," she said, "as long as you are both willing to revisit the price topic if we see thirty days of inactivity."

Mark circled the top number on his paper pad three times and added exclamation points at the end. I could feel his excitement grow with his exclamations—each dot more vigorous than the last.

"Definitely," Mark said. "It sounds like we have a deal."

After Mark hung up the phone, he took the empty paper pad out of my hand and set it on the coffee table along with his own. He turned toward me and gave a look that announced, *Wow!*

"I think that went well," he said, and put his hand on my knee.

"Agreed. I was surprised by everything she was willing to manage in our absence. Maybe I don't need to fly back to California after all."

I had expected Kim to provide a long list of presale tasks for us to complete. Since Mark was accruing days toward his Act residency requirements, I anticipated flying back to California solo to get things sale-ready.

"At least not until it sells," Mark said. "There's only one reason Kim is prepared to do all this extra work. Selling River Acres is easy money. If you fly back early, let's hope it's to pack."

I looked down at my clasped hands. I had been squeezing them so tightly that commas, made from my fingernails, had formed on my skin. I was revising my future on the backs of my hands and here was punctuation for the developing sentences.

I was two people. The me that had heard Kim's encouragement was eager for retirement. She enjoyed watching her husband's excitement and thought selling River Acres was a fantastic move. But the other me—the one that didn't want to sell her home—felt twisted up. She thought about all the birthday parties and sleepovers hosted there, the fresh vegetables she tended to in her garden, and the long walks she took with her dog Lucy along the river. If the place sold, what would become of Lucy? Or the fig trees that ripened with the heat of the summer? Who would invite the neighbors over to pick grapefruits and explain which trees produced the sweetest pink globes?

"It's helpful that Kim's willing to handle these presale chores," I said. "I'm worried I'll spend one night at home and call the whole thing off."

"We've made a lot of good memories in River Acres. But owning homes can mean very different things to different people. I wish you could share in my excitement."

I sighed. "For me, that house symbolizes family and security."

"And probably safety too," Mark said. "You didn't get enough of those things growing up, so our home was like a force field of protection. But a house doesn't give you those things, George; we created those things in our house. You created them inside of you."

"I know. A house is just the container. But River Acres is special to me. I've never lived in the same place for so many years—an entire decade. And the things I feel about this space are the antithesis to my childhood homes. I think I'm fixated on River Acres because the life we've lived there feels magical. I know it's our family and friends that matter—all the love and fun we have shared inside—but we made that house great. I'll miss it."

I looked down and smoothed the nail marks on my hands with my thumb.

Mark watched me rub out the commas. Then he shifted his position on the couch and leaned a little closer to me.

"In my family, selling a home symbolized moving up in the world." His voice was kind. "When my parents sold our home, I knew things were getting better. A 'next home' meant my self-employed folks had crossed into another income bracket; it was cause for celebration and a sign that my parents were doing things right."

"Ironic. I have the exact opposite memories as a kid. Once my parents split up, we kept moving down and moving scared . . . the lesson I learned was that things were about to get harder when it was time to move out."

My throat felt tight. Thinking about my childhood made complicated emotions rise from my gut and travel toward my mouth, but I swallowed them back down.

"Buying and selling homes is just a part of life—and for us, it's a good part," Mark said. "Selling River Acres is about progress and financial independence. Instead of stagnation, instead of lethargy, we are *doing* things. Financially smart things."

Mark relaxed back into the couch. I felt nervous, but he looked confident.

That afternoon I took a walk and thought about the meaning of home—how mine was so different from Mark's. Even though the day was warm and there wouldn't be any shade, I headed to the beach, where I could walk alone in the sand.

* * *

There was a gate that separated our community from the beach. Once I entered, I headed east, past our grassy community gathering spaces and toward miles of sand that joined one coastal neighborhood to another. When I reached the long strip of beach, I took off my tennis shoes and hid them under a palm frond for safekeeping. The afternoon sun made my skin hot, but the cool, wet sand between my toes kept me comfortable.

My earliest memory of home was how hard I struggled to breathe, my skin a pale blue, my chest tight under the weight of an elephant's foot about to squash my tiny frame. As a small child, I was prone to asthma attacks. These most often occurred in the middle of the night. My mom would hear my coughs and gasps, get me out of bed, then help me with inhalers or injections, depending on the severity of the attack. Once the pressure on my chest subsided, she'd rock me in her arms until I fell back to sleep.

When I struggled with asthma, my mom shushed my weak cries and protected me, but I still felt the struggle in my body. This dusty image of me and my mom was like a rope; it braided together feelings of fear and protection. Its sinewy strands tied me tightly to my mother. When I was very young her care kept me breathing.

"Deep, slow, breaths," she'd say in a voice that invited relaxation. "Deep. Slow. Breaths."

My mom's bathrobe was the color of honey and it felt soft against my bare skin. Or maybe I just remember the color that way because she was golden, the skin on her arms and face kissed by the California sun. Mom ran her fingers through my hair while she rocked me back to sleep. We sat snuggled, me against Mom's lap, Mom against the old wooden rocking chair, both of us moving in time to the rhythm she picked for the night. She smelled safe. Her arms held me tight and kept my body angled to reduce pressure on my airways. Her beautiful voice hummed gentle melodies that vibrated in her chest and tickled my ear. This all took place in the first house my parents bought, a ranch-style residence in Tustin, California. This was home those early years.

We moved to our next house when I was six and my brother was four, a place my parents bought in Orange, California. The year was 1975 and this, our second home, had serious bohemian charm. Sage-green appliances lined kitchen walls and there were yellow vinyl chairs around the table. The living room, sunken by a single step, included beige shag carpet with dark brown flecks. Two mango-colored barrel chairs, placed in front of a large picture window, swiveled in complete circles so that the pool in the backyard looked like a giant fuzzy topaz gem with each new spin.

Either something changed between my parents in this house or I grew old enough to finally see what was there all along, but in the Orange house, life turned sour. It was obvious my parents didn't like each other. Not long after we moved in, I was watching TV while my parents argued in the kitchen. As their voices grew louder, I leaned forward to hear the cartoons on the screen. Shaggy and Scooby-Doo were about to unmask an impostor just as Daphne, Fred, and Thelma tumbled out of the Mystery Machine. I tried to focus on Scooby and ignore my angry parents, but they spit threats and bad words at each other like handfuls of tacks tossed across tile. I felt worried. My heart beat faster but I kept staring at the television set. I told myself to stay still.

"Get the fuck out," Mom screamed at Dad. "I'm done!"

The electricity in the room made the small blonde hairs on my arms stand straight up. The cartoon images on the screen started to dim and I could hear myself swallow.

"I'm not going anywhere," Dad said in a tone that communicated Mom was acting nuts.

"Oh yes, you are," Mom screamed. "I want you out of this house right fucking now!"

My mom's voice hurt my ears. It screeched like an accident that was about to happen, sound that explodes before heavy objects collide.

"Stop acting crazy!" Dad shouted back. "You don't have a bank account. You don't even have a credit card. There's no way in hell you can make it out there without me, you ungrateful lunatic!"

I kept watch on my parents from the corner of my eye, their anger heating up worse than usual. I could tell because Dad still hadn't stormed out of the room and Mom wasn't backing down. I scooped a blanket into my arms and squeezed it tight like Mom squeezed me when I struggled to breathe.

My parents' fight got so loud that I couldn't hear anything else and my focus switched from the television to their bodies. I saw Dad grab Mom by the shoulders and shake her hard, her petite frame whipping back and forth. Then his hands moved to her neck and she gasped. Her mouth was stuck open but no sound came out. I felt paralyzed. I couldn't breathe. Dad shoved Mom's head against the big picture window that separated our backyard from the kitchen; my mother's scream, and the sounds of shattered glass, filled the air.

"Stop! Stop fighting! Stop!" I sobbed, finally, but the fight was already over. My dad stormed out of the house and my mom curled up into a ball on the kitchen floor. She lay there, gasping and crying, in a bed of glass and blood.

My pace quickened as I walked along the beach, thinking about this fight between my parents in our Orange house. I had listened to many of their fights from the safety of my bedroom, but watching this one unfold had seared it into my memory. With each step, my toes gripped the wet sand and my arms swung by my sides, fists clenched. I moved further down the beach, traveling deep into my past.

Before my parents finally divorced, their relationship roller-coastered, climbing peaks of promise, then careening into ditches of despair. Watching family life unravel in the Orange house was a whiplash-inducing event that left me nervous and confused. Just when it seemed like they'd never speak to each other again, one of them would proclaim renewed love and marital commitment. Then the cycle would start all over again.

A few months after the broken window fight, to save their struggling marriage, my parents unexpectedly took a vacation to Hawaii. The legend goes that they attended a charity auction and enjoyed too much champagne. When my mom went to use the bathroom, my dad decided to surprise her by bidding on a trip to Maui. As a kid, I loved this story, my dad making a grand gesture to show my mom that he loved her. They kept the large poster board from the auction on display in their bedroom before the trip, a reminder of fun and romance on the horizon.

Once they got back from Hawaii it seemed that whatever troubles had plagued them before their vacation were left behind on the faraway island. They seemingly rekindled the thing that got lost when we moved into our Orange house. A week later, they told my brother and me that Maui was the answer to everything and where we would have our next home, so we moved.

Since moving to Maui didn't stop their fighting, they must have realized that exchanging their Orange home for one in Lahaina wasn't the remedy to the bubbling anger and resentment that had simmered for years.

My mom had married my dad when she was just eighteen to escape my Grandpa Stanford. Instead of solace, she found herself with another man who believed women were the inferior sex and that men were the boss, which was typical of the times.

After more fights, my parents divorced. Mom couldn't afford to keep living in Lahaina, so we moved to more modest neighborhoods on the island, a blur of rentals where door hinges broke, faucets leaked, and carpets needed to be replaced. During that time, I struggled to adapt to school in Hawaii. I was one of two *haoles*—non-native Hawaiians of European descent—enrolled in second grade at King Kamehameha III Elementary School, and I got picked on daily by the other kids for my light hair and blue eyes.

This was the year that I first met and befriended a school crossing guard. She was a strong, imposing woman whose clear directions kept children safe. When school let out, and the bullies chased me, I ran to her for protection. Her bright vest made her easy to spot from long distances. She would blow her whistle and tell the mean kids who taunted me to go home. While she waved her red stop sign and directed traffic, she let me sit at the end of her crosswalk until I felt safe enough to leave the school grounds. Sometimes, when I cried, she gave me a hug. Years later, it was a miniature version of this woman who appeared on my shoulder with her whistle and sign, telling me to straighten up and stop using drugs. When my imaginary crossing guard directed my decision-making, I knew that she was trying to protect me, just as this real woman had done in elementary school.

The fear I felt at school was matched by the fear I felt at home. Mom's single-parent challenges fueled the turmoil that dominated my young life. Like most women in her shoes—divorced from a deadbeat and responsible for the care and keep of two children—Mom experienced compounding financial problems. Single moms like mine only earned about sixty cents for every dollar made by a man in the 1970s. In addition to low-wage jobs, women faced harassment and discrimination in the workplace. I knew about these hardships because Mom was a grand emitter of emotion, a nuclear power plant of feelings. She said exactly what was on her mind, and if she was upset or angry, she said it with unsettling force.

"Life is a bitch. So, when I ask you to do something," Mom yelled at me a hundred times, "I expect you to do it!"

If she came home from work to find a bathroom towel on the floor or trash stuffed in a can that should have been taken out, her fiery temper flared.

I was afraid of my mother and the intensity of her rage. I learned to repent when she was mad. Even when I knew that I hadn't done the thing she accused me of, I held my tongue and assumed a submissive posture. My mother did not tolerate disrespectful children.

"I'm sorry, Mom."

Before she left for work each day, Mom would create a list of chores, and when she got home, she'd evaluate our domestic efforts. If a task hadn't been completed to her satisfaction, she screamed her frustrations and shamed us with insults.

"I don't work my ass off to support you lazy kids so that I can come home and be treated with disrespect. If you plan to live under my roof," she'd yell, "you had better follow the rules!"

Sometimes she made her point while breaking the kitchen dishes I was supposed to have washed or smashing objects, like the toys my brother should have put away. I didn't feel safe at school or at home. I was an anxious kid. I worried about my scrawny frame, but I never had an appetite. I was nervous about my grades even though I earned consistently high marks. I always felt like something bad was about to happen, even when I didn't have a reason to worry. It was my friendship with Shelly, the school crossing guard, and later with Kimberly, the other haole kid at school, that got me through these years.

If my mom was content, our house was calm, but if she was unhappy, so was I. Her fights with the universe—over money, love, substances, work, faith, and her indolent children—were like ten-foot waves that crashed for weeks at a time in the middle of our home. Whenever her emotional surf wiped out my semblance of normalcy, I dog-paddled, trying hard to keep my head above the tide, but it felt like salt water was perpetually burning my throat.

During these tumultuous years, I lived in multiple houses, switched schools often, and moved from California to Hawaii and back to California. My mom's Hawaiian boyfriend moved in with us, then moved out. He moved in, again, and moved out. He was replaced by a stream of boyfriends that were great. Then assholes. Our little family—me, my brother, and my mom—bobbed along in an inflatable boat that kept taking on water. Mom would patch one hole, but another would soon appear. I lived in fear that the next big storm would sink us for sure. A new house was a sign that I should get my bucket ready.

It wasn't until my mom remarried, more than a decade after my parents split up, that she appeared happy again. By then I was nineteen and had been living on my own for two years.

"You're not going to believe it," my mom said. She was radioactive with joy. "I think I finally met a *nice* man."

I was lying on the floor of my apartment, annoyed that I had answered the phone when it rang. This was a period in my life when I avoided my mom. In my late teens and early twenties, I had put her in the "bad mom" category of my mind. I was struggling to pay my own bills, indignant that my university acceptance had been squandered for community college, and resentful over a lack of parental support. I was also quick to judge my mother's mistakes. It took years of growing up, and therapy, before talking to her on the phone didn't spoil my mood.

"What makes this guy so great?" I asked.

My mom tended to date hypermasculine men who drank too much (not unlike Grandpa Stanford). She had a type.

"For starters, I met him at church. And after our first date, which was a very appropriate dinner, he sent me flowers!"

As with boyfriends, Mom had an on-again, off-again relationship with church. When things got hard and it was time for her to turn the page on the latest chapter of her challenging life, Mom and God reunited. I understood her relationship with God to be unpredictable and exasperating, just like her moods and romantic affairs.

"Flowers? This one does sound different," I said. Snide comments started to form in my mind, but instead I added, "Good for you."

Now, when I walked along the beach and thought of selling my beloved home, the part of my brain that stored early memories got activated. All of the purging, packing, and moving conjured recollections of instability, of stepping backward, of losing, of sinking, of struggling to breathe. Each relocation was an elevated tick on the universe's chaos meter. Even though my adult mind recognized that this pattern of thinking belonged to my child self, the feelings and images still came.

When I returned from my walk on the beach, I found Mark sitting on the couch. After our conversation with Kim, I had watched my thoughts but didn't give them a voice. Now, I had clarity about their meaning. They existed, these thoughts, but they no longer trapped me. They couldn't control my decision-making or trick me into thinking they were trying to protect me. I knew it was static. Just noise from the past.

I sat down next to Mark and gave him a kiss on the cheek. He set down the book he was reading and smiled.

"You're right," I said to Mark. "Selling River Acres *is* in our family's best interest. The process is hard for me, but I'm with you, and I agree—this is a sign that we are moving on up. Your dad would be proud. I know I am. Let's sign Kim's contract and get this show on the road."

River Acres was for sale.

CHAPTER 31:

INOCULATIONS

On March 22, 2021, Mark and I drove to the Walgreens in Dorado to get our first dose of the COVID-19 Pfizer vaccine—at last. Wasn't everybody wondering when life was going to get back to normal in 2021? We had all endured too much isolation, worked too many hours in front of a computer screen, and watched way too much television.

On this morning, after receiving my vaccine, I was giddy. I hadn't been aware that I was holding my breath, but the exhale that coincided with my shot was instructive. I started to relax and it seemed like Mark did too.

"That was simple," Mark said to me as we left Walgreens and walked to the car.

"It sure was," I said. "Thank goodness we are finally vaccinated."

I noticed a tension I'd been carrying around between my shoulder blades disappeared. I felt like skipping to the car.

"I wonder how long it will take to get everyone vaccinated in Puerto Rico?" I asked.

It had taken us weeks to get the Walgreens appointment. Every morning, new appointments were released online by designated providers, from convenience stores to hospitals, but the spots were snapped up in minutes. The vaccine had to be shipped from the States, carefully refrigerated because of the tropical weather, and it was in short supply.

"I'm not sure, but given how difficult it was to schedule an appointment, I think most people are motivated to follow the CDC's vaccination recommendation. Everybody knows that the medical system here is a problem—Puerto Rico doesn't have the medical staff to handle an influx of sick people."

Mark started the car and we headed for home.

"I understand why the COVID safety protocols are strict on the island," I said, "but I'll be glad when we're past the pandemic. I am so sick of wearing a mask everywhere I go I could scream. Today feels liberating."

"To modern medicine," Mark said.

"Hear, hear," I agreed. "And just in time for our visitors!" This thought made me smile wide.

Even though we had seen Abby and her boyfriend Sam during the Christmas holiday, we were excited to show our other daughters Puerto Rico and felt grateful to get vaccinated before their arrival. News reports at this time indicated that pandemic fatigue was prompting people to go on vacation. We were not the only parents who had reached the end of their isolation rope and doctors predicted that spring break travel would give COVID numbers a boost.

Our family visitors included our nineteen-year-old daughter, Olivia, who attended the University of California, Santa Cruz; our twenty-three-year-old daughter, Rae; and Rae's longtime boyfriend, Shane, both of whom attended California State University, Sacramento. It had been many months since these sisters had seen each other, and even more time had passed since we had all been together. Mark and I were eager to show them the island and hoped they would love our new home.

On the day of their scheduled arrival, I zipped around the house like a wind-up toy. I tried to trade crypto, but couldn't focus, picked up a book but kept re-reading the same page. Ultimately, I bounced around the condo fluffing pillows and wiping down kitchen counters that already sparkled. I hadn't seen my daughters in four months—the longest I'd ever gone without them—and I was bursting with excitement.

At 3 p.m. Mark grabbed the car keys and headed toward the airport. He had to pick up Olivia, Rae, and Shane without me since their luggage made for a tight squeeze in the car.

Two hours later, when the front door swung open, I cried happy tears and hugged each of our weary travelers.

"I hope you're hungry," I said once the kids settled in. "I made lasagna."

"Starving," said Shane. "A bag of airplane peanuts just doesn't cut it."

Rae and Olivia agreed.

After dinner, Rae announced she had packed much-loved family games and we decided to play an old favorite—Barbie Uno.

"Uno," Mark said. We each laid down one more card before my husband yelled, "Out!"

Olivia rolled her eyes and everyone tossed their cards my way. I shuffled the stack.

"Make sure he's not sitting on cards," Rae said. "You know he cheats."

"Never!" Mark said in a voice that feigned hurt feelings.

Rae looked like Mark. She had soft olive skin, full lips, dark eyes, and thick brown hair. Her smile radiated charisma, just like her dad. And she was fearless; she called bullshit the moment she saw it. Even as a child, Rae was never afraid to speak her mind.

The cards were dealt, and a new game began.

"I want *your* hand," Shane said to Mark, and placed the swap card on top of the pile. "If you're cheating, I want in on the action. Hand 'em over, buddy."

Shane and Rae had started dating in high school. He was on the football team and Rae helped out as a student coaching assistant. She was crazy about him from the start. Traveling to the first team away game, they sat next to each other on the bus. When Rae told me about her new crush the next day, I could tell she was smitten. At six foot four, Shane towered over Rae by a foot. He had the build and the intimidating air of a defensive lineman, the kind of sixteen-year-old who looks like a grown man. Fortunately, he turned out to be the sweetest and most polite high school boy I had ever met. Mark and I grew to love him quickly.

Mark groaned and exchanged his three cards for the fistful that Shane offered.

"Look!" Olivia said, pointing under the table at Mark's foot, "I see cards down there!"

I smirked and raised my eyebrow at Mark, but he just shrugged his shoulders and looked perplexed.

"I must have dropped one—it was an accident!" Mark said. "Yeesh, cut a guy some slack."

Olivia smiled at Rae and Shane, and then the three of them started laughing.

"Framed!" Olivia cheered.

As the youngest, Olivia was most often the target of family pranks, not the instigator, and she looked pleased with her success.

"You deserve it, Dad," Rae said, "for all the times you really did cheat at Uno when we were kids."

"Ah, come on," Mark said. "Someday you girls will play a hundred games of Barbie Uno with your kids—just wait and see all the crazy tricks you'll pull to make it more interesting."

When Mark mentioned grandchildren, our eyes locked for a brief moment. Would we be so lucky?

Everybody laughed and my heart swelled. Living in Puerto Rico, and becoming an empty nester, had awakened a deeper appreciation for time spent with my family. I had been happy in the role of family caretaker, but I was starting to understand that my identity as a mother to adult children looked different than it did when we lived at River Acres in Sacramento. Our family was evolving. I loved my daughters fiercely and if Puerto Rico had taught me anything, it was that change facilitated opportunity.

"I hope you're not in any hurry," Rae said. "I certainly don't plan on starting a family anytime soon."

"Or *ever*," Olivia added, a look of disgust on her face.

"So . . ." Shane began, changing the subject. "What do you think of living in Puerto Rico? Was it worth it?"

"Better than expected," Mark said, and gave me a wink. "And yes, financially, it has been an excellent decision."

"I just wish we didn't have to sell River Acres," Olivia said softly.

"Me too. But change isn't always a bad thing." I looked at Mark. "It took me a while, but I understand that now."

I put my hand on top of Olivia's from across the table and gave it a squeeze. We were at different life stages. Our children's adult lives were just beginning. They were thinking about college graduation, starting careers, travel, friends, and fun. In contrast, we were thinking about retirement, buying and selling homes, and sending our yet-to-be-born grandchildren to college. Our daughters weren't thinking about the legacy they would leave behind, something Mark and I had discussed more often since moving to Puerto Rico. Would our decisions inspire professional creativity in our children? Would they ultimately think us courageous for relocating under Act 20 & 22, or crazy? Some things are impossible for parents to accurately impart because nobody acquires a lifetime of perspective until they have, well, lived a lifetime.

"See you in the morning," I said. The girls helped me put game cards back in boxes and I gave them each a big hug.

"Get some sleep," Mark added, "because tomorrow the fun starts!"

Mark wrapped his arms around my waist as soon as we entered our bedroom. We stood like that, pressed tightly together at the foot of our bed, quiet and happy. It had been a good night and our little condo had felt like a home.

CHAPTER 32:

CRYPTO PREDATORS

The next morning, as our kids awoke and meandered downstairs for coffee, Mark and I were waiting.

"Good morning," I greeted Olivia. She was followed by Rae and Shane.

I had set out a large platter of sliced mango and pineapple that looked like a child's drawing of the sun. Our kids grabbed a cup of coffee, one after the other, and sat down at the kitchen table.

"So today we get to plan our activities for the week," Mark began. "Puerto Rico is a perfect vacation spot and there's lots to do. I thought we should go over options and put together a schedule."

Mark reviewed highlights: snorkeling at beaches in Dorado, strolling through Castillo San Cristóbal and El Morro in Old San Juan, boating off the coast of Fajardo, hiking through caves in Arecibo, and surfing in Isabela. We also offered them an introduction to our crypto community.

Rae rubbed her eyes and looked toward the ocean. "I just need sunshine, so anything that gets us outside is good with me."

Olivia nodded.

"It all sounds awesome," Shane said. "And I definitely want to learn about crypto while I'm here."

"Me too," said Olivia. "The crypto thing sounds interesting. I'm game."

Olivia was a finance major and Shane was a business major, so we suspected a Crypto Tuesday event would pique their intellectual curiosity. Like many previous events, the Crypto Tuesday scheduled during their visit was held in the large outdoor space at Delavida restaurant. The speaker was Yaron Brook, chairman of the Ayn Rand Institute and host of *The Yaron Brook Show*. Even though I knew this speaker was likely to focus on political ideas in addition to finance, I hoped that exposure to our crypto community would give our kids a taste of the new things we were learning and a little more context for our life.

On the night of Crypto Tuesday, Rae had a college Zoom class to attend, so Mark and I climbed into the car with Olivia and Shane and drove to San Juan for our next adventure. Once we arrived, we found an empty picnic table on the outer edge of the deck and sat down. The weather was balmy. A light breeze blew at Olivia's long dark hair. She wore it straight, and it draped over her shoulder in a silky mass. When I sat across the table from Olivia, I felt stunned by her beauty. She looked, suddenly, like a woman, not my baby girl. Her crystal-blue eyes were bright against skin richly tanned from a day at the beach. Her hands, strong from many years of playing the violin, looked gentle with nails painted lavender. And my favorite feature, her Stanford-recessive-trait dimpled chin, added a bit of mischief to her otherwise perfectly delicate features.

"Would you like something to drink?" a waiter asked as he approached our table.

"I'll have a margarita," Olivia answered first for our group. I shot my daughter a mom look. The drinking age in Puerto Rico was eighteen, a fact that delighted my nineteen-year-old. I wanted her to enjoy her vacation, but I wasn't keen on her increased access to alcohol.

The rest of us ordered, then a crypto community member approached our table.

"Hi, I'm Derek," he began. "Do you mind if I take a seat at your table?" The venue was quickly filling up.

"No problem," I answered. "It's nice to meet you. I recognize you from past Crypto Tuesdays. I'm Georgine, and this is Mark, Shane, and Olivia."

I scooted over to make room for Derek, but he sat down next to Olivia.

Derek turned to my daughter. "It's a pleasure to meet you." He took her hand in his for what looked like a caress instead of a shake.

"I try not to miss these weekly events," he said. "This community is amazing, and I want to show my support as much as possible. I work closely with Brock Pierce now. We are starting a new bank and I am also working on a documentary. We'll debut at Sundance this year and we just locked up sponsorship deals with Cartier, Rolex, and Tesla."

"Sounds like the masses will relate well to your sponsors," Mark said, his tone mocking Derek. "Here's to DeFi democracy."

Derek clearly thought a lot of himself. The pride with which he dropped elite company names, and bragged about his crypto documentary, was a little nauseating. He radiated the crypto-super-rich vibe we had gotten used to in Dorado. I suspected that one of the Lamborghinis parked out front belonged to him. His clothing was European designer chic, his shoes looked handcrafted, and he carried an array of space-age electronic devices, perhaps to complement his expensive man-jewelry. He was in his early thirties and the muscled biceps that stretched the arms of his black T-shirt, and his chiseled jawline, were impressive. By the time Derek had finished outlining his latest banking venture with Brock Pierce, he had locked eyes with Olivia.

"So, what about you?" he asked my daughter.

Olivia led with a self-conscious giggle. "I'm here visiting my parents. I'm a student at UC Santa Cruz. I'm studying finance and economics."

"I got my degree in mathematics from Vanderbilt," Derek said. "But if I knew then what I know now, I wouldn't have wasted my time and money on college. If you want to be successful, everything you need to learn is right here." Derek conducted a visual scan of the Crypto Tuesday audience.

Great, I thought. *That's just the academic guidance every mother wants an attractive, wealthy hipster to give her youngest child.*

"A college degree never hurts," I said, but Derek and Olivia weren't paying attention to me.

Scott Windsor, the man who had hosted Crypto Tuesday from his penthouse terrace a few months back, was the MC for this Crypto Tuesday event since Julio was in Dubai working on a crypto deal. Scott welcomed the crypto community and then introduced Yaron Brook. Once the cameras signaled "ready," Scott held up his fingers for the 1, 2, 3 countdown and Crypto Tuesday began.

Yaron Brook was born and raised in Israel. His Wikipedia page proclaimed that he rejected socialism, embraced by his Jewish parents, for objectivism. This philosophy was explained by the Russian American writer Ayn Rand in her book *Atlas Shrugged* and posits that rational selfishness is a moral virtue and that altruism is evil. This paradigm explained Brook's opening sentiments, which criticized religious values and celebrated radical capitalism.

Brook had my attention, but not in a good way. I found his free-market ideology off-putting and his admiration for "radical capitalism" unsettling. Radical capitalism, I thought, sounded great if everyone started the game on the same playing field, but I didn't believe that was the case. I taught at one of the most diverse community colleges in the United States and was convinced that poverty and racism were woven into the fabric of our country. Fair was an illusion. I believed the same forces that Brook celebrated actually institutionalized white privilege in ways that made government structures, financial systems, and access to wealth unjust. This seemed especially true for Puerto Rico.

I leaned over to Mark and whispered, "What do you think my Re-Emerging Scholars students would say to this guy?"

"Hmm . . . Probably that white privilege is bullshit and that radical capitalism has really worked out well for them," he answered sarcastically. Then he let out a long, disgusted sigh.

I squeezed my husband's hand, grateful that like me, he found Brook's comments offensive.

"This guy!" I said into my husband's ear. "Makes my blood boil."

After Scott's interview with Yaron Brook began, Olivia excused herself for a restroom break. A few minutes later, Derek headed in the same direction. When Olivia returned, she slid into the seat next to me, snuggled up, and rested her head on my shoulder.

"Would it be all right if I went out with some friends after this is over?" she asked.

"What friends?" I questioned. "You don't know anyone in Puerto Rico."

Pangs of irritation made my jaw tighten. Even though the evening had cooled down nicely, I was suddenly hot.

"Derek and some friends are going out after this. Mom, this is the chance of a lifetime. When am I ever going to get an invite to party in San Juan with crypto millionaires?" she pleaded. "Besides, I'm nineteen. I'm legally an adult."

"You may be nineteen," I said, "but the answer is absolutely no."

The maternal warmth I felt when she first snuggled next to me turned into full-on parental frustration. Derek's aggressive pursuit of my daughter ignited a mama bear response.

Olivia's back stiffened and she crossed her arms tightly in front of her chest.

"You're being ridiculous," she said.

"Perhaps." Then I went to pay our tab at the bar. When I returned, I gathered my things.

"I think we should get out of here," I whispered to Mark.

"Agreed," he said with enthusiasm, and I knew he had overheard my exchange with our daughter.

"Shane," Mark said to Rae's boyfriend, "I think we're going to head out."

Olivia was silent on our drive home. Her outrage added heat to our already stuffy car.

"I have another proposal," Olivia told me privately back at home. We were standing in the kitchen before heading to our rooms for bed. "And you can even be there so you don't have to worry about my safety."

"Okay," I said, tentatively.

"Derek and I were texting and he invited me to a fire dancing lesson tomorrow night in La Perla. Apparently, his wife teaches fire dancing lessons and he and his girlfriend will both be there. You could come too. Just think about it before you say no. How fun would it be to take a fire dancing lesson?"

I remembered the naked fire dancers promoted at Julio's crypto camping weekend and thought about the incestuous nature of our crypto community.

"You do realize Derek just invited you to an event with his wife *and* his girlfriend," I repeated.

"So what?" she said. "I think it would be super fun."

YOLO was a refrain we heard often from Olivia. It was the acronym for "You only live once." In our family, it was Olivia who was the most driven to seek out excitement and adventure, the most like me as a young woman.

"Olivia, Derek is a jerk," I snapped. "He's a predator. What kind of thirty-something-year-old man invites a nineteen-year-old to hang out with his wife *and* his girlfriend? There is no way that I am going to facilitate a date between you and that entitled crypto asshole."

Olivia left the room, her heels stepping hard on the floor.

Most mothers were wired to save their daughters, to protect them from harm. I saved Olivia's kindergarten finger paintings, curly locks from her first haircut, plaster impressions of her little-girl hands, Mother's Day coupons and cards, prints of her tiny newborn feet, her favorite books, blankets, stuffed animals—I saved pieces of her young life and put them in a special box for safekeeping. But this kind of saving—from experiences I feared she was not yet prepared to manage—wasn't something mothers always got the chance to do.

Was I overstepping? Olivia handled herself well at college, but Derek wasn't some typical college boy. Derek's fire dancing invitation was an attempt to groom my daughter, and I wanted to save her from predatory forces even more than the fragments of her childhood in my keepsake box. At nineteen, I hoped she wasn't yet familiar with the precipice upon which she teetered, that knife edge of pornographic excitement, that space where a body is collected, splayed, and used like a commodity by others, where a young woman's confusion can be manipulated by men like Derek. My daughter was not just another cryptocurrency to be owned or traded. I wanted her body to serve her. I wanted her to feel empowered, free to explore her sexuality and own her decisions. *And* I wanted to protect her from the predatory behavior of this rich, entitled man.

This contradiction—the desire to protect my daughter from Derek while empowering her to make her own decisions about sexuality—resulted from my past. I knew the dark side of being naive yet thrust into compromising situations. I learned this lesson on a winter evening from a man named Stewart.

CHAPTER 33:

WINDOWS

I was nineteen and Stewart was twenty-nine when we went on our first date. We had met at a club, danced, ordered tequila shots, kissed, and agreed to go out. The next night, Stewart and I met at a bar called the Pine Cove. I liked his confidence, how he looked directly into my eyes, and his deep, husky voice. The way his attention landed on me, like warm water, felt thrilling.

The Pine Cove was dark and smoky but decorated inside with little red and orange twinkle lights that made the atmosphere feel festive. Stewart and I were drinking screwdrivers when Tammy, my cocaine-snorting, ex-high-school-boyfriend's sister, walked in with her date. After mostly living with my high school boyfriend and his family for a few months during my senior year, I knew that wherever anyone in the Rollins family went, cocaine followed. I hadn't had any in a few weeks and the thought of the white powder in Tammy's purse flooded me with eagerness. I invited them to join us.

After another round, Stewart suggested Tammy and her date hang out with us back at his apartment.

"Come with me," Stewart offered. "I don't live far from here and we can pick up your car later."

"Sure." I jumped in Stewart's car. Tammy and her date followed.

"How's your family doing?" I asked Tammy. We were sitting in Stewart's living room around a worn coffee table. "I miss seeing them."

"This is excellent," Stewart said after he snorted a line of cocaine off a rectangular piece of mirror sitting on top of the table. "Do you have an eight ball to spare?"

"No problem," Tammy said to Stewart. And then she said to me, "We miss having you around, Georgine, but Danny told us you're in college now and I'm happy for you. Sounds like a better decision than partying all the time at my house."

"Well, maybe a little partying doesn't hurt," I said, and snorted the next line off the mirror.

Flush with drugs, we split up—Stewart and I retreated to his bedroom and Tammy and her date took the living room. I didn't know Stewart well, but he was a great kisser and told hilarious stories about snowboarding in Lake Tahoe. Plus, I was high on cocaine and vodka, so familiarity seemed relatively unimportant.

"I'm going to use the restroom," Stewart said. He gave me a slow, focused smile and moved his eyes from my bare toes to the top of my head. "Why don't you lose some of those clothes before I get back?"

Take off my clothes? I hesitated and scanned Stewart's room. Records in old milk crates were stacked three crates high by the stereo system that blared INXS. A plastic pink hamper full of dirty clothes sat in one corner, a snowboard in another. Band posters were pinned to the walls and a musky-smelling mattress on the floor was his bed. Even though Stewart was a decade older than me, his furnishings screamed frat boy.

I debated Stewart's request to take off my clothes. Sleeping with a guy on the first date broke a rule in my imaginary book on dating. When I had broken this rule before, I regretted it; the sex had proved to be particularly unsatisfying and I spent the days following the encounter feeling bad about myself. Even though I found Stewart sexy as hell, what I really wanted was more cocaine, vodka, and kissing. I hadn't decided if Stewart was destined to be my next sexual partner, but I didn't want it to happen on our first date. I took a hairbrush, lipstick, and a mirror from my purse and refreshed my look. Even if I didn't have sex with Stewart—yet—I wanted him to want to have sex with me. Sometimes, the wanting was the best part.

I sat down on Stewart's bed, leaning back on one elbow, in a pose I thought provocative. Michael Hutchence sang about lovers never getting torn apart, the music so loud it made the mattress vibrate.

When Stewart didn't return from the bathroom, I stood, opened his bedroom door, and walked into the hallway, nearly tripping on the tangle of naked bodies at my feet.

"We've been waiting for you to join us," Stewart said, looking up at me from the inside of Tammy's wet thighs, his voice sultry, his face shiny. The order of people on the floor was Stewart, Tammy, and then Tammy's date. They were a three-person toppled-down totem pole, each one attached in some way to the other. Tammy's date, the body farthest from mine, lay stretched out on his belly; his white buttocks glowed in the dim light. He was propped up on one elbow so that he kissed Tammy's mouth and moved his other hand over her large breast. It took a minute for me to register what I was looking at, to make sense of the way arms, legs, and body parts connected in the narrow shadowy space.

"Well . . . huh . . . that's nice of you," I said.

My cocaine-infused heartbeat picked up the pace like a race car engine pushing the redline. I had never been in the presence of other people having sex before, let alone three people having sex together. I didn't have much experience with pornography. Drugs, alcohol, and singing "Happy Birthday" in my underwear? Yes. But watching people fuck? No. The graphic, feral-smelling, wet suction-sounding event flung my brain circuitry into overdrive.

I stood there, stunned, watching Stewart, my ex-boyfriend's sister, and some other guy, tearing it up like chimpanzees in an apartment hallway.

"Just give me a minute," I said as I headed back into Stewart's room and shut the door. My flesh was on fire, ignited by the sexual energy that leaked like smoke from underneath the shut door. I would never have to see these people again, I reasoned. I could satisfy the urge I had to rip off my clothes and jump into the middle of the writhing mass, and nobody would ever have to know. Nobody, except me.

At nineteen, sexual titillation wasn't the only thing that raged in my body while watching a live sex show in a hallway. I also felt sick, insecure, and frightened. I decided to escape out of the window in Stewart's room.

With shaking hands, I pushed out the screen and squirmed through the opening, scraping my knee and twisting my ankle. I must have hobbled more than three miles before I saw the green and white Pine Cove sign blinking in the distance—the spot where my night first began.

Please. Let my car be there.

I limped faster, wondering why I'd agreed to go out with Stewart in the first place. He was a creep. What kind of man leaves his date for the bathroom and starts having group sex in a hallway?

With each agonizing step, I told myself I had fucked up. I was too high to attend my 8 a.m. college class and would probably be too sick to make my restaurant shift that afternoon. Something was definitely wrong with my ankle, and I didn't have the money to go to a doctor. I was in a mountain of trouble.

At last, I saw it—my dented, rust-eaten Ford Fiesta. The car sat alone in the Pine Cove parking lot, covered with a thin layer of frost. Shivering, I unlocked the door and climbed into the driver's seat. My swollen ankle bulged above my right shoe, so I reached down to unbuckle the leather strap. Then I rested my pounding head on the steering wheel and cried.

The stink of stale vodka wafted from my mouth as a brutal hangover gripped my body like a straitjacket. Every inch of my skin hurt. I imagined the black ghost of death in the back seat of my chilly car, hovering and hungry, and cried harder.

That's when I heard her for the first time—my crossing guard. She said in a loud, clear voice, "Enough!"

I rubbed my throbbing temples while she continued, "You are responsible for your own choices. If you want a different life, you need to get it together, starting now."

It was like being snapped from a trance. What I had believed to be true one second was proven ridiculous in the very next. I wasn't building the successful future I had fantasized about in high school. I wasn't maximizing the potential my teachers said they had seen in me. Instead, I was a disaster. I had justified one risky decision after another. I had to stop!

Waking up from this dream state, I wondered if the ghost that hovered in the back seat was real. What if *I* was my own worst enemy? Neither the sexual assault I had endured nor the lack of parenting I had received was to blame for my drinking and drug use. It was me. I knew better.

New questions filled me: *Would I let secrets define my life? Would I repeat the cycle of poverty? Would I learn to face my demons?* Running icy fingers through my matted hair, I considered the kind of woman I would turn out to be if I continued climbing out of windows.

I took a deep breath and forced myself to turn toward the back seat and face the ghost whose presence haunted me. But there was nothing there.

No more, I promised. *No more drugs. No more wasted nights with men I don't know. No more dangerous jobs. No more escaping out windows.*

* * *

A few days after Olivia, Rae, and Shane headed back to California, I played pickleball with Deborah, and I asked her if she knew Derek, the man who had pursued my daughter at Crypto Tuesday.

"Handsome? Spiky hair? Always wears black?" she asked.

"That's the one," I confirmed. "Do you know him?"

"Well enough," she said, holding her racket.

Deborah seemed like she had more to say so I waited.

"Look. He's probably a nice guy and all, but he's not my cup of tea." She looked at the ground and adjusted the cap on her head.

"Scratch that," she continued. "To be honest, I think he's a snake. He wrote a book on tribal living, and I think all that tribal living bullshit is just an excuse for these crypto-rich guys to feel less guilty about the fact that they have sex with lots of different women. Call me old-fashioned but that lifestyle is bothersome. From what I've witnessed, it's much better for the rich men than it is for the women living in their harems."

I nodded in agreement.

When I finished my pickleball game with Deb, I went straight home and opened my laptop. The term "tribal living" had varied definitions, but I learned that Derek's definition promoted Western men forming polyamorous households or communities. Just like Julio, Derek collected women, and I was grateful that my daughter wasn't among them.

I closed my computer and zipped it into a black fabric case. Then I sat back in my chair and looked out the window at the ocean. Cryptocurrency had been good to me, I thought. Learning about cryptocurrency had served as an important distraction when I felt like a sad mother hen, stranded on an island, desperately missing her chicks. It ignited my fiscal curiosity, challenged my childhood scripting around money, and sparked interesting economic conversations with Mark. It introduced me to new technologies, like blockchain. And finally, it was profitable. In the first three months of trading cryptocurrency, I had doubled my money, taken profits, and knew that future wagers were on the house, so to speak. Buying and selling crypto was an important part of my financial life. I didn't plan to stop anytime soon.

Still, there was a lot about cryptocurrency, and the crypto community, that weighed heavily on me. For example, when I analyzed crypto white papers, I'd ask questions like, "What does this crypto do?" and "What problem does it solve?" But the answers weren't always clear. In contrast to Bitcoin, it seemed to me that a significant number of altcoins had make-believe value and weren't much use to people outside of select crypto cult-like groups.

I also experienced "frozen funds." One time, when I tried to sell tokens that had shot up in price during intense trading activity, Coinbase gave me an "apologies . . . but we are experiencing temporary technical problems" message. This happened at a moment when the price of my tokens was soaring; the trade would have been outstanding. Instead, I had my own private Robinhood moment.[15] And the news of crypto fraud? Literally endless. Perhaps these things would change with time, but after all my trading experience I still worried about market volatility, platform pitfalls, and security. Some days I thought investing in crypto was equivalent to putting my chips on red and watching the wheel spin!

Okay. I was being dramatic. It did feel a little like that in the beginning, when I first started trading crypto, but not now. Like any new skill, it got easier with practice, and adding crypto to one's financial portfolio was smart. I believed that there were important uses for Bitcoin and other cryptocurrencies, especially for people who lived in countries with unstable banking systems. There was undeniable risk, but the odds of making money trading crypto certainly exceeded those of betting on roulette. For myself, and other women operating in crypto spaces, this meant vigilance, not avoidance; informed decision-making, not reckless impulse.

More disturbing to me than observing crypto's demand for caution was what I uncovered about the misogynist attitudes that bubbled up in the cryptocurrency community I'd encountered, especially among the male leadership. Finance was a male-dominated, hyper-masculine industry, and this was especially true for cryptocurrency—not good for women.

The sexism was concerning and I didn't believe in rational selfishness or that altruism was evil, like Yaron Brook. I didn't agree with the libertarian ideals that underpinned crypto community conversations. I didn't appreciate the promotion of excessive drug use at community camping getaways. And after Derek tried to prey on my nineteen-year-old daughter, I was done with Crypto Tuesday events in Puerto Rico. There were many kind and interesting people in this community,

---

15. In February of 2021, Robinhood, an online commission-free brokerage trading platform, made the decision to halt GameStop buying activity.

but I'd met others who prioritized self-interest over the common good.

After my initial crypto enthusiasm—after inhaling the hopeium dust for months—I felt inoculated. It wasn't magic. Learning how to trade crypto changed my financial future, and it could certainly do the same for others, but it wasn't as mysterious as I originally thought. The primary requirements were a willingness to learn a new skill, assess crypto company white papers, and critically evaluate the historical trends of coins, tokens, and crypto commentary.

I hoped that in the future, more women would emerge as leaders in crypto spaces. Learning to trade crypto could change women's financial lives for the better, and I wanted us to support one another in this effort. Unlike the advice I gave my daughter, Abby, regarding her O Chem efforts, I would look back on learning how to trade crypto as one of the *best* decisions I ever made.

I left my kitchen table, the spot where I had been sitting, and walked onto my patio to take in the spectacular day. A pair of pelicans soared above the water hunting fish, each catch executed with deadly precision, while parrots gossiped in the nearby palm trees. Even though my feelings about cryptocurrency had shifted—from curiosity to awe to awareness—my life in Puerto Rico with Mark was only just beginning. And it was beautiful.

CHAPTER 34:

PERSPECTIVE

It all happened fast. After we hired Kim as our Sacramento real estate agent, she quickly transformed our vacant, dusty River Acres house into a showpiece. Before the month's end, she procured two purchase offers and we scheduled a phone meeting to discuss the potential buyers.

Mark and I were sitting next to each other on the living room couch when the phone rang. After we exchanged pleasantries, Kim got straight to the point. She communicated offer amounts and I looked at Mark with shocked wide eyes.

"Even though the second submission is above asking, I think the first offer is the strongest," Kim went on. "An all-cash buyer willing to pay your asking price is golden. With this proposal, loan-related appraisals are a non-issue."

Mark grabbed a pad of paper off the coffee table and scribbled oversized digits in bold red ink; the numbers he wrote down comprised most of the space on the sheet.

My jaw dropped. "I can't believe these offer amounts. Holy cow!"

I thought about the numbers Mark had written down when we first spoke with Kim: a dream price, a likely price, and a rock-bottom option. I had hoped to land in the "likely" zone and considered Mark's dream price ridiculous, but to my surprise, that's where we ended up.

Mark put his paper pad back on the table next to his phone, looked at me, and smiled. Then he wove his fingers through mine.

"This is terrific news, Kim. Thank you for all your hard work." Mark gave my hand an enthusiastic squeeze.

"You're welcome," she said. "It's not just me, however—I have an amazing team."

The red numbers on Mark's legal pad were intoxicating.

"Well, please thank your team on our behalf," I said, overwhelmed by the news.

"I will." Kim cleared her throat. "But getting back to your options . . . It's been a while since a house sold along the river, so comps could be a problem with the second offer. I think the peace of mind that accompanies an all-cash process is valuable."

"What about responding to the cash buyer with a counter offer?" Mark asked. "We have an above-asking price possibility, so it's a legitimate question."

Kim hesitated. She explained that with a counter we risked offending the cash buyer because he offered full price. If that happened, she warned, he might walk out the door.

"Understood," Mark said. "George and I need to talk, but we'll get back to you by the end of the day."

Mark ended the call and gave me a hug.

"I guess this is really happening," I said. My feelings were hard to pinpoint, a mix of sorrow over selling our family home and exhilaration over the money we were about to realize. I embodied equal and opposite ends of an emotional yardstick.

"Just goes to show you what houses are selling for in parts of California," Mark said, "since both of our offers came from people relocating, one from San Francisco and another from Los Angeles. Home prices in the Bay Area and So Cal are obscene, but they make River Acres look like a bargain. That's why I think we should counter. I don't know this person's story, but if he has that much cash lying around, money isn't an issue. If he wants the house, he'll cough up the extra dollars."

Mark sounded like he was ready to mediate a case settlement.

"What about what Kim said?" I asked. "Do we want to risk offending him?"

"I doubt that's a serious concern," Mark said. "The worst thing that's likely to occur is that he'll reject our counter. If that happens, we'll circle back and accept his original offer."

Mark shifted on the couch and paused for a moment to look out at the ocean. He had a pleased look on his face, like he had just put his chess opponent in checkmate.

"In some respects, I like that scenario even better," he said. "The buyer knows his all-cash offer carries weight and if he thinks he avoided a bidding war, he's less likely to nickel-and-dime us after inspections. People are more cooperative if they think the other side has already made concessions. Everybody wants to be a winner."

"According to that logic, we win either way," I said.

Mark's negotiating expertise relaxed me. I took a deep breath and looked into my husband's dark eyes.

"Okay. I trust your instincts," I said. "It seems worth the gamble."

Mark leaned over and gently kissed my lips. Butterfly wings tickled my stomach.

"I think we should celebrate," he said, and kissed me again, longer this time. "It's not every day you make enough money to afford an early retirement, Professor Hodgkinson."

"If this is an attempt to keep me from whining about the fact that I already miss my house, it's working," I said, and kissed him back.

"Are you suggesting I have ulterior motives?" Mark asked in a playful voice.

"Sounds like you win either way," I teased.

"That's my specialty," he replied.

I followed Mark upstairs, toward our bedroom, thinking about love and money. My favorite stories pitted one force against the other: The protagonist had to make a choice. Would she choose the object of her desire, a love match and a life where she was poor but happy? Or would she relinquish love in the name of duty to appease her family, her kingdom, and secure wealth instead of a soulmate?

The protagonist was not supposed to get both, but that's how I felt, like a storybook rogue whose good fortune shone in both directions. I had grown up believing that regular people didn't get to live such a life. After all, the odds of winning a lottery jackpot were one in 300 million. It was twice as likely that a person would get struck by lightning. When I considered the winding, pothole-filled road my life had traveled—down the long highways of poverty, off the dangerous cliffs of adolescence, and through the dry deserts of divorce—I couldn't believe that I had ended up at this extraordinary destination. It took perseverance, luck, and a willingness to take risks.

* * *

"Stay out of trouble," Mark said. At the airport, he pulled my suitcase from the trunk, gave me a hug, and kissed my

COVID mask. Then he joked, "I've seen the mischief you can cause when you're visiting your mom."

"No promises," I said. "You know my mother. If she has her way, we'll be drinking margaritas with sombreros on our heads by lunchtime tomorrow."

Mark smiled. He got a kick out of my mother's spunky personality and she adored my husband.

"Seriously, enjoy this time with your mom. I know she has really missed you since we moved to Puerto Rico."

"I've missed her too," I said. "Good luck with Sal. If anyone can get a deal with an old mobster across the finish line, it's you, counselor."

Mark gave me a final hug and I headed inside the airport terminal. The all-cash buyer came through and we had closed on the River Acres house. We were five days into a thirty-day escrow. Mark was a few weeks shy of meeting his Act 20 & 22 residency requirements, so I was going back to California to manage the packing tasks while he stayed on the island. After packing up River Acres, I planned to stay at my mom's house a few miles away.

I wasn't the only one who would be busy in the coming weeks. Mark had tasks of his own to complete. He and Sal had finally agreed on the terms of the condo sale and were working with attorneys to finalize paperwork, but one hurdle remained: the transfer of funds. Sal was miffed that Mark wouldn't fly the cash to Panama and they hadn't agreed on a funds transfer process.

I checked in, boarded, and headed for Miami, the first leg of my flight back to Sacramento. Out the window I watched my island home get smaller until it was a chunk of brown rock in a turquoise sea. The pilot announced the altitude over the intercom, and I pulled my window shade down, closed my eyes, and thought about how the passage of time changed relationships. Decades could take the broken shards of the past, melt them down, and set them into a new design.

"Thanks for helping me, Mom," I'd said on the phone the week prior. I had just purchased a plane ticket to California.

"Of course!" Mom responded excitedly. "You're always invited to stay with me. I'm happy I'll get you all to myself for a few weeks. We have months' worth of lunch dates to catch up on."

Maggie and Zoey barked in the background and Mom shushed them sweetly.

"I'm sure I don't say it enough, but I really appreciate you. Dealing with the sale of River Acres is so much easier with your help. Plus, I know I can always count on you for support. That means more than you know."

My voice cracked and my eyes felt wet. I couldn't wait to see my mom.

"Oh, I get it. And you're welcome. Life was so damn challenging when your dad and I split up. We've both come a long way, Georgine." She paused. "And I'd do anything for you. You know that, right?"

After I'd hung up the phone, I saw those early challenges like movie clips: the sexual assault I hid, the cocaine I greedily snorted, and strip shows I gave at birthday and bachelor parties. For years I blamed my troubled adolescence on poverty and a lack of parental guardrails. Now, when I thought of those times, I simply watched them. They were just what happened; the assignment of fault didn't matter. Not really. There was no universe in which my poor choices were weighed against a lack of resources or my mom's post-divorce parenting. A mythical tally only served to keep me distanced from my mother and myself.

I saw this phenomenon with my RES students. When they let go of blame, when they were able to talk about their past as something that simply happened, they seemed freer. As long as their story oozed with shame, or self-righteous indignation, they stayed trapped by the events that had landed them in prison. Life had pulverized my Re-Emerging Scholars, but self-loathing, or a desire for revenge, blocked their journey to a different, better life. A neutral witness perspective created space for these students to reconnect with themselves and form new healthy relationships with others.

Relationships fascinated me. Some people said that academics studied the thing that challenged their early life, the thing they needed to figure out about themselves. Hypothetically, the anxiety-ridden child turned toward psychology, and the youngster who got cancer, medicine. I taught communication studies because human connection, and how we become who we are, helped me to understand my adolescent patterns. My relationship with my mother became a case study I devoured for years. Its complexity and unpredictability kept me searching for deeper understanding. Over time, however, my scholastic awareness turned into something much more valuable: acceptance. My mother was a complicated character in the story of my life, but she was mine and I loved her.

I have had three different mothers during my fifty years. The first was just eighteen when she married my father and barely twenty when I was born. This mother had grown up a Stanford, a family that wielded power and social clout instead of compassion. To make up for the slights she endured, this mother showered me with kindness. She knew the importance of holding me close because, as a child, she had not been held. She embraced her role as my protector because she had not been protected. This mother tended to me when I was sick, rocked me when I couldn't sleep, and wrapped me tight in maternal warmth. She promised to love me in all the ways she wished she had been loved by her parents.

When I was nine years old, this mother began to disappear, and a frustrated, ill-tempered, and unpredictable woman took her place.

"I work all goddamn day and come home to this mess?" she'd scream.

The familiar scene made me feel sick. I'd come home from high school to find my mom drinking wine and tearing around the kitchen. I could see anger rise from her head like steam off an active volcano.

This second mother, the one that struggled after her divorce, was angry and desperate. She forgot about her pledge to reinvent the ugly family traditions of her Stanford clan. Like her progenitors, this mother turned to alcohol, drugs, and sex for distraction and relief. She wanted more for herself than the poverty that accompanied her single-parent life, and she struggled to balance the responsibility of guardianship with insatiable desire. The urges this mother repressed in her adolescence, responses to a domineering, alcoholic father, erupted with volcanic intensity when she got divorced. Like a toddler who craved attention, she acted out against perceived injustice. Against scarcity and wanting. Against a life that proved more difficult than she had anticipated.

I didn't meet my third mother until she became a grandmother. By then, she was in her fifties and had married the man who sent her flowers after their first date. She was correct that day she called to tell me her news, the day I regretted answering the phone. This man *was* different from the others she had dated; he was better in every way. The moods and vices my mother brandished during my adolescence didn't dissolve with a second marriage, but they decreased. She still yelled plenty, but throwing food, dishes, and toys was a thing of the past. Or maybe it just seemed that way. I didn't live with my mother's new family, her husband and his kids. I was already living on my own. But from my perspective, my mom had started to transform.

I was nineteen when my mother walked down the aisle for the second time and another family was made. Mom's new husband had two young children, a girl and a boy, almost the same ages my brother and I were when she divorced my father. Before she remarried, she confided in me that she didn't much like raising children the first time, and that she hadn't planned on doing it again. While her orientation toward parenting complicated her choice to remarry, making this new family was the best decision my mother had made in a very long time.

"It's finally just us!" my mother had exclaimed when my youngest sibling left for college. "Me and my husband."

My mother and I had met for lunch, and sandwiches in red plastic baskets sat between us on a wobbly table.

"I guess I just realized you've never had that before. A 'just us' stage of life. You got married and became a mother so soon after. You've only ever been a woman who's divorced with children or married with children. But always—with children." I thought about that timeline. Mom had parented or co-parented for almost thirty-five years. "What are you guys going to do to celebrate?"

"Enjoy each other. And the quiet." She was silent for a moment. "Then travel. Take weekend biking trips. Have more dinners out with friends . . . I don't really care. But it feels great to start our empty nester life together."

I took a sip of water and rubbed my large belly. This transition, when my mom and my stepfather became empty nesters, happened at the same time I was about to give birth to my first child.

"Plus," she continued, "it will give me more time to help you with your baby. I never really knew my grandparents, but I want my grandchildren to know me."

We finished our lunch and hugged in the parking lot, my middle smashed between us like a beach ball. This was the moment my third mother appeared.

This grandmother-mother, and her loving second husband, were exuberant when my daughter Abby was born. They rearranged their work schedules to help me and my first husband with childcare, read Abby all her favorite stories, and delighted in each new baby step and stage. This grandmother-mother rocked Abby like my first mother had rocked me, in arms that radiated love and safety. After marrying her second husband—a damn fine man, I liked to say—my mother's ability to love others increased exponentially.

This grandmother-mother has been mine for more than twenty years now. Her Stanford flair—marked by a zest for life mixed with stubborn determination—has enriched my adult life. And even though this mother lost her true love to cancer, the impact of my stepfather lives on in my mother's kinder, gentler ways.

I've heard self-identity described as a rubber band: Life stretched us, but our natural tendency was to bounce back to our original shape. That may be true when we're young, I thought, when we're likely to snap back into what feels comfortable without thinking, but at a certain point that metaphor fell apart. Most of us snapped. Maybe we were more like a ball of yarn? The years knitted us into sweaters, hats, gloves . . . then unraveled us. After each unraveling, we were wound up into balls of grief or joy, over and over, until we understood that impermanence was woven into the fiber of our being. We came to understand that change was inevitable, not just in life but in ourselves.

I wondered if this experience—watching one's parent transform into a different person—was what people meant when they said you don't appreciate your parents until you become one yourself. Perhaps a little. But mostly, I believed my mother grew up and changed. She finally got lucky in love and she left her frustrated, unhappy single-parent self behind. I understood evolving identities. None of us were the same person we were at twenty or thirty or forty. I was no longer a cocaine-snorting singing-stripping-telegram-girl, and she was no longer an angry divorcée. We knew each other's secrets and loved each other in spite of our past bad decisions. I hoped like me, she felt lighter, and freer, for having let her old identities transform into new ones.

CHAPTER 35:

LETTING GO

"Hi, Mom! It's so good to see you." I dropped the handle on my suitcase and rushed into my mother's arms in the loading zone of the Sacramento airport.

"Oh, sweetheart, it's good to see you too! Dear God, have I missed you."

Travelers bustled around us, a rush of energy. I just wanted to be with her alone. I wanted to reconnect.

"Let's get out of here," I said. "Can I throw my bags in your trunk?"

Mom hit a button on her car keys and the trunk popped open.

"Thanks," I said. "It feels good to be in California."

Mom headed for the I-5 and I relaxed into the passenger seat.

"How's Mark?" she asked, easing into traffic.

"Good. But he's still wrestling with Sal over a few final condo purchasing details. That old mobster wants everything his way."

All the hoops we had to jump through to appease Sal were maddening. He walked away from sale negotiations with Mark multiple times before he finally signed a contract. He was a bully until the end.

"Sounds like my father. And your dad. I think it's probably how most men from my generation are. They grew up believing they were the boss. Still do."

"It's exasperating," I said.

"At least there's hope for men in the next generation. Thank God for #MeToo." Mom turned on the car radio and pop music poured out of the speakers. "Speaking of the next generation, the girls should be here in a few hours. Just like old times!"

When I was a single parent, Mom and I would take Abby and Olivia on what we called "mini G-ma vacays." We'd screamed together on the Matterhorn at Disneyland and caught crawdads on the shores of Lake Tahoe. My daughters were close with their grandma, just as she had predicted when I was pregnant with Abby.

"Thanks for organizing dinner, Mom. Eden and Rae have to work, but I'm grateful to have Abby and Olivia's help packing River Acres, especially since it requires they miss a day of classes and drive here from the Bay."

I gazed at my mom and smiled. She looked much younger than her seventy-two years and I hoped I'd look as youthful at her age. The love I felt for this grandmother-mother was vast. We'd weathered plenty of rough seas, but now our relationship felt inviting, just like the gentle waves on the shores of my new island home.

At Mom's house, a few hours later, Abby and Olivia arrived.

"Hey, girls," I cheered when they walked through the door.

I hugged them both and kissed their cheeks. Before I got weepy, I encouraged them to grab pizza and salad from the counter.

"You'll need all those carbs tomorrow for packing!" I joked.

Abby laughed. "This looks delicious."

"I'm starving," said Olivia. "Thanks for dinner, Grandma."

The girls filled their plates while Mom and I cleared boxes and books from the table.

"What's all this?" Abby asked.

"Photos of our family," Mom replied. "I've been meaning to organize these old pictures for ages and your mom was helping me."

We'd spent the afternoon sorting scrapbooks and loose photographs into piles. The images spanned generations of Stanford life. I found myself drawn to the black-and-white portraits, the ones that smelled damp and had yellowed with age. The people in these pictures served as portals to another family dimension. The images didn't make me feel warm, like the mother and daughters eating pizza by my side, but they did connect me to an ancestral web and added to my expanding definition of home.

Home, I came to realize, was wherever my people were. It was a place inside me that lit up, that actually ignited, in the presence of familial connection. Home existed when I was with the family to which I was born, the family I made, or the family I blended with Mark. Home got to be in all the spaces I occupied with the people I loved. It was where I belonged. When it came to going home, neither the location nor the container mattered.

* * *

"I think that's the last of it," I said. Mark helped me squeeze the final boxes into our storage pod. "I'll let my mom know we'll make it to her house by dinner."

The storage pod had been delivered the day before Mark arrived in California and it sat like a mini garage in the driveway of our home. I decided to keep a few pieces of furniture, some carefully wrapped art, and a dozen boxes containing personal effects and family photos. Everything else? Gone. I had expected to agonize over a downsizing process of such magnitude, but it was easier than I anticipated. Abby and Olivia had made the experience fun.

"Take whatever you want," I'd offered, opening closet and kitchen cupboard doors. "I'm having an estate sale next week and the rest gets donated."

"Yes!" Olivia cried. "Dibs on the vacuum cleaner. My roommates are gonna be stoked! Sweeping the rug doesn't exactly work all that well."

"Gross! None of your roommates has a vacuum cleaner?" I laughed. "Abby, what about you? No, wait. Let me guess. Baking supplies!"

"Absolutely!"

We organized, packed things into boxes, and sang along to our favorite songs, which we blared at high volume throughout the house. Compared to all the other times I'd moved in my life, this was the first that didn't seem ominous, like walking down a dark hallway toward inevitable doom.

It turned out that a year in Puerto Rico, a period in which I lived in a small condominium, had lessened my need for the trappings of a large home. It made me want less, not more. *What sane person even needed this many things?* I wondered as I stuffed bag after bag with Salvation Army donations. I hadn't planned to accumulate so much stuff, but there it was: proof of where I had put my attention for a decade. Getting rid of it felt good. Thanks to my crypto earnings, my bank account had never looked better, so it was ironic—this desire I had to declutter and dematerialize my life.

Standing in front of River Acres, I told Mark, "I didn't know we had so much stuff before I started packing, but it feels satisfying to downsize into a single Pod."

He pulled the Pod door down with a thud and secured it with a padlock.

"It gets picked up tomorrow," I added, "and then we really are free."

"I know that living out of a suitcase until Sal's condo is remodeled isn't ideal," Mark said, "but it's exciting to think we can travel for a while, visit family and stay in towns we've always been curious about. Being empty nesters in a world of remote work is an adventure."

"Will we ever stop calling the condo 'Sal's place'?" I asked.

"I'm sure we will, but we have a long way to go on the demolition front before it will feel like ours," Mark said. "I'm just relieved the sale process is over. You're not going to believe the threatening voicemails Sal left for me during the forty-eight hours he had to wait while the money transferred from my bank account into his lawyer's. He's not used to waiting for cash, doesn't trust the Internet, and I think he was worried I'd try to pull a fast one."

"Makes sense. Just look at the folks he's done business with all his life."

"Even though that guy is old," Mark said, "he can still sound damn scary."

We walked over to the hose. It was hooked to a spigot in the front yard so we rinsed off our dirty hands. River Acres was clean and empty, ready to turn over to the buyer. Now that the last of the boxes were out of the garage, it was time to say goodbye.

"I have loved this house," I said, shaking water from my hands and looking up at the beautiful home. "I hope the new owner finds as much joy here as we have over the years."

Mark put his arm around me and I could feel the wet imprint of his hand on my shoulder.

"Except for finding our dog a new family," Mark said, "everything about this year has gone darn near perfect for me."

"I'm glad you're happy and I think Lucy will forgive us," I said. "She was lonely after the kids left, and now she is surrounded by people who love her."

"And *that's* what matters," Mark said and kissed my messy hair.

We stood side by side in the driveway of our home. We were quiet for a moment, each of us saying a private, nostalgic farewell.

"It was good for me to come here alone and pack up this house," I said, breaking the silence.

"Yeah?"

"It gave the girls and me a chance to spend time together and all the purging felt like some kind of new age letting-go ritual," I explained. "There were moments of sadness, but by the end, I was singing and packing at the same time. And now that it's done, I've never felt lighter."

I remembered the stipulations I had levied before agreeing to Mark's Puerto Rico relocation plan. I had insisted that selling this house was a deal-breaker. When I thought about this conversation, I imagined another version of myself, one that was driven by a fear of change and a desperate need for security. I didn't believe all my shortcomings had evaporated into thin air. It wasn't like my need for control simply vanished because I moved to Puerto Rico and learned how to trade crypto. But I felt less attached to my to-do list, closer to my husband, and willing to take risks.

Separation from my family home, professional environment, and patterned daily behaviors had loosened my wiring. The little girl me, the one raised by an angry, overworked single mom, felt held by the woman I was becoming. She felt safe in her own skin. And the adolescent me, the part that ran wild and was filled up with secrets and shame, felt worthy of forgiveness. The skeletons she hid when it came to drugs and taking off her clothes in front of leering men were just what happened.

The woman who stood in the driveway of River Acres was openhearted. Her spirit felt spacious. She appreciated her scrappy adolescent self and cherished her identity as a mother. She welcomed her crypto trader self and valued her roles as professor and wife. All of these selves seemed auspicious in their own way. They were old and new pieces of a messy, authentic life and as they matured, they transformed or fell away. This created space for all the identities yet to come. I was all of these women and none of them, since each passing moment changed everything.

Mark pulled me close. We gazed at River Acres, my body pressed against his, listening to the sounds of squirrels running up the walnut trees behind us.

"This might look like the end of an era," he said, "but it's just the beginning for us."

"A year ago, I didn't think I wanted our lives to be different, but now I'm grateful that they are."

I felt the truth of these words in my body and knew that accepting change was the only way to really live.

EPILOGUE

As I write this, looking out at the Atlantic from my patio, I feel the salty freedom that comes from living at the ocean's edge. Almost five years have passed since the conclusion of this memoir and I am reminded of how we are never the same people we once were. The point in time that this story takes place—a year in which I struggled with geographic relocation, changes to my mothering identity, and learned to trade crypto—is in the rearview mirror. Even though my fifties began with an earthquake in San Juan, they have become my favorite decade. It is a joy to watch my daughters mature into fascinating women and exhilarating to ask, "What's next?" Midlife is truly an adventure—a trek through uncharted territory where the maps of youth no longer apply, and we navigate by different stars. While my days of climbing out windows are long gone, the doors before me hold promise.

Mark and I continue to split our time between Puerto Rico and California. In the beginning this lifestyle seemed geographically demanding, but with practice, it has developed into a comfortable rhythm. Starting the early retirement program at my college helped—I teach during the fall semester, which leaves me free to write the rest of the year while living in the Caribbean. Not bad for a poor kid who used to hunt through couch cushions for loose change. Thanks to my husband's support and to my own cryptocurrency accomplishments, I finally have my dream job: writer. My days are filled with meandering words, and my weeks burst with the stories they make.

Like my personal and professional changes, legislation in Puerto Rico has matured. Act 20 & 22 have turned into Act 60, with expanded tax incentives for those interested in minimizing federal tax obligations while maintaining US citizenship[16]. If you're curious, Puerto Rico's Department of Economic Development posts this legal code on their website, but you can also find plenty of articles online that summarize Act requirements.

The world of crypto has also transformed. With the election of the "Crypto President" in 2024, cryptocurrency popularity and acceptance have exploded—so much so that for the first time in history we have a US president with his own crypto ($TRUMP is a meme coin housed on the Solana blockchain platform[17]). While these and other developments in the world of crypto raise challenging regulatory and other questions, they also suggest that the future of global finance includes crypto.

Another important crypto change since writing this memoir happened in the years-long SEC v. Ripple legal case. Ripple

---

16. For more information about Act 60, visit Puerto Rico's Department of Economic Development and Commerce at https://incentives.ddec.pr.gov or read the legal code at https://bvirtualogp.pr.gov/ogp/Bvirtual/leyesreferencia/PDF/2-ingles/60-2019.pdf.

17. A meme coin is a type of cryptocurrency that is inspired by Internet memes, jokes, or popular culture. Unlike other cryptocurrencies that might aim to solve specific financial or technological problems, meme coins often begin as satirical projects. Their value is primarily driven by social media buzz, community engagement, and speculation.

(whose cryptocurrency, you'll recall, is XRP) reached resolution in 2025. The outcome? Ripple agreed to pay a $125 million civil penalty, significantly less than the SEC's initial request. Pundits argue that the outcome of this case signifies a friendly shift in the digital currency landscape, and I agree. Just as Mark had predicted, the result of this lawsuit was a slap on the wrist. In July of 2025, XRP's value had increased by 1,605 percent since the day I started The Experiment in 2020. Wow!

One development since writing this book has caused me feelings of melancholy. Our dear friends and neighbors, Alberto and Ana, moved to Florida. This occurred a few months after they were married in a lovely ceremony at sunset in San Juan. Alberto's family sold their home in Playa Tortuga, for a record price, to an Act 60 transplant. Alberto and Ana have joined other young, educated Puerto Ricans—part of the ongoing Puerto Rican diaspora—who have relocated to the mainland because of devastation from Hurricane Maria and limited professional employment opportunities on the island. They are missed.

Finally, the way I understand the island of Puerto Rico has evolved. Its status as a US territory became a powerful symbol for me during the writing of this book. Puerto Rico embodies the liminal spaces my memoir explores—neither fully one thing nor another. Just as the island exists between statehood and independence, I found myself between my past and future, between my growing privilege and a developing awareness of economic inequality that impacts the island. This complexity continues to inspire writing, reflection, and a desire to support the island and its native inhabitants.

The first half of my fifties has been a sweet mix of self-acceptance, discovery, and financial opportunity. Life as an empty nester feels liberating, unexpectedly fruitful, and lively. I enjoy my relationships and my work more deeply, and at a pace that seemed less available when I was a full-time college professor and busy mom. If you're familiar with this middle stage of life, I hope you're knitting your current self into a form that fits, and if you're not quite there, I highly recommend unraveling. Beautiful patterns of possibility await.

RESOURCE GUIDE:

QUESTIONS TO CONSIDER BEFORE YOU BUY, TRADE, OR SELL CRYPTO

I am not a financial advisor or a cryptocurrency whiz. I am, however, a professor of communication studies, which means I teach classes that focus on the relationships we have with others and ourselves. I understand how scary it feels for a gal to push herself out of her comfort zone. When it comes to crypto (or love, for that matter), I advise taking things slowly and checking in with yourself along the way.

If you're like me and interested in trying new things (especially when those activities have the power to change one's financial life for the better), I think there are some initial steps to consider. First, do your homework. There are lots of books, articles, videos, and podcasts on trading crypto, and I'd encourage you to spend some time getting familiar with the basics of this environment (e.g. blockchain, trading platforms, security, etc.). Before you transfer your hard-earned dollars to Coinbase, or someplace else, prepare by doing some research.

Second, conduct a self-analysis of your risk tolerance. With all investments, there is risk, but the crypto environment is particularly volatile. If the mere thought of market volatility makes you vomit, cry, or scream, you might not be well-suited to this environment. Tell yourself, "Crypto is not my thing and that's okay!"

If you've read this far, and you're still thinking about buying some crypto, here are a few questions I'd encourage you to ask yourself first:

1. What amount can I afford to lose? Covering your essential expenses and adding to your personal emergency fund take precedence over adding "crypto trader" to your list of personal accomplishments.
2. Am I prepared for market volatility? Buying crypto isn't like investing in a mutual fund. With mutual funds, someone else is responsible for buying/selling/trading stocks that comprise the fund. When it comes to crypto, you are your own fund manager.
3. What percentage of my investment portfolio will constitute crypto? The answer to this question may be complicated by age as well as risk tolerance.
4. How long do I plan to hold the crypto I buy? The crypto landscape is changing at a rapid pace. While Bitcoin might make sense to hold for the long term, the majority of cryptocurrencies demand a watchful eye.
5. Do I understand the crypto I'm buying? Is it a coin or a token? What purpose does it serve? What did I learn from reading its whitepaper?

6. What are the tax implications of selling crypto in my state and country?
7. Do I have a plan for when to sell or take profits?

DISCUSSION QUESTIONS

1. This story begins with an earthquake that makes Georgine wonder if she experienced a nimitta—an omen or sign of things to come. Georgine interprets this message to mean her life is about to change dramatically. Do you believe in nimittas, or do you have superstitions?
2. Moving to Puerto Rico under Act 20 & 22 is challenging for Georgine but exciting for her husband, Mark. How would you navigate a challenge like this in a relationship? Would you consider moving to a Caribbean island for tax advantages?
3. When Georgine visits Sierra Gardens, the house where she lived during high school, she remembers the details of being sexually assaulted. She also feels angry at her younger self for keeping silent. Regarding sexual violence, how have social attitudes and resources for victims changed over time?

4. What are your experiences with cryptocurrency? If you don't already own crypto, would you consider owning this digital asset?
5. Georgine studies cryptocurrency as a distraction from missing her daughters and her life in California. What strategies have you used to survive challenging times in your life?
6. Have you ever learned a new skill that was outside your comfort zone? If you had the opportunity to start learning a new skill today, what would it be?
7. Throughout this book, Georgine meets formerly incarcerated people and works with formerly incarcerated students at her college. What are your experiences with justice-impacted people in your family or community?
8. When Mark offers to help Georgine financially—so the couple can purchase Sal's condo and Georgine can start an early retirement program—the couple's previous financial agreements are revised. Is this good for their marriage? Why or why not?
9. The devastating impacts of Hurricane Maria are explored when Ana and Alberto share their experiences. Have you ever experienced a natural disaster? What lessons do natural disasters teach us? How are the impacts of natural disasters different for economically disadvantaged communities?
10. Throughout this story, Georgine struggles with selling her family home and downsizing. Once this happens, however, she feels freedom in letting go. Have you ever downsized? What was this experience like for you?

11. Mother-daughter relationships are explored in this story. Georgine feels that she has had three mothers during her lifetime. What distinct phases have you experienced with your parents or caregivers?
12. On the topic of identity, Georgine believes that "impermanence is woven into the fiber of our being" and that we are not the same person at twenty, thirty, or forty. How would you categorize major shifts over the decades of your own life?

ACKNOWLEDGMENTS

I would never have completed this memoir without a tremendous amount of support. I am grateful to friends who cheered me on, writing teachers who helped me develop my craft, and the family members who encouraged my efforts and gave me their blessing to share these stories. There are many people who deserve acknowledgment:

Heather and Michael Blair, Chris Brown, The Cool Chicks of Puerto Rico, Brenna Curtis, Barbie and Phil Elsasser, Stacy Holman Jones, Jennifer Simms, J.D. and Mary Lasica, Tany Nguyen, The Regency Book Club, Rasha Salama, Felix and Eimee Seda, Mia Shepherd, Micki Singer, Pauline Stahl, Nadene Uys, Eddie Vasconcellos, and Sandra Wheeler-Abeyta, thank you for encouraging me when I told you I was working on a memoir and for giving me empathy when I complained of my challenges. I appreciate the advice and the adventures—in California and in Puerto Rico.

To my RES students, thank you for inspiring me. Your commitment to your education, in spite of the challenges you face each day, makes being your teacher an honor.

To Brooke Warner and Linda Joy Myers, thank you for teaching your memoir class. It was an incredible experience and just the inspiration I needed to write this story. Your instruction, support, feedback, and ability to create community are fantastic.

To Addison Gallegos, Melinda Andrews, and my SWP team, thank you for your editorial support and for helping me keep this project on track. I appreciate your efforts and guidance.

To my beloved early manuscript readers, Lori Goodin, Tammy Montgomery, Julie Oliver, and Sherrie Thompson, thank you for your willingness to give time and energy to this project. Your feedback helped to make this book better and your support sincerely touches my heart. You are all amazing women and your friendship has blessed my life.

To my writing buddy, Casey O'Connell, thank you for going on this writing journey with me! Chapter by chapter we traveled together and it made all the difference. Thank you for reading everything from the roughest drafts to the final manuscript, sharing your own work, and being the best accountability partner a gal could ever wish for.

To my daughters and their partners—Eden, Rae, Shane, Abby, Sam, and Olivia—thank you for your support of this book. You applauded when I said I wanted to be a writer and that has helped me live into this next phase of my professional life. I'm both proud and grateful.

To my mom—I was shaking with nerves the day I called to talk to you about the stories I included from our past. Despite your discomfort, you encouraged me. You put my happiness above your own uneasiness. You have taught me many lessons over the years, but I'll hold this one about generosity close to my heart forever. I'm grateful to be your daughter.

To my husband, Mark—Where do I even begin thanking you? There are too many possible starting points, so here goes: Thank you for your adventurous spirit and imagining a life that included Puerto Rico. Thank you for learning about crypto with me, martini lunches with old mobsters, and all the voice memos we made along the way. Thank you for your unwavering belief in my ability to write this story. Truly, this memoir exists because you've given me the encouragement to grow as a writer, the inspiration to live a professionally meaningful life, and the space to see if I could do it. Thank you for these things and a thousand breakfast salads. You are wonderful and I feel so incredibly lucky to share this life with you. I love you with all my heart.

ABOUT THE AUTHOR

Georgine Hodgkinson is a professor of communication studies at Cosumnes River College in Sacramento, where she also served as program coordinator for Re-Emerging Scholars, a program for formerly incarcerated students. Her published scholarship includes book chapters, journal articles, and essays exploring politics, gender, and spirituality. In 2025, she was a People's Choice Winner for the Amy MacRae International Memoir Award. A certified yoga instructor who loves to run and play pickleball, Georgine splits her time between Dorado, Puerto Rico, and Folsom, California, with her husband, Mark.

Author photo © Rudy Meyers

Looking for your next great read?

We can help!

Visit www.shewritespress.com/next-read
or scan the QR code below for a list
of our recommended titles.

She Writes Press is an award-winning
independent publishing company founded to
serve women writers everywhere.